CONFRONTING MALPRACTICE

CONFRONTING MALPRACTICE

Legal and Ethical Dilemmas in Psychotherapy

Kenneth M. Austin
Mary E. Moline
George T. Williams

SAGE Publications

International Educational and Professional Publisher
Thousand Oaks   London   New Delhi

For information address:

SAGE Publications, Inc.
2455 Teller Road
Newbury Park, California 91320

SAGE Publications Ltd.
6 Bonhill Street
London EC2A 4PU
United Kingdom

SAGE Publications India Pvt. Ltd.
M-32 Market
Greater Kailash I
New Delhi 110 048 India

Printed in the United States of America

Library of Congress Cataloging-in-Publication Data

Austin. Kenneth M.
    Confronting malpractice : legal and ethical dilemmas in
  psychotherapy / Kenneth M. Austin, Mary E. Moline, George T.
  Williams.
      p.   cm.
    Includes bibliographical references and index.
    ISBN 0-8039-3081-X. — ISBN 0-8039-3978-7 (pbk.)
    1. Psychotherapists—Malpractice—United States.
  2. Psychotherapy—Moral and ethical aspects. I. Moline, Mary E.
  II. Williams. George Taylor. III. Title.
  KF2910.P753A97   1990
  346.7303'3—dc20
  [347.30633]   90-8742
                                                                        CIP

94 15 14 13 12 11 10 9 8 7 6 5 4 3 2

Sage Production Editor: Diane Foster

Contents

Foreword

Psychotherapy is a complex process. Its definitions are multiple, beginning with a narrow focus on the technique known as psychoanalysis and extending to most any kind of psychological intervention by a trained specialist for a patient's emotional and psychological problems.

Common to all psychotherapeutic approaches is the general goal of helping the patient reach greater effectiveness in living life. What *effectiveness* means varies from one psychotherapeutic approach to another. Still, the common goal is for the patient to become able to meet basic human needs more effectively within a complicated and ever-changing world.

In early psychotherapeutic endeavors, the contract between the psychotherapist and the patient was fairly straightforward. The psychotherapist offered expertise and time for a fee, and the patient agreed to the set time and fee as well as to talk about innermost thoughts, feelings, and experiences. From this arrangement, the goal was to help the patient gain insight and understanding into personal conflicts, thereby reducing anxiety and enabling the patient to live a more productive life.

Psychotherapy used to be limited to the select few who could afford its cost and time demands. Now, between 10% and 15% of Americans will utilize some form of psychotherapy sometime during their life span. As the number of consumers increases, so do consumers' knowledge and expectations about psychotherapy increase. Basic elements of the early psychotherapeutic contract remain the same, but there are many new requirements.

The patient has a right to be treated by a psychotherapist who is competent and adequately qualified to provide the services offered. A patient has a right to have an adequate assessment made of his or her psychological condition, including a working diagnosis.

A patient has a right to be informed about the offered psychotherapeutic treatment including its process, goals, assets, limitations, and risks. Alternate treatment approaches as well as risks if no treatment is followed must be discussed as part of psychotherapeutic informed consent.

A patient has a right to have an adequate record kept of the therapeutic intervention, to know the information in that record, and to have that record transferred upon written and signed request. A patient has a right to have all information exchanged in the therapeutic interaction remain strictly confidential, except in the case of a few specific legal exceptions. A patient has a right to know what these exceptions are *before* treatment begins.

With more consumers of psychotherapy and greater consumer knowledge about psychotherapy, patients expect more from the experience and are more willing to protest when expectations are not met. This leads to an increasing number of complaints against psychotherapists in the form of malpractice suits and complaints filed with ethics committees and licensing boards.

This volume is an excellent handbook for the psychotherapy practitioner at any level. By studying it, students and young psychotherapists will gain an early understanding of the legal and ethical complexities involved in their profession. More seasoned and senior psychotherapists will find the reference a useful update on case law and the changing legal and ethical demands upon the practicing psychotherapists. Teachers of both general psychotherapy and specific psychotherapeutic approaches will find this volume to be an excellent aid in instructing trainees in the realistic task of protecting their psychotherapeutic practices.

Although there are a number of books for individual mental health professions, this is the best example I know—and perhaps the only one—in which the ethical principles of all the mental health professions have been analyzed and integrated with case law to form common standards of psychotherapeutic care and service delivery across mental health professions.

The authors have adopted a chapter format, which makes reading and understanding the material easy. Elements of both legal and ethical requirements are clearly defined and discussed. Individual chapters explain specific actions for malpractice.

Within the individual chapters on malpractice, there is an opening statement regarding the overall issue of the chapter, a listing and review of relevant court cases, a discussion of the implications for psychotherapeutic practice, and a summary statement regarding the issue. After summarizing the issue, the authors provide a professional commentary, which integrates relevant literature, offer their own conclusions with guidelines for practice relevant to the issue, give a vignette, and ask a series of questions every practitioner should be able to answer to aid his or her own safe and effective practice.

In the following chapters, the authors have taken ethical requirements out of the realm of the unobtainable and have translated them into a practical guide for competent psychotherapy practice. The volume might also be called *A Safety Manual for Psychotherapists and Patients*.

I wish I had had a reference like this when I began my career as a psychotherapist 22 years ago. I am thankful for it now and strongly recommend it as required reading for every professional who calls him- or herself "psychotherapist."

—Sherry L. Skidmore, Ph.D.
Diplomate, Forensic Psychology,
American Board of Professional Psychology

Preface

Each of the three authors has equally contributed to the writing of this book, so there is no senior author. Although we each had primary responsibilities for certain chapters, we collaborated while planning and revising the contents of each chapter and other sections of the book. The three of us have spent hundreds of hours with one another sharing ideas and restructuring the organizational format of this book. Numerous rewrites have preceded this finished product. We anticipate future revisions of this text as malpractice suits continue to be filed against psychotherapists.

The idea of doing a book in the area of malpractice and ethics began in 1982. It started with the material developed for a "Law and Ethics" class in a marriage, family, and child counselor training program. All three of us felt that this information should be made available to mental health professionals in general.

Because all three of us are teachers in the field of mental health, we hope that students and interns matriculate and comprehend this information. It is not only important to understand these legal issues so that professionals can practice with high standards when dealing with clients and protect themselves from malpractice suits but it is also important to the field in general. It is important that we practice with the highest standards available so that our care is of the quality that will provide clients with the treatment they deserve. We believe that the material presented in this book can assist the mental health professional to do just that.

This book is limited in scope because of space and time constraints. Therefore, we chose not to explore in detail malpractice issues in other areas of psychotherapy such as group work, family practice, and medication.

We also want to say that we are not members of the legal profession and that our comments and evaluations of the legal cases presented are from the viewpoint of mental health professionals. We also recognize that the implications of the cases and categories presented differ from state to state and that, if you want additional information, you need to consult your lawyer, professional credentialing agency, or professional organization.

Acknowledgments

The preparation of this book has taken a great deal of our time and co-ordinated effort. We are grateful to our families for their support and patience during this period. We also wish to thank all our friends for their encouragement. Special thanks go to (listed alphabetically) Jerry Corey, Ed.D.; Marianne Schneider Corey, M.S.; Barbara Herlihy, Ph.D.; Sandy Jacobs, M.S.; Martha Jo Patterson, J.D.; Kenneth S. Pope, Ph.D.; Theodore P. Remley, Jr., J.D., Ph.D.; and Bonnie R. Williams, M.A., for their valuable assistance in reading various drafts of the manuscript and offering many suggestions that have been incorporated into the final text. Our main satisfaction in writing this book has been the knowledge and friendship we have gained from the experience.

Several of our graduate students also deserve special recognition for helping to generate some of the ideas contained in the "Implications" and "Questions to Consider" sections of many of the chapters. These students at California State University, Fullerton, include Lupe LaCoste, Mary Lindsey, Sandra Paul, Sandra Poulson, Peggy Pelonis, and Roderick Paterson. Students at Loma Linda University include Christina Nicolora, Jeanine Parsons, and Cindy Voight.

Overview

In Chapter 1, we provide some general information designed to supplement your understanding. Specifically, we discuss the legal process as it affects the psychotherapist without a comprehensive examination. We hope, however, it will give you, the reader, some basic (yet limited) understanding of what the legal process might be if you found yourself involved in a lawsuit.

In Chapters 2 through 16, we discuss ways that a mental health professional can become the target of a lawsuit. We examine 15 issues (categories) that can be targets of malpractice suits (e.g., records and confidentiality) and review legal cases associated with each of these issues. In our opinion, by careful review of these cases, you can learn a great deal about how to avoid a malpractice suit. In addition, we present implications from the cases, develop questions regarding the case, provide vignettes, introduce recommendations developed by professionals in the field regarding the issues, and conclude with our recommendations on avoiding malpractice litigation. It was our intention to organize and discuss these various malpractice issues in a way beneficial not only to the practicing professional but to the student in an educational setting. The categories/issues include, according to chapter, (a) records, (b) confidentiality, (c) privacy, (d) defamation of character, (e) failure to warn and protect, (f) failure to take precautions against suicide, (g) sexual contact with a client, (h) injury from nontraditional therapy, (i) diagnosis, (j) inadequate termination or abandonment, (k) releasing or obtaining information and informed consent to treat, (l) illegal detainment, (m) wrongful release, (n) undue influence, and (o) negligent supervision.

In Chapter 17, we differentiate between *ethics*, *morality*, and *law*. Reasons for adopting a professional code of ethics, limitations of ethical codes, and the historical development of ethical codes are discussed. Attention is given to ethical decision making. A major focus of this chapter is on the similarities and differences between six of the major professional organizations' codes of ethics, those of the (a) American Psychological Association (APA), (b) American Psychiatric Association (AmPsyA), (c) American Association for Counseling and Development (AACD), (d) American Association for Marriage and Family Therapy (AAMFT), (e) National Association of Social Workers (NASW), and (f) Association for Specialists in Group Work (ASGW).

In Chapter 18, we have included material we thought would be useful, including questions that cannot be answered from reading the legal cases presented, but are there for you to consider and discuss among colleagues or classmates.

References used in the preparation of this book are provided. In the Appendixes you will find: (a) legal citations of cases discussed in the book, listed by chapter and state; (b) sample forms; (c) names and addresses of professional organizations; and (d) some professional organizations' ethical codes. The appendixes are followed by the Glossary.

The audience for this book includes licensed mental health professionals, unlicensed mental health professionals, and mental health interns who are working toward a mental health license. This book is suitable for professionals in the fields of psychology; psychiatry; marriage, family, and child counseling; human services; social work; psychiatric nursing; and other areas in the mental health professions. Professionals in the legal field might also be interested in this book.

PART I

1

Introduction

One striking characteristic of Americans today is the frequency with which they go to court. The trend of suing one's psychotherapist is also increasing. The April 1986 issue of the *Monitor* (published by the American Psychological Association) indicated that psychology was in a liability crisis. As an example, a Maine psychologist would have to pay nine times his or her prior year's malpractice insurance premium. Another illustration presented was a liability policy purchased in 1984 for $450 by a New Hampshire psychological association that would, by 1986, cost $4,000.

Most mental health professionals carry professional liability insurance. However, few read their policies to find out exactly what is covered. For example, does your policy protect your office or property? If a patient slips in your office, will medical expenses be covered? Is your insurance void if damages are caused by the negligent supervision of your assistant? Some therapists do not obtain coverage believing that they will then be less attractive targets for a suit. Other therapists decide not to buy protection because they work in an agency that has sovereign immunity or one policy for all employees. However, sovereign immunity may not protect the employee but may only protect the

Table 1.1
Ten Greatest Causes of Successful Cases Against Psychologists: Malpractice
Costs, 1976 to mid-1986

Rank	Cause	Percentage of Cases
1	sexual contact	18.5
2	treatment error	15.2
3	loss from evaluation	9.6
4	death (patient/others)	8.6
5	breach (confidentiality/privacy)	6.9
6	faulty diagnosis	5.9
7	countersuit over fee collection	5.9
8	defamation (libel/slander)	4.4
9	violation of civil rights	2.9
10	assault and battery	1.1

SOURCE: Pope (1986).

governmental entity. Whenever a policy covers all employees, it may
be to the insurance company's advantage to show that the employee's
behavior fell outside the scope of the coverage so that it can avoid legal
liability.

In 1976, the American Psychological Association signed up with
American Home Insurance. In 1984, the number of claims against
psychologists was 171. More important to insurance officials is the
amount of money paid out. In the eight years from 1976 to 1983, a total
of $5.4 million was paid out. One year later, the figure was $9.7 million
and, by 1985, the total had become $17.2 million.

Figures released covering malpractice costs between 1976 and mid-
1986 show the 10 greatest causes of successful cases against psychologists (see Table 1.1). However, remember that what is more important
to the insurance industry is the amount of money paid out. The 10
highest causes by amount paid are shown in Table 1.2.

In these litigious times, you may someday find yourself as the
defendant in a malpractice action. To prepare you for such an event, we
will discuss the type of cases that could be brought against you, the
legal process as it might occur, and some hints about what you can do
to make the process easier for yourself. We are not lawyers, and what
we will be presenting is a simplified version of what might actually
occur. The best advice would be for you to consult your lawyer, who

Table 1.2
Ten Greatest Causes According to Amounts Paid by Insurance Companies:
Malpractice Costs, 1976 to mid-1986

Rank	Cause	Percentage of Dollars
1	sexual contact	44.8
2	treatment error	13.9
3	death (patient/others)	10.9
4	faulty diagnosis	7.9
5	loss from evaluation	3.2
6	breach (confidentiality/privacy)	2.8
7	failure to protect (warn)	2.7
8	bodily injury	2.4
9	countersuit over fee collection	2.2
10	assault and battery	1.8

SOURCE: Pope (1986)

should be qualified to tell you exactly what will occur during the legal
process as well as the course of action you will need to take.

The Legal Process as
It Affects Therapists

MALPRACTICE

The burden of proving that harm occurred is the plaintiff's (client's).
The client needs to prove (a) that a professional relationship existed;
(b) that the therapist deviated from the "standard of care," that is, the
therapist breached his or her duty in not providing what is determined
as the "standard practice in the community" (a therapist can be regarded as competent by his or her profession and still be found liable,
but the likelihood is small), (c) that proximate cause of injury is
determined, that is, the breach must be the only cause of the injury
(therapists who give directives for concrete action make it easier for the
court to find them liable); and (d) that an injury was sustained. Some
of the kinds of injuries that might be claimed by a plaintiff (client) are
increased presenting symptoms; new symptoms; misuse or abuse of
therapy; overextending him- or herself, leading to failure; reliance on
directives leading to divorce, job loss, emotional harm, suicide or death) · · ·

of third party, or self-inflicted injuries; deprivation of constitutional rights; and/or loss of liberty or privacy.)

SUBPOENA

Probably one of the most disturbing things to happen to a psychotherapist is to be served with a subpoena. You may receive either a criminal or a civil subpoena. A criminal subpoena is likely to be titled "People of the State . . . v. . . ." or you could receive a "subpoena duces tecum," which requires you to bring records.

There are various issues that may be raised regarding the service of and response to a subpoena. Some of those are as follows:

(1) Don't release any information unless you are sure you have been authorized in writing to do so.

(2) If you do not know whether the privilege has been waived, you must claim the privilege to protect your client's confidentiality.

(3) Should you employ a registered assistant or trainee, it would be wise to claim the privilege to protect confidentiality even though the court might rule that unlicensed practitioners are not covered by the privilege.

(4) You need to determine who served you with the subpoena. You need to arrange for any witness and travel fees before going to court.

(5) At a deposition, where there is no judge, you might have your own attorney present or choose to follow the advice and direction of your patient's attorney.

(6) If you feel your information about your patient is embarrassing, damaging, or immaterial, you might consider getting written permission to discuss the situation with your patient's attorney.

(7) Unless you are required to produce records only, and are providing all your client records, you must appear at the location stated in the subpoena.

PRETRIAL

For those of you who have recently entered the practice of psychotherapy (especially in California) the odds are increasing that someday you will open your mail to find that you are being served with a complaint filed in the superior court or to find a letter from the plaintiff's lawyer advising you that a suit charging you with negligence has been filed. Your initial reaction is likely to be shock. "How could someone I have tried to help do this to me?" More often than not, this will be followed by anger. It is best to remember not to do something you may later regret. Don't telephone the client to argue, plead, or threaten. Instead, you should "immediately" contact your insurance carrier, or an attorney if you don't have insurance, and send a copy of the attorney's letter, or complaint filed with the court, and wait for further instructions. Do not discuss the case with anyone. Your insurance carrier will assign you an attorney. Personal meetings with your attorney and/or insurance representatives will be needed to prepare a defense. Expect to furnish copies of your records (see Chapter 5 to determine what a good record should include). Resist any impulse to change or alter your records. Your insurance carrier may ask you to fill out forms or submit a copy of your vita. Any request for information by the plaintiff or the plaintiff's attorney should be referred to your attorney. (If you do not carry malpractice insurance but have been dependent on your employer to protect your interest, you might wish to retain your own counsel because your employer's attorney will be representing your employer.) Under "discovery" rules, the lawyers involved are legally obliged to keep each other abreast of certain information relating to the case so that both sides can adequately prepare for trial or enter into an out-of-court settlement. During the discovery process, you are likely to be asked or subpoenaed to give a deposition. A *deposition* is a sworn statement that is taken from you before the trial. A legal stenographer will record the proceedings verbatim. Make sure that you allow yourself enough time to prepare for your deposition. You should have the facts of the case clearly in mind. Nothing in your deposition should contradict what you plan to say in court. Your lawyer will be present at your deposition. Although this is not the trial itself, the importance of the deposition cannot be overemphasized. Therefore, some guidelines are offered.

(1) Wait before you answer a question. This gives you time to think about your answer as well as providing your legal counsel with time to raise any objections. If your lawyer advises you not to answer a question, then don't answer, even if you think it might help your case.

(2) Speak slowly and stop talking if your attorney interrupts. Should the opposing attorneys get into an argument, keep out of it. However, listen to what is said, especially to the point your counsel is trying to make.

(3) Be as honest as you would be under oath, tell the truth at all times. If it can be shown that there are any falsehoods in your statements, your credibility will be called into question and there may be charges of perjury.

(4) If you do not understand a question, ask for clarification.

(5) If you do not know the answer to a question, do not be afraid to say, "I don't know." Do not guess.

(6) Unless 100% certain about a fact, use qualifiers like "as best I can recall," "my recollection is," or "I think."

(7) Any time during the deposition, you may ask to have a private conference with your attorney. Also, you may ask for a break to go to the restroom or if you become fatigued.

(8) Never volunteer information. Short answers are best and "yes" or "no" when possible.

(9) If you are asked to review any document the plaintiff's attorney has in his or her possession, read it carefully before replying to any question.

(10) Be courteous and professional at all times. Do not let an attorney provoke you.

(11) If the plaintiff's counsel attempts to summarize what you have said, listen carefully. Do not let him or her put words in your mouth. If in doubt, ask to have that portion of the transcript read back to you.

At any point in the pretrial stage, or even during the trial, the attorneys for all parties involved can agree on a dollar amount for which they will settle the claim out of court. You may be upset with the insurance company's willingness to settle out of court. Resist the impulse to clear your name. If you proceed with a trial, you may be responsible for any monetary award above the dollar amount for which the insurance company would settle the case out of court. Although settlement is not in the best interest of the professional, most malpractice cases are settled out of court at the pretrial stage due to the prohibitive cost of trial proceedings. In some states, there is a mandatory meeting of the lawyers before the trial judge to discuss the evidence. This meeting is designed to explore or encourage an out-of-court settlement. Also, a judge may dismiss an action in response to various kinds of motions to dismiss or rule that the litigation had not been initiated within the time limit set by the state.

THE TRIAL

In state courts, civil cases can be tried by either a judge or a jury. Usually jury trials are preferred by plaintiff attorneys because members of the public are apt to identify more with the wronged client rather than with the powerful professional. A pool of prospective jurors is drawn

from voter registration lists and/or other sources such as auto licenses
or tax rolls. Attorneys are allowed to question prospective jurors
(known as *voir dire*) to determine their competency. Of course, each
attorney wants to keep those who will be sympathetic to his or her case.
A limited number of prospective jurors may be rejected. After the jury
has been selected, they are given the role of "trier of fact," that is, they
will decide the questions of fact while the judge will decide the questions of law.

The trial begins with the plaintiff's attorney and the defense attorney
making opening statements. Each points out what he or she plans to
prove and how he or she will attempt to prove it. The legal liability
affecting a psychotherapist is covered by a tort. A *tort* is "a wrong," it
is a harm done to an individual in such a manner that the law can order
the person who does the harm to pay damages to the injured party. The
"burden of proof" (responsibility) is on the plaintiff to show by the
majority of the evidence that (a) there was a patient-therapist relationship, that is, a "duty of care," (b) the therapist's conduct was below the
"standard of care," (c) the patient was injured, and (d) the therapist's
conduct directly caused the harm.

A duty of care begins when the psychotherapist agrees to treat the
patient. (The element of payment is not necessary for a therapeutic
relationship to exist.) This is usually the easiest of the four elements to
prove. The "standard of care" is the level of proficiency against which
the psychotherapist's behavior will be measured. Professionals are held
to the same standard of care as other professionals in similar localities
and circumstances with comparable qualifications, background, and
experience except where the standard is prescribed by statute. Put
another way, a psychiatrist, a psychologist, a social worker, or a marriage, family, and child counselor has a duty to exercise the standard of
care of the average (meaning ordinary, reasonable, prudent) member of
that specialty. Therefore, malpractice is usually decided upon the basis
of expert testimony. However, there are situations in which "the act
speaks for itself" and expert testimony is not needed.

The harm or injury can include exacerbation of symptoms, new
symptoms, or some type of loss such as of liberty, privacy, constitutional rights, life, money, or companionship. In other words, the plaintiff must suffer some specific damage, either emotional or physical.
Probably the most difficult to establish is that the psychotherapist's
wrongful act was the direct (proximate) cause of the patient's injury.
On the other side, it can be expected that the defense attorney will argue

that the treatment offered conformed to accepted practice, or that the patient was not damaged, or that the damage resulted from some other cause.

Following the attorney's opening statements, the plaintiff's counsel will call witnesses whose testimony will support the plaintiff. The questioning of these witnesses is called *direct examination.* Immediately following, the defense attorney may cross-examine each witness in an attempt to question his or her credibility, expertise, and so on. The cross-examination is followed by redirect examination and re-cross-examination to elicit the best possible understanding of the testimony.

After the plaintiff's attorney has presented his or her case, the defense attorney calls the defense's witnesses. This follows the same format as before: The defense attorney conducts direct examination and the plaintiff's attorney conducts cross-examination followed by "redirect" and "recross."

Throughout the trial, either attorney may object to a question, and the judge will either sustain or overrule each objection. Also, the judge may be asked by either attorney to direct a verdict. Depending on the state, after each side has made its presentation, the judge will explain to the jury which laws are involved, the legal facts of the case, which testimony should be ignored, and how to compute the dollar amount if the defendant is found liable.

When the jury reaches its verdict, the attorney for the losing side may immediately make various motions. In some states, if the judge feels the jury's award was too small or too large, he or she may modify its findings. At the end of the trial, either side may appeal the outcome to a higher court. Most state courts have a three-tier system: the trial court, then the court of appeals or appellate court, and the highest court (usually the state's supreme court). An appellate or supreme court is usually made up of panels of three to seven judges. They have the power to reverse a decision made by a trial court, affirm the trial court's decision, modify the judgment of the trial court, or send the case back to the trial court.

Questions to Consider

(1) What is a *tort*?   Vita

(2) What should you do if you are served with a subpoena?

(3) What are the four elements the plaintiff must prove in malpractice litigation?

(4) How do the guidelines for giving a deposition differ from those presenting courtroom testimony?

(5) If you were called to court now, how prepared would you be?

(6) How concerned are you that you could be involved in a malpractice suit?

PART II

2

Records

"Record keeping, from a liability perspective, is a compilation of evidence of the adequacy of care a patient has received" (Schutz, 1982, p. 51). You need to be aware of how your record-keeping procedures can determine the outcome of a legal case brought against you. Although such a case is not likely to be due to inadequate record keeping, such practice could negatively affect the outcome of your case. Some students and therapists view it as unwise to keep detailed records about their clients. However, should you be involved in a lawsuit, you are likely to be deemed as behaving unprofessionally if you have not kept adequate records.

> Given that records are the most reliable evidence of proper treatment and diagnosis and as such are the basis for review in peer review activities and in questions of unethical or negligent behavior, it is incumbent upon psychologists [and other psychotherapists] to be concerned with their own record-keeping, the record-keeping of their supervisees/employees and with their clients' access and review of the accuracy of those records. (Hall, 1988, p. 4)

Some states define two different categories of client records: (a) agency records and (b) clinical case notes. Agency records include such information as the name and address of the client, the name of the therapists, dates of appointments, fees charged for services, and a record of payments. Clinical case notes contain information necessary for the therapist to serve the client, including tests, diagnoses, hunches, doubts, possibilities, and questions to be dealt with at another time. The agency owns agency records, but the clinical case notes belong to the treating psychotherapist. Remley, (1989) in his essay on record keeping in the new *Ethical Standards Casebook* of the American Association for Counseling and Development (AACD), asserts that courts have determined that client records are like medical records in that the information belongs to the client and the therapist is only the keeper. A lawful subpoena may request agency records, clinical case notes, or both.

The following two cases demonstrate the point that you won't be cited because of inadequate record keeping. However, if a suit is brought against you, and it is discovered that your records do not conform to the "standards of the profession," then you may increase your probability of losing the case. The "standards of the community," or the "locality rule" (i.e., "holding one only to the standard of practitioners in one's community"), has been replaced by national standards of practice (Schutz, 1982, p. 4). Because there are different theoretical orientations in psychotherapy, the "standards of the profession" would be judged by expert witnesses in the courts according to the psychotherapist's professed school of thought for practicing therapy. Also, in a minority of states, expert testimony is supplemented with published professional standards as an assessment measure, particularly if they are the standards of the professional group with which the psychotherapist identifies (Schutz, 1982).

Court Cases

(1) **Whitree v. State of New York (1968)**
(2) **Peck v. Counseling Service of Addison County (1985)**

Case Reviews

Victor J. Whitree, Claimant, v. State of New York, Defendant
Court of Claims of New York
290 N.Y.S. 2d 486 (May 14, 1968)

Inadequate record keeping contributed to the wrongful confinement of
a psychiatric patient, Victor J. Whitree, at Matteawan State Hospital for
over 12 years. During the claimant's wrongful confinement, he suffered
moral and mental degradation and sustained pain and suffering caused
by attacks and beatings from patients and guards at the hospital.

On March 25, 1945, at the age of 46, Victor J. Whitree, the claimant
in this case, was arrested in New York City on the charge of stabbing
John O'Connor. Following court hearings, he pleaded guilty to assault,
third degree, on December 6, 1946. The court of general sessions
suspended sentence and placed Whitree on probation. An assault, third
degree, was a misdemeanor in 1946. Thus Whitree's probation, according to the state's "Code of Criminal Procedure," and assuming no
violations, could be no longer than three years from December 6, 1946.
Whitree violated his probation and was taken into custody on April 7,
1947, and two days later was ordered to Bellevue Hospital for formal
psychiatric examination. On April 11, 1947, he was committed to
Bellevue Hospital for observation and, on April 29, 1947, as directed
by the court of general sessions, he was formally examined by two of
the hospital's psychiatrists. The two psychiatrists reported to the court
of sessions that Whitree "was in such a state of insanity that he was
incapable of understanding the charge, or of making his defense"
(pp. 491-492). The diagnosis for Whitree was "paranoid condition in a
chronic alcoholic." Incidentally, the maximum jail term Whitree could
have received if he had been psychiatrically evaluated to be "sane"
would have been three years beyond the examination date (i.e., April
29, 1950).

Whitree was transferred to Matteawan State Hospital on May 19,
1947, on the basis of the court order and the diagnosis of the Bellevue
Hospital psychiatric examination. After spending the first week in the

admission ward, Whitree was first placed in Ward 7, a quiet ward where he remained for two and a half years, and was then transferred to Ward 9, an essentially open ward for more difficult patients. He was later transferred to a seclusion ward on January 29, 1955, after he had assaulted another patient, and then to another seclusion ward, where he remained until May 11, 1960, when he was transferred back into Ward 9. Thus, for over four years, he had been placed in maximum security confinement, where each patient was kept in a locked cell except for exercise and toilet requirements. Due to an altercation with two other patients on December 4, 1955, Whitree was placed in a "camisole" for one day, even though hospital policy was to place a patient in a camisole for not more than two or three hours.

When serving Whitree's type of sentence, the New York statutory law "required that a prisoner receive thorough psychiatric examination not less than once every two years" (p. 497). However, hospital records revealed that Whitree had not been afforded adequate psychiatric care as evidenced by his having "been psychiatrically examined 7 times in 6 years, of which only 3 examinations were of any depth and those in the first 4 months of this 6 year period" (p. 498). On September 10, 1947, the hospital's staff of psychiatrists held the only diagnostic staff meeting at which Whitree was present during his entire fourteen and a half years at the hospital. His diagnosis at that time was reported to be "psychosis with psychopathic personality, paranoid trends." The medical record revealed that Whitree had not been treated with any of the modern tranquilizing drugs or any of their less effective antecedents during his entire hospital stay and that such drugs were not prescribed to him until 1959. Moreover, Whitree was never exposed to psychotherapy or to psychological testing during his confinement.

Whitree sustained numerous injuries during his incarceration. For example, on one occasion, after he had endured a beating administered by the attendants, he was stripped and placed in the "Blue Room," "a small dark room without toilet facilities, without water facilities, and, without a bed or mattress" (p. 502). He was confined to the "Blue Room" for about eight days and given only bread and water plus a meal every three days. Other injuries sustained by Whitree included many fractures to various body parts, which healed with deformity, as a result of other patients and the attendants striking, kicking, and beating him. On one occasion, he received first-degree burns to his face and chest after another patient poured hot coffee on him, and, "on several occasions, while he was sleeping, he was struck by other patients and his testicles were squeezed" (p. 504). In addition, he sustained permanent, chronic peritonitis of the right shoulder from all of the beatings.

Whitree was denied three applications for writ of habeas corpus (i.e., to determine the legality of his custody) before his application for a fourth writ was granted on March 3, 1961. It is worth noting that Whitree was represented by counsel for the first time during the court of general sessions hearing when the writ was granted and he was subsequently discharged from the hospital. "This demonstrably indicates the awareness that without counsel the average litigant does not possess sufficient acumen or training to present his side of the issues" (p. 494). Also, "courts do not look with favor on successive applications for the writ which raise no new grounds or supply no new facts, and they may give weight to a prior refusal to grant the writ" (p. 493). On September 8, 1961, Whitree was discharged from Matteawan State Hospital with the diagnosis of "psychosis with psychopathic personality, paranoid trends. Condition on Discharge: Improved" (p. 500). He was later administered a thorough and complete psychiatric examination on September 25, 1961, at Bellevue Hospital and diagnosed as "schizoid personality with paranoid features" and further that "he is not in such a state of idiocy, imbecility or insanity as to be incapable of understanding the charge, indictment, proceedings or of making his defense" (p. 500).

COURT DECISION

At the court of claims trial on May 14, 1968, the claimant, Victor J. Whitree, was 68 years of age. The judge dismissed two of Whitree's four claims but ruled in his favor for two of his other causes of action. Whitree was awarded $300,000 for damages suffered: moral and mental degradation implicit in such confinement, sustained pain and suffering caused by attacks and beatings from patients and guards at the hospital, and lost earnings over the period of incarceration.

The main item of damage related to Whitree's false imprisonment for more than 12 years of his 14 year, 3 month, and 20 day confinement (i.e., May 19, 1947 to September 8, 1961). Evidence established that "with proper and adequate psychiatric treatment, claimant should have been released no later than May 19, 1949" (p. 488).

The other cause of action was based on the alleged injuries he had received during his confinement.

The defendant was negligent in failing "to conduct regular treatment and periodic comprehensive examinations of the claimant" and "in failing to provide ordinary medical care in addition to failing to attend to and to treat the personal injuries which the claimant sustained from the beatings he suffered at the hands of fellow patients and attendants in the employ of the defendant at said State Hospital." (p. 490)

The court recognized that "prison physicians owe no less duty to prisoners who must accept their care than do private physicians to their patients who are free to choose" (p. 488). In addition, the court reported that "the hospital record . . . maintained by the State for claimant was about as inadequate a record as [they had] ever examined" (p. 495). They found that the "said record did not conform to the standards in the community; and, that the inadequacies in this record militated against proper and competent psychiatric and ordinary medical care" (p. 495) for the patient during his stay at the hospital. The court held "to the extent that a hospital record develops information for subsequent treatment, it contributed to the inadequate treatment this claimant received" (p. 495).

The court recognized that the failure of the state to call several of its employed physicians, psychiatrists, and attendants as witnesses warranted "the inference that their testimony would not have substantially contradicted the testimony of Butler [the only lay witness for Whitree who had been a patient during a large part of Whitree's confinement] and Whitree" (p. 503). That the "attendants received an absolute minimum of training in the proper handling of patients with psychiatric problems" (p. 503) was evidenced by a revealing answer given by one of the attendants during the trial: "They are irritable, eighty per cent of my fights, or trouble is at 6:30 in the morning. If there is a movie coming on, or if there is a good meal—I don't know if I should say this—but they are like an animal, they know when to be fed, they are like dogs wagging their tail" (p. 503). Despite this observation, however, the court found that the "State [was] not necessarily liable because of sudden assault by one patient in mental hospital upon another" (p. 499).

Charles and Margaret Peck v. the Counseling Service of Addison County, Inc. **Supreme Court of Vermont**
499 A.2d 422 (Vermont, 1985)

This case involves two parents, Charles and Margaret Peck, who brought action against a mental health counseling agency to recover damages for their property loss after their son, John, who was being treated as a mental outpatient, burned down their barn. The Superior Court of Vermont (trial court) dismissed the action with prejudice because it determined that, under current Vermont law, there was no basis indicating that the counseling service owed a duty to take action to protect the parents. Mr. and Mrs. Peck appealed and the case was then heard in the Supreme Court of Vermont on June 14, 1985.

John Peck had attended weekly psychotherapy sessions with the same therapist at the Counseling Service of Addison County, Inc., between September 1976 and October 1977. He had been treated for a history of impulsive assaultive behavior and past alcohol abuse. Concurrently, John had been treated by physicians outside the counseling services for his medical problems of epilepsy and the possibility of a brain disorder associated with his epilepsy. Then, from October 1977 until June 1979, John was no longer a client of the counseling service and was employed in a vocational workshop.

At the time of the incident, June 27, 1979, John Peck was 29 years old and living at home with his parents. Seven days earlier, John had resumed his psychotherapy sessions as a voluntary outpatient at the Counseling Service of Addison County, Inc. On June 20, 1979, during an argument, John's father called him "sick and mentally ill" (p. 424) and told him that he should be hospitalized. John packed his suitcase, went to see his therapist, and reported that "he had a fight with his father, that he was upset with his father, and that he didn't think his father cared about him or respected him" (p. 424). The therapist arranged for John to stay at the home of John's grandparents and scheduled a counseling session for the following day, during which time John was still angry toward his father. During the next counseling session, five days later, John told his therapist that "he wanted to get back at his father" (p. 424). In response to a question by the therapist about how he would get back at his father, John stated, "I don't know, I could burn down his barn" (p. 424). After a discussion of the possible consequences of such an act, John, at the request of the therapist, made a verbal promise not to burn down his father's barn. The therapist believed in "good faith" that John would abide by his promise and, therefore, did not disclose John's threats to any other staff member of the counseling service or to John's parents. The following day, John set fire to the barn, located 130 feet from his parents' house, and it was completely destroyed. Several years later, John's parents brought action against the counseling service concerning two counts. The first count alleged negligence on the part of the counseling service in failing to take steps that were reasonably necessary to protect them from the threat posed by their son. The second count alleged professional malpractice.

COURT DECISION

The trial court (i.e., Addison Superior Court) dismissed the case with prejudice, because it determined that, under Vermont law, there was no basis to indicate that the counseling agency owed a duty to take action to protect the parents of one of its voluntary outpatients. However, "the trial court concluded that if the law of Vermont did require a duty to warn, then a warning would be required on the facts of this case even though the threat to the plaintiffs was one of arson to their property rather than a physical harm to their persons" (p. 424). Also, the trial court held that the defendant was not liable for negligence to the plaintiffs, Mr. and Mrs. Peck. The Pecks appealed the superior court ruling and the case went before the Supreme Court of Vermont.

The Supreme Court of Vermont determined that "the therapist was negligent, and did not act as a reasonably prudent counselor, because her good faith was based on inadequate information and consultation" (p. 425). Psychiatric expert testimony given on behalf of the plaintiffs served as sufficient evidence for the court. The testimony made reference to John Peck's past history of impulsive behavior and his epilepsy, possible brain disorder, and past alcohol abuse. This historical information about John underscored the importance for the therapist to reveal John's threat, and failure to do so was deemed inconsistent with the mental health profession.

The court summary report noted that the investigation process included an examination of the clinic's written records of the client, the cross-referencing system between its therapists and physicians, and the hospital's written policy regarding staff procedures for dealing with clients. The process the court used to investigate these three forms of documentation addressed the issue of conforming to the "standards of the community." Evidence revealed that, at the time of John's threat, the counseling service did not have a cross-referenced system between its therapists and the physicians who were treating the same clients for medical problems. The counseling service also lacked any written policy concerning formal intrastaff consultation procedures when a client presented a serious risk of harm to another.

The defense highlighted the fact that John Peck was a voluntary outpatient and that the relationship between a community mental health agency and a voluntary outpatient does not include a duty to protect third persons. The defense also argued that a therapist seeing an outpatient does not have a duty to control the patient. However, the court indicated that, "whether or not there is actual control over an outpatient in a mental health clinic setting similar to that exercised over institutionalized patients, the relationship between a clinical therapist and his or her patient, 'is sufficient to create a duty to exercise reasonable care to protect a potential victim of another's conduct' (*Tarasoff v. Regents of the University of California*, 1976)" (p. 425).

Although there was no duty to warn under the current state law in Vermont, the supreme court reversed the judgment of the trial court. The mental health agency was held negligent for failing to warn the client's parents concerning their son's threats to burn down their barn. The court stated that a mental health professional should know the standards of the mental health profession for exercising reasonable care and protecting identifiable victims whenever a client poses a serious threat. Although the parents argued that the trial court had erred in finding them 50% comparatively negligent in causing their barn to be destroyed, the supreme court agreed with the trial court. The court remarked that, at the time of the incident, the parents already had knowledge of their son's predisposition to violent behavior.

Implications

a. The hospital, agency, or individual practitioner should have clear, written procedures to follow. This constitutes an important dimension of "record keeping."

b. It is especially important to be familiar with the laws of the state as well as with the policies pertaining to the mental health professional's employing agency. For example, if you practice as a mental health professional in New Orleans, the court will assess the case according to the law of Louisiana. Similarly, if you practice in Cincinnati, Ohio, the case will be reviewed according to the law of Ohio.

c. Evidence of good record keeping can be interpreted as evidence of providing high-quality, competent care. In any case coming before a court, it is likely that the court will look at the treatment. Failure to keep records or keeping inadequate records *may* contribute to your losing a malpractice lawsuit.

d. Professional counselor organizations could organize committees in local areas to keep mental health professionals updated on laws concerning adequate record keeping (Kenneth S. Pope, APA Ethics Committee chair, personal communication, February 24, 1989).

e. Records can help protect the psychotherapist as the court may review records to determine how the therapist handled cases involving duty to warn, duty to report abuse, and/or potential danger to self or others. The courts may also examine whether the therapist deviated from average care and/or whether authorization was given by the client.

f. All therapist consultations with other persons, including correspondence (Schutz, 1982) regarding a client, should be documented in the client's file.

g. Records should include all treatment contracts made with a client, either in person or by phone, including descriptions of significant events (Schutz, 1982).

h. The diagnosis of a client should be reviewed and revised regularly and documented in the client's record.

i. Destroying client case notes is a felony in some states. If you are under court order to appear concerning one of your clients, do not destroy the client case notes. "Anything in the records is going to be less incriminating than having erased or destroyed the records" (Kenneth S. Pope, APA Ethics Committee chair, personal communications, February 24, 1989).

j. Kenneth S. Pope discourages therapists from keeping two different sets of client records. As reported by Pope, "with keeping two sets of records, you perjure yourself."

k. Soisson, Vandecreek, and Knapp (1987, p. 501, cited in Hall, 1988, p. 3) indicate that the record should not only document the treatment but "facilitate the coordination and continuity of services, assist in the evaluation of the client's condition and progress, and evaluate the success or failure of treatment." Therefore, the record-keeping requirement is to provide "meaningful information should the patient transfer to a new practitioner or should the treating practitioner be unavailable for any reason" (Hall, 1988).

l. Written and signed client consent forms should be included in the client's record file (Schutz, 1982).

m. Financial records should be kept separate from treatment records to help maintain the confidentiality of clients in those instances where the therapist must submit the record of payments to authorities (Hall, 1988).

n. When the psychotherapist leaves for vacation or for an unexpected emergency, Hall (1988) recommends that "a sealed copy of a list of clients' names, addresses and phone numbers may be sent to the designated licensed professional" (p. 3). This form of abbreviated record will help guard confidentiality.

Commentary

Possibly one of the most important aspects of treatment is a clinician's records. They serve as a defense against malpractice claims, but, according to Soisson, Vandecreek, and Knapp (1987, p. 501), they should also *serve the clients* by documenting "that treatment occurred, . . . facilitating the coordination and continuity of services, assisting in the evaluation of the client's condition and progress, and by evaluating the success or failure of treatment."

Record keeping *serves you, the therapist,* by providing proof that treatment occurred, that treatment plans were appropriate, that diagnosis and evaluation occurred, that your treatment was consistent with the "standard of care," and that, if you should leave the profession, become deceased, retire, or move, your records would assist the referred therapist to provide quality and continuity of treatment for the client.

Although to date we have not located any court case in which a suit occurred because of poor records, there have been cases where a therapist was found negligent of professional care because of poor or absent record keeping. As stated by Slovenko (Soisson, Vandecreek, & Knapp, 1987, p. 499), "an inadequate record of itself is taken to be indicative of poor care." Most frequently missing among records are treatment plans and medication assessment notes (Soisson, Vandecreek, & Knapp, 1987).

To protect your client and avoid legal malpractice, this section on record keeping will examine (a) guidelines for content and (b) retention, storage, and disposition. Record keeping involves not only what specifically should be recorded about a client (content) but how long records should be kept (retention and storage/disposition) and, "although state laws typically mandate record keeping in mental health settings, the laws provide few guidelines for record content" (Soisson, Vandecreek, & Knapp, 1987, p. 49), retention, storage, or disposition. Guidelines have been provided by professional organizations and other professionals in the field. We will examine these guidelines and in addition provide some guidelines of our own.

CONTENT

The following professional organizations have some general policies concerning the contents of a clinician's records:

A. The American Psychological Association adopted the *Specialty Guidelines for Delivery of Services* in 1981. These guidelines state:

> 2.3.3 Accurate, current, and pertinent documentation of essential clinical psychological services provided is maintained (p. 9).

According to these guidelines, records should include the following: "identifying data, dates of services, types of services, significant actions taken and outcome" (p. 9). All must be recorded within a reasonable time. In more than one malpractice case, the above guidelines have been successfully cited as the "standard of care" in the profession of psychology.

B. The National Association of Social Workers (NASW) *Standards for the Private Practice of Clinical Social Workers"* (Washington, DC National Association, draft of April 22, 1981) states that

> Y.E. Private clinical practitioner *shall keep up-to-date, accurate records on treatment of the client. (Records should protect confidentiality while recording subjects discussed in sufficient detail to justify therapeutic action.)*

Professional organizations seem to provide only brief guidelines as to what clinicians should write in their clients' records. We did not find any specific directions as to what good records should contain in the six professional organizations' codes of ethics (see Chapter 17 of this book).

Professional writers such as Cohen; Woody; Schutz; and Soisson, Vandecreek, and Knapp have suggested the following regarding record content. Compare and contrast their recommendations. Whatever method you decide to follow regarding the content of your records, it will be an excellent defense to demonstrate that you followed a method prescribed by a well-known professional in the field.

Cohen (1979) recommends that records should include "a descriptive summary of all contacts, regular summaries of progress, available psychological test data, notations of informed consent to all aspects of treatment, notes concerning phone contacts and conversations with significant others in the client's life, and copies of all correspondence with the client" (Soisson, Vandecreek, & Knapp, 1987, p. 500).

Woody (1988, p. 140) points out that "there is no definitive list of materials that must be included in a client's record." However, he does state that the "main guidelines are to fulfill the purpose of records—namely, planning and evaluating the services for the benefit of the client, recording communications between health care personnel and the client, and establishing legal safeguards for the practitioner and employer."

Schutz (1982, p. 52) gives a list of nine items that need to be included in the records, as follows:

1. Written and signed informed consents for all treatment.
2. Written and signed informed consents for all transmissions of confidential information.
3. Treatment contracts, if used.
4. Notes of all treatment contracts made, either in person or by phone, including description of significant events.
5. Notes of all contacts with significant others, or consultations, including correspondence.
6. A complete history and symptom picture leading to a diagnosis, including past and present psychological and psychiatric evaluations, medical history, and a current physical examination. The diagnosis should be reviewed and revised regularly.
7. All prescriptions and a current drug usage profile.
8. A record of the therapist's reasoning as he [she] made all decisions in the diagnosis and treatment of the patient.
9. Any instructions, suggestions, or directives made to the patient that the patient failed to follow through on. (Such records can be used to establish contributory negligence—a powerful defense to any negligence suit).

Soisson, Vandecreek, and Knapp (1987) suggest what *not to include* in records, such as "emotional statements and other personal opinions. Information about illegal behavior, sexual practices, or other sensitive information that may embarrass or harm the client or others are rarely appropriate for the record" (p. 500). "Records should document the decision and treatment processes and the patient's response to treatment" (p. 498).

RETENTION AND DISPOSITION

How long do you keep your records? Have you decided what you will do with your records when the time comes to dispose of them? To answer, you will need some rationale based on an agreed standard of care. The time may come when your records will be subpoenaed. You could be held liable if you have no records for a client and cannot give a reason, based on some standard, for the disposal of the requested records. We have provided some of the suggestions provided by national mental health associations and other experts in the field.

The American Psychological Association set guidelines for retention and disposition in their *Specialty Guidelines for Delivery of Services* in 1981. These guidelines have been cited in court cases as the "standard of care" in the profession of psychology.

> 2.3.4 Each clinical psychological service unit follows an established record retention and disposition policy.
> Interpretation of these guidelines are that policy must conform to state statutes where applicable. When there are no statutes 1) records should be retained for 3 years, 2) either the full record or a summary be maintained for 12 more years and 3) no record be disposed of until 15 years after services were completed.

Judy E. Hall (Ph.D., executive secretary to the New York Board of Psychology) recommends that "if the recipient of services is a child, it may be more advisable to maintain records until the developmental period is over (e.g., age 18 in some states)" (Hall, 1988, p. 4).

The American Association for Marriage and Family Therapists (AAMFT) *Code of Ethical Principles for Marriage and Family Therapists* (1988) states:

Marriage and Family therapists [should] store or dispose of client records
in ways that maintain confidentiality (2.3).

Counseling psychology specialty guidelines recommend following
state regulations, and, if there are none, the policy is (a) that the full
record be maintained intact for at least 14 years after the completion of
planned services or after the date of last contact with the user, whichever is later; (b) that, if a full record is not retained, a summary of the
record be maintained for an additional 3 years; and (c) that the record
may be disposed of no sooner than 7 years after the completion of
planned services or after the date of last contact, whichever is later.

How long one should maintain records varies from location to location. If one considers only "hospital records," then the following states
have given guidelines:
  (1) California—7 years after discharge (patient 21 years or older)
  (2) Massachusetts—30 years after discharge
  (3) New York—6 years after discharge
  (4) Pennsylvania—15 years and permanent case file
  (5) South Dakota—permanently
  (6) Texas—10 years

You need to have made arrangements in your will or with your lawyer
concerning what to do with your records should they outlive you. In
dealing with private practice, state laws are not specific. All readers are
advised to consult with an attorney familiar with the statutes that apply
to their practice.

Conclusions

The following is what we endorse as a desirable way to structure the
contents of your records. Examples of some of the types of forms we
think ought to be included in your records appear in Appendix B.
Records belong to the psychotherapist or agency involved, depending
on the setting. Only the information contained in the records belong to
the client. However, the Privacy Act of 1974 (Public Law 93-579) gave
clients access to their health-related records and this includes the right
of the client to see his or her records, copy them, and request corrections

or amendments (Woody, 1988, p. 139). Therefore, the contents of your records may be subject to disclosure provided the client's consent has been obtained or a court has ordered such disclosure. The prudent psychotherapist will keep notes on every case as if there will be disclosure. Keeping this in mind, we believe a "good record" should include several components. We have subdivided the contents into two categories: (a) essential (i.e., contents we believe you must have in your records) and (b) strongly recommended (i.e., contents that you could delete but that would give you and your client more protection).

Essential

(1) Written and signed *informed consents* for treatment (see Appendix B)

(2) Written and *signed consents* for all transmissions of *confidential information* (see Appendix B)

(3) *Written treatment plans and treatment contracts*, if used; we suggest the following:

    (a) stating problems reflecting necessity simply and clearly based on observable behavior, including the frequency with which they occur

    (b) stating objectives that show a measurable change in the frequency of the problem behavior and the date that this change is expected to occur

    (c) stating a plan of intervention that includes the mode (e.g., individual, couple, family, group) and the focus (e.g., supportive, confrontive) of the intervention as well as the frequency and duration of contact with the client (see Appendix B)

(4) *Notes on all therapy sessions* including a description of significant events; we suggest the following:

    (a) the type of contact (e.g., individual, couple, family, group)

    (b) the exact date and times of the beginning and end of each session

    (c) the progress or lack of progress in the problem(s) as stated in the terms used in the treatment plan

    (d) the remaining degree of psychological impairment as described in observable behavior to document the continuing need for the current level of treatment—using the frequency statement and progress (as opposed to process) notes—to demonstrate accountability; there are a variety of methods one can use, such as comparing test scores and mental status exam results

(5) any past or present *psychological/psychiatric evaluations* (it is crucial in a court of law that this include any evaluations done in the past 12 months)

(6) *Diagnosis*—the *Diagnostic and Statistical Manual of Mental Disorders-III R* (*DSM-III R*, 1987) and the *International Classification of Diseases-9-CM* (*ICD-9*-for clinical modification in the United States, 1978) are acceptable references for diagnosing a client's mental health problem

(7) any *instructions, suggestions, or directives* made to the client that the client failed to follow

Strongly Recommended

(1) written documentation of all no-show or canceled appointments

(2) written documentation of all phone calls (including dates and times), whether received or initiated, and all written correspondence

(3) written documentation of all consultations with other therapists (which can be helpful to establish "standard of care") and you should document any supervision that you do

(4) *social/psychological/medical history* (e.g., suicidal thoughts/attempts, notes, and current physical or referral for a physical)

(5) *Current medications used* (*specify physician's name*)

(6) *Prognosis*

ADDITIONAL COMMENTS

We believe you also need to consider the following:

(1) Records should be retained in accordance with your state law. Where no state law exists, you should follow your professional association's guidelines. In addition, you may want to consult with an attorney who is familiar with mental health laws and cases.

(2) Records should be shredded when the required time limit for storage has been reached.

(3) It would be wise to leave a will including plans for the disposition of your practice and records in the event of death or incapacitation. You should consider the following for your will:

  (a) Provide for an executor or trustee to maintain records for a period of 30 days.

  (b) At the end of 30 days, the practice (including all records) will be sold for the sum of $1.00 to a designated colleague.

(c) All active cases should be contacted before their next appointments and notified concerning who will take over their cases and records, unless they wish to choose someone else.

(d) All inactive cases can be sent a letter indicating who will maintain their records, unless they choose another party.

(e) An advertisement will be placed in the newspaper indicating who will be maintaining records unless another provider is selected.

(f) Leave specific instructions regarding accounts receivable and current financial records.

(4) Don't erase/alter your records when you have erred. Place a line through the misprinted material and write in the correction.

Summary

Controversy exists among some mental health professionals about what information to include in client records or whether records should be kept at all. Although it is not likely that psychotherapists will have a lawsuit filed against them for inadequate record keeping, such practice could affect the outcome of a case. It is important that therapists adhere to the "standards of the profession" for keeping records. A psychotherapist's record keeping would be judged by expert witnesses in a court of law according to the professed school of thought for practicing therapy. Furthermore, psychotherapists should refer to state statutes, federal laws, professional organizations' ethical codes, and policies established by the employing agency or institution for keeping records. Destroying client case notes is considered a felony in some states.

Although it is important to maintain a client's privacy in keeping records, it is also important to have client information readily available in agency records for cases of emergency or if the treating therapist is unavailable. Agency records need to be kept in a secure place such as a file cabinet under lock and key and need to include documentation of essentially objective information, such as name, address, and telephone number of client, name of treating therapist; name and telephone number of person to contact in case of emergency; dates of appointments; client's signed release and consent forms; fees charged for services; and a record of payments. Also, any treatment contracts made with the client, either in person or by phone, including significant events should be included. Clinical case notes, which are usually kept in the possession of the treating therapist, include essentially subjective information, such as the therapist's diagnosis, hunches, doubts, prognosis, and questions to consider in future sessions. These guidelines are frequently cited as the "standard of care" by expert testimony.

Vignette

After reading this chapter about record keeping, here is a vignette. See what you would do with this case.

Five years ago, you terminated therapy sessions with a client named Tracy. During the year she was in therapy with you, she had attempted suicide twice. It was upon your recommendation that she went to an inpatient facility. After going to this facility, she terminated treatment with you. While you were seeing Tracy, you kept very brief records about the sessions. You included in your records the date, time, length of session, payment of fees, and brief progress notes. You have just received a letter from Tracy's lawyer, who has subpoenaed her records from you. The lawyer explains that Tracy had committed suicide while in the inpatient facility. The facility informed Tracy's parents' lawyer (who is filing suit against the facility) that you had never sent the facility your records regarding Tracy. The facility claims they sent you a copy of Tracy's consent form for release of her records. How do you respond to the subpoena? Could you be found legally responsible for Tracy's suicide? Were the records you kept sufficient to protect you from a lawsuit?

Questions to Consider

(1) Why should therapists receive signed consent forms from their clients for treatment?

(2) What should be in a written treatment plan?

(3) Should a therapist obtain signed consents for all transmissions of confidential information?

(4) What information should be recorded for each therapy session?

(5) Should failed or canceled appointments be recorded?

(6) Should notes be made of consultations with other professionals?

(7) Why record any failures on the part of the client to follow instructions or directives made by the therapist?

(8) Why record any medications the client might be taking?

(9) What might be the advantages and disadvantages of a therapist taking a client's history during an "intake session"?

(10) What do you do with a client's file after termination? For what period of time following termination might you retain your client's file? What do you do with your client's file if he or she dies during the course of your professional relationship? If your client dies within a few months after you terminate therapy?

(11) What happens to your clients' files if you, the therapist, decide to professionally retire? If you die during the course of your professional relationship?

(12) What do you do with your client's files if you decide to relocate to practice in another state?

(13) What would you do if a client requests to see his or her records?

(14) What would you do if there was a fire that destroyed all of your clients' records?

3

Confidentiality

One of the most important elements of any psychotherapeutic relationship is the confidentiality of communication between client and therapist. Both ethical codes of mental health professional organizations and state laws deal with the concept of confidentiality. The laws define "Confidential communication" and delineate the scope of therapist-client privilege. For example, the California Evidence Code defines a psychotherapist as (a) psychiatrist, (b) a licensed psychologist, (c) a licensed clinical social worker, (d) a credentialed school psychologist, or (e) a licensed marriage, family, and child counselor. "Confidential communication between client and therapist" includes information transmitted in the course of therapy.

There is a difference between confidentiality and privileged communication. *Confidentiality* refers to the "the ethical responsibility of mental-health professionals to safeguard clients from unauthorized disclosures of information given in the therapeutic relationship" (Corey, Corey, & Callanan, 1988, p. 177). However, this confidential relationship is not absolute. Court decisions have pointed to the responsibility of therapists to warn and protect others even though doing so involves breaching confidentiality. Although states vary with regard to the limitations of confidentiality, *all* states agree that, "when the welfare of a child is in danger, reporting of the incident to the proper authorities is now mandatory" (Miller & Thelen, 1987, p. 707).

Privileged communication is granted by statute, and it protects clients from having their communications revealed in court without explicit permission. It is important to note that statutory privilege belongs to the client, not the therapist. A therapist must claim the privilege on the client's behalf when information is being sought unless the "client" or legal representative "waives the privilege" (Corey, Corey, & Callanan, 1988, p. 177). "Counselors [and other mental health professionals] need to be aware that privileged communication statutes, even when they do exist, do not represent absolute guarantees" (Sheeley & Herlihy, 1986, p. 145). For instance, if a judge orders a therapist to divulge information about a client in court and the therapist refuses, the therapist will be held in contempt of court (Theodore P. Remley, Jr., personal communication, April 22, 1989). In such a case, the therapist may file an "interlocutory appeal," although only the issue of the judge not honoring the statute of privileged communication could be appealed in a higher court. The therapist who was held in contempt of court would likely be imprisoned for a long period of time before his or her release could result from an appeal to the higher court.

If there is a statute for absolute privileged communication, court judges are likely to honor it and not force disclosure by the therapist (Theodore P. Remley, Jr., personal communication, April 22, 1989). It is important to note, however, that some of the statutes of privileged communication for licensed mental health providers have specific exceptions. For example, in the state of Virginia, the statute for licensed professional counselors specifies that privileged communication exists, except when the judge rules otherwise.

Several court cases relating to the issues of confidentiality and privileged communication will be discussed in the following section.

Court Cases

(1) *In re Joseph E. Lifschutz on Habeas Corpus* (**1970**)

(2) *Schaffer v. Spicer* (**1974**)

(3) *Caesar v. Mountanos* (**1976**)

(4) *State of Arizona v. Vickers* (**1981**)

(5) *People of the State of California v. Gomez* (1982)
(6) *In re Subpoena Served Upon Jorge S. Zuniga, M.D., et al.;*
     In re Subpoena Served Upon Gary R. Pierce, M.D., et al. (1983)
(7) *In re Donald Pebsworth*, Appeal of Dr. Kersey Anita (1983)
(8) *Tumlinson v. the State of Texas* (1983)
(9) *Sims v. the State of Georgia* (1984)
(10) *State of Oregon v. Miller* (1985)
(11) *Johnson v. Lincoln Christian College* (1986)
(12) *The People of the State of Colorado v. District Court* in and for the
     City and County of Denver, Colorado (1986)
(13) *State of Minnesota v. Gullekson* (1986)
(14) *State of New Jersey v. McBride* (1986)
(15) *Cutter II v. Brownbridge* (1986)

Case Reviews

In re Joseph E. Lifschutz on Habeas Corpus
Supreme Court of California, In Bank
467 P. 2d 557 Cal. (April 15, 1970)

Dr. Joseph E. Lifschutz, a California psychiatrist, presented a novel challenge to the court by initiating questions concerning privileged communication and constitutional law that had not been formerly addressed. This case recognized that no previous cases had applied the patient-litigant exception to the psychotherapist-patient privilege. Dr. Lifschutz was imprisoned after he was ruled in contempt of court for refusing to obey a court order instructing him to answer questions and provide records relating to his communications with former patient Joseph F. Housek. Dr. Lifschutz applied for writ of habeas corpus to secure his release from the custody of the sheriff of San Mateo County.

The series of events leading to this court case arose out of a suit filed by Joseph F. Housek against John Arabian on June 3, 1968. Housek sought to secure damages, claiming that, as a result of an assault by Arabian, he experienced "physical injuries, pain, suffering and severe mental and emotional distress" (p. 559). Housek had received psychiatric treatment from Dr. Lifschutz over a six-month period about 10 years earlier.

After learning during a deposition that Housek had received psychiatric treatment from Dr. Lifschutz, defendant Arabian subpoenaed Dr. Lifschutz and all of his medical records for deposition relating to the treatment of Housek. Dr. Lifschutz appeared for the deposition but refused to produce any of his medical records or answer any questions relating to his treatment of his patients. In fact, the psychiatrist would not even disclose whether or not Housek had consulted him or had been his patient. Neither Housek nor his attorney attended this deposition or any of the subsequent hearings related to this proceeding.

Because Dr. Lifschutz refused to cooperate, "Arabian moved for an order of the superior court compelling the production of the subp[o]ended records and the answers to questions on the deposition" (p. 559). The superior court made reference to the patient-litigant exception of section 1016 of the Evidence Code for this case and determined that the statutory psychotherapist-patient privilege did not apply. Section 1016 indicates that "there is no privilege under this article as to a communication relevant to an issue concerning the mental or emotional condition of the patient if such issue has been tendered by: (a) the patient" (p. 567). In other words, because Housek had introduced the issue of his mental and emotional condition while beginning the legislation for this case, the statutory psychotherapist-patient privilege did not apply, even though he had neither claimed a psychotherapist-patient privilege nor waived such a privilege.

On December 20, 1968, Dr. Lifschutz was ordered by the superior court "to comply with the subpoena and to answer questions posed during deposition" (p. 560). Lifschutz was given 30 days to respond to the request, and he still refused to cooperate. A year later, on December 5, 1969, another superior court hearing was held and Dr. Lifschutz again refused to comply with the order. Consequently, Lifschutz was judged in contempt of court and confined in the custody of the sheriff of San Mateo County. On December 8, 1969, the court of appeals denied Lifschutz's petition for habeas corpus and the case was heard by the Supreme Court of California on April 15, 1970.

Dr. Lifschutz stated his belief that a psychotherapist has a constitutional right to absolute confidentiality in his communications with, and his treatment of, patients. He argued that compelling a psychotherapist to disclose confidential information under some circumstances "unconditionally impair[s] the practice of his profession" (p. 562). He made reference to the California law, which states that "clergymen could not be compelled to reveal certain confidential communications under these circumstances" (p. 559) and that "so distinguishing between clergymen and psychotherapists, has denied psychotherapists the equal protection of the laws in violation of the Fourteenth Amendment" (p. 565). In addition, he submitted affidavits of psychotherapists who had concurred with his assertion that total confidentiality is essential to the practice of their profession.

COURT DECISION

The Supreme Court of California concluded that, although absolute clergymen-penitent privilege exists, "no constitutional right enables the psychotherapist to assert an absolute privilege concerning all psychotherapeutic communications" (p. 573). The court reported that the trial court's order was valid, requiring Dr. Lifschutz to produce the records and answer the questions regarding whether or not former patient, Joseph F. Housek, had consulted him or had been his patient. The patient-litigant exception to the psychotherapist-patient privilege was determined to be at issue in this case. The court reported that "the provisions are intended to serve the important state interest of facilitating the ascertainment of truth in legal proceedings" (p. 564). Therefore, Dr. Lifschutz was properly adjudged in contempt of court. Dr. Lifschutz's petition for writ of habeas corpus was once again denied.

Betty L. Schaffer, Plaintiff and Appellant, v. Edward R. Spicer, Defendant and Respondent
Supreme Court of South Dakota
215 N.W. 2d 135 (1974)

The plaintiff, Betty Schaffer, was granted a divorce from Virgil Dornbusch on July 16, 1965. The divorce decree granted Betty custody of the couple's three children. Over the next four years, the couple disputed child custody. On January 23, 1969, while the children were in Virgil's custody, Betty attempted to show cause to the court why custody of the children should not remain with their father. During this court case, Betty brought action against her psychiatrist, Dr. Edward R. Spicer, for breaching the physician-patient privilege.

    Psychiatrist Dr. Spicer, who was serving as the defendant in this case, presented an eight-page, single-spaced typed affidavit describing his

treatment of Betty Schaffer. This included an extensive, detailed discussion of the communications involved in the physician-patient relationship while Dr. Spicer consulted and treated Betty between
September 5, 1964, and September 17, 1964. Betty's hysteria, the
events that led to her three nervous breakdowns, and the shock therapy
she had received were all discussed in the affidavit.

Defendant Dr. Spicer asserted that Betty, his patient, had waived any
claim of privileged communications with him because she offered
herself as a witness concerning her mental condition in the prior divorce
trial and that the information should be published in the best interest of
the children. Dr. Spicer quoted the South Dakota statute: "If a person
waives such a privilege, as to any particular communication, [s]he
cannot thereafter claim it" (p. 139).

COURT DECISION

The Supreme Court of South Dakota had never before considered how
far a patient's testimony may extend before the patient may be deemed
to have waived the physician-patient privilege. The court reported:

> It is one thing to say that a doctor may be examined and cross-examined
> by the defense in a courtroom, in conformity with the rules of evidence
> . . . it is quite another matter to permit, as alleged here, an unsupervised
> conversation between the doctor and his patient's protagonist. It is the
> opinion of this Court that the mere waiver of a testimonial privilege does
> not release the doctor from his duty of secrecy and from his loyalty in
> litigation, and no one may be permitted to induce the breach of these
> duties. (p. 137)

The court ruled that the defendant psychiatrist was not permitted to
waive or consent to the publication of the information in the affidavit.
The supreme court determined that the trial court had erred in its
judgment for the defendant. Therefore, the judgment was reversed in
favor of Betty Schaffer, so that she successfully sued her psychiatrist
for violating the physician-patient privilege.

The supreme court recognized: "It is true that when a court is called
upon to determine custody of children in a divorce or other proceeding,
it must consider all circumstances, including the relative fitness of each
parent to further the children's best interests and welfare" (p. 137).
However, in this case, the affidavit was first published to a third party,

the attorney of Betty Schaffer's husband, on the attorney's request, and not to a court upon its order.

George R. Caesar, M.D., Petitioner-Appellant, v. Louis P. Mountanos,
as Sheriff of the County of Marin, State of California et al.,
Respondents-Appellees
No. 74-2271, U.S. Court of Appeals, Ninth Circuit, (September 13, 1976)

This case involved a California psychiatrist, Dr. George R. Caesar, who was held in contempt of court for refusing to answer questions concerning his former patient, Joan Seebach, while giving court testimony. Doctor Caesar petitioned for a writ of habeas corpus on the ground that his communications with his former patient were protected by the psychotherapist-patient privilege. However, the California Superior Court, Marin County, judged Dr. Caesar to be in contempt on the basis of the "patient-litigant exception" to the psychotherapist-patient privilege. The background information of this case follows.

Following an automobile accident on December 4, 1969, Joan Seebach was referred to psychiatrist Dr. Caesar for examination and treatment. The treatment involved about 20 psychotherapeutic sessions. Ms. Seebach filed two suits to recover personal damages incurred from the December 4, 1969, accident and another automobile accident in which she was involved on August 30, 1968. She "alleged that the accidents caused her personal injury and pain and suffering not limited to her physical ailments" (p. 1065). She also asserted that "she had incurred medical expenses and loss of income in amounts not fully ascertainable at that time" (p. 1065). Ms. Seebach and her counsel stated in a deposition on June 15, 1971, that "some of the care and treatment" administered by psychiatrist Dr. Caesar "may be involved in this lawsuit" (p. 1065). A deposition from another psychiatrist indicated the attending physicians had recommended that Ms. Seebach see Dr. Caesar based upon the belief that there was "an emotional overlay to her problems" and that she was "magnifying her distress" (p. 1065). The other psychiatrist also testified she understood that Dr. Caesar had attributed some of Ms. Seebach's emotional problems to her early childhood.

On April 5, 1972, Dr. Caesar testified that he had forwarded his notes concerning Ms. Seebach to her counsel. He declined to answer several questions regarding his treatment of his patient, asserting that he believed "answering further questions and revealing her confidence could be harmful to her psychologically, and detrimental to her future well-being" (pp. 1065-1066). Dr. Caesar also said that he had not received "valid consent" from his former patient to testify. Ms. Seebach's counsel then informed Dr. Caesar that there had been some confusion concerning Ms. Seebach's consent; however, she had granted all authority to her counsel stipulating consent. Dr. Caesar would not acknowledge this form of consent and further stated that he would not divulge the confidential information, even if Ms. Seebach granted consent in writing. Ms. Seebach then submitted a written statement, abolishing the psychotherapist-patient privilege.

On October 18, 1972, Dr. Caesar was ordered to present his deposition as Ms. Seebach had waived the psychotherapist-patient privilege when she related her "mental and emotional condition" to the pending court issue by "claiming damages for mental and emotional distress" (p. 1066). During a second deposition on November 27, 1972, Dr. Caesar reported having treated Ms. Seebach for injuries resulting from the automobile accidents and having diagnosed her as being depressed. However, he refused to respond to 11 questions concerning the relationship of Seebach's emotional condition to the accidents.

COURT DECISION

On December 12, 1972, Dr. Caesar received a court order stating that he was held in contempt of court for not answering questions pertaining to his former patient. Subsequently, he submitted a petition to eradicate the contempt adjudication and it was denied. The California Court of Appeals held that the statute pertaining to the right of privacy does not provide privilege for psychotherapeutic communications. As noted by the court: "There is no privilege under this article [i.e., California Evidence Code § 1016] as to communications relevant to an issue concerning the mental or emotional condition of the patient if such an issue has been tendered by . . . the patient" (p. 1066). Furthermore, the court reported that "the constitution . . . permits limited intrusion into the psychotherapist-patient privilege when properly justified" (p. 1067). Therefore, psychotherapist "disclosure can be compelled only with respect to those mental conditions the patient-litigant has disclosed . . . by bringing action in which they are at issue" (p. 1069). The court stated that there needs to be "a proper balance between the conditional right of privacy encompassing the psychotherapist-patient relationship and [California's] compelling need to ensure the ascertainment of the truth in court proceedings" (p. 1070). Because the plaintiff (i.e., Ms. Seebach) had already related her mental and emotional condition to the issue of the court case, she herself had breached the confidential relationship with Dr. Caesar. The court of appeals affirmed the judgment of the district court denying Dr. Caesar's petition for habeas corpus.

State of Arizona v. Vickers
Supreme Court of Arizona, 633 P.2d 315 (1981)

In this case, the defendant, 21-year-old Mr. Vickers, was convicted of first-degree murder for choking and stabbing his cell mate, Mr. Ponciano, at the Arizona State Prison and was sentenced to death. The defendant appealed the case, relying on an insanity defense, specifically arguing that Ponciano was killed while the defendant was suffering an epileptic seizure. The defendant contended that statements made to an unlicensed professional, Kent Spillman, a Psychological Associate II, were considered to be privileged.

Responding to the request of the prison administrator, Spillman had conducted a mental status examination of defendant on the day of the killing. At the beginning of the interview, the defendant asked Spillman if the interview was being taped. Spillman showed the defendant an unplugged tape recorder and told him that tape-recording the interview would be illegal. Apparently reassured of confidentiality, the defendant described to Spillman how he had murdered Mr. Ponciano with premeditation. The defendant reported being mad at the victim because the victim did not awaken him for lunch and because the victim drank the defendant's Kool-Aid.

COURT DECISION

The supreme court held that "the physician-patient privilege was not applicable in regard to mental status examination of defendant by a person employed as a 'Psychological Associate II' at state prison" (p. 315). The key here is that physician-patient privilege was waived because the information was given to an unlicensed professional. The judgment of guilt and sentence of death were affirmed.

People of the State of California v. Gomez
185 Cal. Rpt. 155 Cal. Ct. Pap. (1982)

This California case held that the "psychotherapist-patient privilege" does not extend to student interns, even interns placed with the Family Court Services Office. The privilege only extends to those situations involving a psychiatrist, a licensed psychologist, a licensed clinical social worker, a credentialed school psychologist, and a licensed marriage, family, and child counselor (MFCC).

In June 1978, defendant John Gomez and his wife Celia Maldonado initiated a marital separation. Ms. Maldonado had become involved with another man, Al Herrera, who became the victim of first-degree murder in this case. After the couple separated, Mr. Gomez told Ms. Maldonado that, unless she stopped taking their son with her to Herrera's house, he would kill Herrera.

A petition for dissolution of her marriage was filed by Ms. Maldonado in July 1978. Four months later, she and Gomez met with Royal Copple, a student intern who was working with the Fresno County Family Court Services (FCS). During the session, Gomez told Copple that he would kill Herrera when the right opportunity arose. After the session, Copple informed Judge Kessler, who had referred Gomez and Maldonado to FCS, about the threat made by Gomez.

Several months later, in January 1979, Gomez met with another student intern, Jerry Rauschman, who was also serving with the FCS. While meeting with Rauschman, Gomez said that he was going to kill Herrera. Afterward, Rauschman notified both Herrera and the Fresno police of the threat.

The divorce was finalized in July 1979 and afterward there were several incidents in which Gomez made threats to his ex-wife Ms. Maldonado that somebody was going to get killed and that she would be sorry. On May 3, 1980, Gomez went to Celia Maldonado's house and shot Herrera on the front lawn.

Gomez testified in his own defense. He contended that the trial court erred in permitting the student interns to testify concerning his threats against Herrera made to them because "psychotherapist-patient privilege" of communications should apply. In regard to "criminal proceedings," Gomez also contended that the limitation of privilege to psychiatrists and psychologists but not interns invaded his constitutional right to privacy and denied him the equal protection of the law.

COURT DECISION

The defendant's appeal of his first-degree murder charge was not upheld. The court held that none of the defendant's contentions had merit. First, privileged communication does not extend to student interns as the privilege includes every licensed classification of "psychotherapist" in the State of California. It was reported that the "defendant is unable on this record to provide reason that the privilege should include 'psychology students' or 'student interns.'" The court reported that privileged communication would not apply in such a case even if the defendant's theory of applying privilege with student interns were true. Evidence Code section 1024 states that there is no privilege "if the psychotherapist has reasonable cause to believe that the patient is in such mental or emotional condition as to be dangerous to him[her]self or to the person or property of another and that disclosure of the communication is necessary to prevent threatened danger" (p. 159). Furthermore, the defendant's argument that his right to privacy was invaded was evaluated as being without merit.

Since the case of Gomez (1982), two legislative bills have been passed in the state of California. The passage of these bills changes the findings of *California v. Gomez*. These bills are (a) AB 2402 (1987), which extends the psychotherapist-patient privilege to marriage, family, and child counselor (MFCC) registered interns for both civil and criminal proceedings, and (b) AB 4168 (1988), which extends the psychotherapist-patient privilege to trainees in civil proceedings who are engaged in meeting their practicum requirements.

In re Subpoena Served Upon Jorge S. Zuniga, M.D. et al.;
In re Subpoena Served Upon Gary R. Pierce, M.D. et al.
U.S. Court of Appeals, Sixth Circuit (1983)

Two practicing psychiatrists, Jorge S. Zuniga and Gary R. Pierce, who were licensed to practice medicine in the State of Michigan, appealed orders of the Sixth U.S. District Court ruling them in civil contempt for failing to appropriately respond to a subpoena *duces tecum* (which required them to produce documents) issued to them by the Grand Jury of the Eastern District of Michigan. The two separate appeals filed by Zuniga and Pierce were consolidated into the same court hearing because their issues and arguments pertained to the same investigation. In both cases, the grand jury was investigating alleged schemes to defraud with billings submitted to Michigan Blue Cross/Blue Shield. Enforcement of subpoena duces tecum commanded both Zuniga and Pierce to produce information as to the identity of their patients, the dates on which they were treated, and the length of treatment on each date.

COURT DECISION

The U.S. court of appeals recognized that communications between a psychotherapist and a patient are privileged. However, the court also held that enforcement of subpoena duces tecum, which commanded the psychotherapists to produce information as to their patients' identities and the dates and lengths of their treatment, did not unconstitutionally infringe upon their patients' privacy rights. The identity of the patients was already known to the grand jury from insurance forms in its possession while investigating the insurance fraud. In addition, the information sought would be protected by the veil of secrecy attending grand jury proceedings. The court concluded that the refusals of Zuniga and Pierce to comply with the grand jury subpoena were unjustified and the lower courts' judgments of contempt were, therefore, proper. In other words, grand juries investigating insurance fraud may lawfully require psychotherapists to provide information on the identity of their patients, the dates on which they were treated, and the length of each treatment.

In re Donald Pebsworth
Appeal of Dr. Kersey Anita
No. 82-2726, U.S. Court of Appeals, Seventh Circuit (1983)

An Illinois psychotherapist, Dr. Kersey Anita, was investigated for possible criminal misconduct in fraudulently obtaining reimbursement from medical insurance companies through submission of false psychiatric patient care records. Donald Pebsworth, the authorized representative of Blue Cross/Blue Shield of Illinois, was subpoenaed to produce "any and all records concerning Dr. Kersey Anita. . . . Such records to include but not limited to physician service records, claim submission records, checks, bank drafts and other records of payment" (p. 262). Furthermore, the questioned information included the names of some of Dr. Anita's patients, a listing of their visits, and some of the patients' diagnoses.

Blue Cross and Dr. Anita as intervenor-appellant opposed the government's request on the basis that the production of such materials would violate the psychotherapist-patient privilege. Dr. Anita strenuously argued that the result of psychotherapists' waiver would cause prospective psychotherapy patients to have to make an unreasonable choice between not receiving treatment or receiving treatment at the cost of making public their illness. The court acknowledged this unpleasant dilemma inherent in the system of third-party medical reimbursement.

COURT DECISION

The district court held that "even assuming *arguendo* such a privilege existed, it was waived through the patients' explicit authorization of disclosure of such records to medical insurance carriers, and their consequent expectation that the confidential character of the records would necessarily be compromised pursuant to the reimbursement process" (p. 262). The Seventh Circuit U.S. Court of Appeals upheld the district court's determination that the psychotherapist-patient privilege was waived once the patients authorized disclosure of their records to medical insurance carriers. As reported in this particular court case, "a crucial element of the privilege is intent" (p. 263). Therefore, if a patient/client makes a communication expecting it to be disclosed to other persons, or even to insurance companies, there is no privilege.

William Michael Tumlinson, Appellant, v. the State of Texas, Appellee
663 S.W.2d 539 (Tex. Ct. Am p. 1983)

This criminal case relates to psychotherapist-patient privilege. The defendant, William Michael Tumlinson, a staff sergeant in the U.S. Air Force, was convicted for the offense of murder and he appealed the decision.

On March 30, 1982, the defendant checked in at the emergency room of the Air Force Regional Hospital at Carswell Air Force Base in Fort Worth, Texas, complaining that "he was nervous, anxious, and had been contemplating suicide" (p. 541). Tumlinson was then directed to speak with the chief of psychological services at the hospital, Dr. Michael

Murray, a Texas licensed psychologist. Tumlinson disclosed to Dr. Murray his fears that he might have killed a woman in Dallas, Regina Pruett. He explained that he had spent two or three days with her during the past week and he described a vision of the woman's face covered with blood, with a rope around her neck. Sergeant Tumlinson gave Dr. Murray the address and phone number of Ms. Pruett. Dr. Murray revealed Tumlinson's identity to the police as well as the details of his conversations with him. Later, following an investigation and court hearing, Tumlinson was found guilty of the offense of murder and sentenced to 99 years in the Texas Department of Corrections.

At his jury trial, Tumlinson objected to the admission of the statements he had made to Dr. Murray, on the basis that the communications applied to psychologist-patient privilege under Texas statute. The trial court overruled the defendant's objections and permitted Dr. Murray to testify regarding the conversation with Tumlinson and the information that was shared with the Dallas police. Tumlinson claimed that the trial court erred in admitting the testimony of Dr. Murray and filed an appeal.

COURT DECISION

The court of appeals held that the conversation between the defendant and the psychologist was professional and confidential. Therefore, the trial court had erred. It was agreed that the defendant's verbal agreement with Dr. Murray to call the police did not waive privileged communication. Texas statute requires that, in court proceedings, the waiver must *be in writing*.

Sims v. State of Georgia
3211 S.E. 2d 161 (Supreme Court of Georgia, 1984)

This case involved a woman, the defendant, who was convicted of murdering her husband, Marshall Sims, and sentenced to life imprisonment. The evidence at trial indicated that the couple had a turbulent relationship during their three years of marriage and that the defendant had sought private psychiatric counseling sessions for the depression and treatment of her marital problems. Occasionally, her husband would accompany her to these sessions for joint treatment. The scenario that led to the husband's death was described during the court trial as follows.

The defendant testified that, on the evening of her husband's death, she returned home around 5:30 p.m. following an appointment with her psychiatrist. Her husband requested that she prepare dinner and she declined, responding that she needed to go back to her office to complete some work. Within a few minutes, she completed the work and on her way home passed her husband, traveling in his car, in the direction of his office.

Once arriving at home, the defendant's 11-year-old son informed her that he and his dad had argued about the child's failure to complete assigned household chores. As a punishment, the child's father told the child that he could not spend the night with a friend, despite the mother having already granted permission.

The defendant reported how she went to her husband's office to discuss their differences regarding disciplining their son. She found her husband in his workshop, located on the floor above his office. She said that he was "in rage" because of the impending breakup of his law firm and described how he threw her to the floor, striking her head "four or five" times while saying that he was seeing, and would continue to see, other women. He then told her, "go home and get the gun. I'll put you out of your misery" (p. 163).

The defendant testified that her psychiatrist had previously instructed her to "obey . . . the absurd demands [the victim] made when he would go into a rage" (p. 163) on the theory that he would realize how "stupid" his demands were and "would calm down." Reflecting upon this advice, the defendant went home to get her husband's .38 caliber pistol and returned to his office. After arriving at the office, she reported that her husband was still angry and, consequently, pinned her down on her back against the top of a tablesaw while raising a large board, preparing to strike her. As she raised her arm to defend against the blow, the gun discharged.

A firearms examiner reported that the fatal shot had been fired from a distance of at least 30 inches. The medical examiner testified about the passage of the bullet through the victim's body. The state argued, recognizing the trajectory of the bullet, that it was not possible to have fired such a shot from a supine position. The jury determined that the defendant was guilty beyond a reasonable doubt.

The defendant argued that the trial court erred in refusing to permit her psychiatrist to testify about the statements her husband had made during their joint counseling sessions. She maintained that privileged communications between her husband and the psychiatrist did not exist because a third party was present during their discussions.

60   CONFRONTING MALPRACTICE

The court indicated that the presence of a third party will sometimes destroy privileged communication. However, with this particular case, the court determined that the communications between the husband and the psychiatrist were privileged, even though the wife was present during joint marital counseling. Furthermore, the court stated that the psychiatrist-patient privilege survives the death of the communicant. The judgment of the defendant as guilty in murdering her husband was affirmed.

State of Oregon, Respondent on Review v. Jerry Lee Miller, Petitioner
709 P.2d 225 (1985)

This case was heard in the Supreme Court of Oregon and relates to the scope of the psychotherapist-patient privilege in Oregon, under OEC 504. Below is a summary of the facts that were presented to the court.

The defendant telephoned his brother in California just before midnight on August 6, 1982, and said that he had just "strangled a kid." The brother advised him to talk to someone who could help him or call a mental hospital. Minutes later, the defendant telephoned Dammasch State Hospital and spoke with the secretary-receptionist, Ms. Smith, requesting to speak with a doctor. In identifying himself, the defendant gave Ms. Smith a false name. In response to questioning about "what the problem [was]," the defendant replied, "Murder. I just killed a man." She asked the defendant for the telephone number from which he was calling and told him that she would have a psychiatrist call him. The defendant told Ms. Smith the number and stated that he was at a public telephone booth.

Ms. Smith then telephoned the Clackamas County Sheriff's office, explained the situation, and told them the telephone number of the public telephone booth. Next, Ms. Smith contacted Dr. Wendy Saville, the psychiatrist on duty that night at the hospital. Dr. Saville was asked by Ms. Smith to keep the defendant on the phone so that the sheriff's office could "trace the call."

Dr. Saville talked with the defendant for 10 or 15 minutes, conducting a structured dialogue similar to those she usually had with her patients during a psychiatric interview (i.e., asking him for background information). When she asked the defendant his name, he questioned whether their conversation was confidential. Assured that Dr. Saville would not disclose any information, the defendant told her his true name and made a number of incriminating statements about his homosexual encounters with the victim, his fantasies, and how he had killed the victim.

During the telephone conversation between Dr. Saville and the defendant, a police officer from the Portland Police Bureau arrived, after having traced the call. Once the officer determined that the defendant was the person talking to Dr. Saville, he physically removed the defendant from the telephone booth, frisked him for weapons and found none, removed defendant's wallet, and placed him in the locked rear passenger area of his patrol car.

The officer returned to the telephone booth to talk with Dr. Saville. Initially, Dr. Saville declined to provide the officer with any information because she believed that the communications were confidential under the psychotherapist-patient privilege. The officer then became "angry" and insisted that she tell him what had happened. Dr. Saville then told the officer that the defendant had informed her that he had murdered someone.

The officer returned to the patrol car and continued to ask the defendant whether he had hurt someone and the whereabouts of the person. The defendant then admitted that he had "hurt someone," that he "couldn't wake him up," and said that the person was in the defendant's residential hotel room. The officer then took the defendant's room keys, called an ambulance, and drove one block to the hotel room, where he discovered the victim's body. The officer returned to his patrol car and for the first time advised the defendant of his *Miranda* rights.

COURT DECISION

The defendant was convicted of first-degree manslaughter. The court also held that "the psychotherapist-patient privilege protects the communications made in an initial conference for the purpose of establishing a psychotherapist-patient relationship, even if such a relationship is never actually formed" (p. 234). Furthermore,

> Where a patient consults a psychotherapist for professional assistance for a mental or emotional problem and reasonably believes that the psychotherapist is willing to embark upon a professional relationship, the fact that the psychotherapist has a secret ulterior purpose for the interview or

examination [as in this case] will not prevent the patient from claiming
the privilege as to confidential communication. (p. 235)

The facts of this case revealed that the defendant specifically requested,
and was assured of, confidentiality. It was only following such reassur-
ance that the defendant divulged his true name. The fact that Dr. Saville,
the psychiatrist, had an ulterior purpose (i.e., keeping the defendant on
the telephone line until the police arrived) did not justify her breaching
the psychotherapist-patient privilege, according to the court's ruling.

As a result of this court hearing, psychotherapists are to be cautioned
whenever divulging information to the police, even when danger exists.
In most cases, the public interest could be served by notifying the police
and divulging only that information indicating why a clear and immediate danger exists. A psychotherapist would rarely be justified for the
full disclosure of a client's confidences to the police.

Gregory Johnson v. Lincoln Christian College
501 N.E. 2d 1380 (1986)

Gregory Johnson was enrolled as a student at Lincoln Christian
College (LCC), Illinois from September 1976 to March 1981. His
five-year program of studies was to prepare him for a career teaching
sacred music. Although he had fully paid his tuition each year and had
completed all of his course requirements, LCC, to this day, refuses to
grant Johnson a diploma on a charge that he might be homosexual.

The charge of homosexuality arose during Johnson's last semester at
LCC. Another student, Linda Heppner, told LCC's Dean of Students
Thomas Ewald that Johnson might be homosexual. Relying solely on
the student's accusation and without further investigation, Mr. Ewald
told Johnson that he would graduate only if he sought counseling from
Kent Paris. Johnson believed that he would graduate if he complied
with LCC's demands and consequently attended private counseling
sessions with Paris. He disclosed many personal facts during their
sessions with an understanding that the information he shared with Paris
would be kept confidential. Although Johnson never consented to the
disclosure of any information discussed during these counseling sessions, Paris reported to Dean Ewald in March 1981 that Johnson had
not changed and was not progressing.

As a result of the information received from Paris, Dean Ewald contacted Johnson to say that LCC would hold a hearing in less than 24 hours at which Johnson would be required to defend himself against the rumor that he was homosexual. Dean Ewald also told Johnson that he would be dismissed from LCC because of his alleged homosexuality and that the reason for his dismissal would be stamped across his transcript. In addition, Dean Ewald telephoned Johnson's mother and informed her that LCC was dismissing her son because he was homosexual.

More than three years later, on November 29, 1984, Johnson filed a seven-count circuit court complaint against LCC and Paris, his counselor, for breach of contract and violation of the Mental Health and the Developmental Disabilities Confidentiality Act. With respect to Paris, Johnson stated three allegations: (a) that Paris breached a confidentiality contract with him and violated the Mental Health and Developmental Disabilities Confidentiality Act, (b) that Paris's disclosure of the confidential information tortuously interfered with Johnson's college student contract with LCC, and (c) that Paris invaded Johnson's privacy by disclosing confidential information.

COURT DECISION

The Circuit Court of Logan County, Illinois, dismissed the case, and Johnson appealed. The Appellate Court of Illinois then heard the case and the order of the circuit court was affirmed in part, reversed in part, and remanded. The appellate court held that five of Johnson's seven complaints were improperly dismissed and that two of the complaints were properly dismissed. The two complaints that were again dismissed pertained to Johnson's allegations that Paris (a) breached a contract with him and violated the Mental Health and Developmental Disabilities Confidentiality Act and (b) invaded his privacy by disclosing essential information. The one complaint filed against Paris by Johnson that was reversed in the appellate court decision was that Paris's disclosure of the essential information tortuously interfered with Johnson's college student contract with LCC. It is important to recognize that this particular appellate court decision in Illinois determined that an individual who is perceived by a client to be a psychotherapist, even if he or she does not hold professional licensure credentials, is bound by the "psychotherapist-patient privilege" of confidentiality.

The People of the State of Colorado, Petitioner, v.
District Court in and for the city and county of Denver, Colorado
719 P.2d 722 (1986)

This criminal case involved a defendant who was charged with first-degree sexual assault. As a result of the emotional trauma experienced, the victim of the offense sought professional counseling treatment with the organization Ending Violence Effectively (EVE). The client's therapist at EVE practiced under the supervision of a licensed psychiatrist, Dr. Jeffrey Corwin.

The defendant issued a subpoena to the therapist requesting production of the victim's psychological treatment records, hoping that information disclosed to the therapist would differ from the information divulged to police officials. At a hearing on the return of the subpoena, the prosecution objected to the defendant's request on the grounds that such practice would violate the victim's psychologist-patient privilege established by the State of Colorado. However, the respondent court reasoned that the defendant's constitutional right of confrontation surmounted the statutory privilege. Therefore, the respondent court ordered that the records be reviewed in camera (i.e., in proceedings that take place privately in the judge's chambers or in court without spectators) for relevant information pertaining to the case or to the credibility of the defendant's complaints.

COURT DECISION

The supreme court later ruled that the respondent court exceeded its jurisdiction in granting the defendant's request to investigate the records. The respondent court contended that the psychologist-patient privilege was not applicable to the victim's treatment records because the victim's therapist was not a licensed psychologist and there was no written contract between EVE and Dr. Corwin, the therapist's supervisor. The supreme court disagreed with the contention and quoted from the statute:

> A licensed psychologist shall not be examined without the consent of his client as to any communication made by the client to him . . . nor shall a licensed psychologist's secretary, stenographer, or clerk be examined without the consent of his employer concerning any fact, the knowledge of which he has acquired in such capacity; nor shall any person who has

participated in any psychological therapy, conducted under the supervision of a person authorized by law to conduct such therapy . . . be examined concerning any knowledge gained during the course of such therapy without the consent of the person to whom the testimony sought relates. (p. 724)

The supreme court reported that "the purpose of the statutory psychologist-patient privilege is to enhance the effective diagnosis and treatment of illness by protecting the patient from the embarrassment and humiliation that might be caused by the [psychologist's] disclosure of information imparted to him [her] by the patient during the course of a consultation for purposes of [psychological] treatment" (p. 724). It was also noted that whether Dr. Corwin's (i.e., the licensed psychiatrist serving as the supervisor for the therapist who was not licensed) services were performed while having a written or oral contract was immaterial. The court concluded that the psychologist-patient privilege was applicable to the therapist's records of the victim's psychological treatment. The fact that the sexual assault victim's therapist was not a licensed psychologist did not preclude the victim from asserting psychologist-patient privilege because the therapist was supervised by a licensed psychiatrist.

State of Minnesota, Respondent, v. Toby Lynn Gullekson, Appellant
383 N.W. 2d 338 (Minn. Ct. Pap. 1986)

The Minnesota Court of Appeals held that statements made by a third-degree murder defendant, Toby Gullekson, to a psychologist and program administrators were not privileged because the meeting was not indicated to be confidential. The facts pertaining to the court hearing follow.

Gullekson was charged with second-degree criminal sexual conduct. As a condition for probation, he entered the Intensive Treatment Program for Sexual Aggressives (ITPSA) at the Minnesota Security Hospital in St. Peter. Gullekson and other program participants were encouraged by the hospital staff to disclose any secrets that were bothering them that might interfere with their treatment. On September 15, 1984, following an unsupervised group therapy session, Gullekson and three other group members contacted Finn Ford, the therapy group's counselor. Gullekson volunteered information to Ford about how he had entered a building two years earlier in Fertile, Minnesota, with the intent of burglarizing it. However, after entering the building, he decided not to burglarize it and, on his way out, set some refuse on fire. He read in the newspaper the following morning that a man had died in the fire.

Ford informed Gullekson that he would have to report the information to the program director, Richard Seeley, and that the information would also probably be reported to Gullekson's probation officer and "legal officials." Gullekson said that he understood.

Ford communicated the information to Seeley and Anne Amundson, the assistant program director. A meeting was then held on September 17, 1984, for Seeley, Amundson, and Bruce Hawkinson, a staff psychologist, to hear Gullekson repeat the statements he had made two days earlier to Ford. Gullekson was verbally informed by Hawkinson at the beginning of the meeting that anything he said would be reported to the authorities. Gullekson replied that he understood and then proceeded to repeat the information he had earlier told Ford.

The information was then reported to law enforcement authorities. Following an investigation, it was determined that there had been a fire in Fertile, Minnesota, on November 20, 1982, in which a man had been killed. Subsequently, Gullekson was charged with third-degree murder.

Gullekson moved to exclude the statements he made on September 15 and 17 on the basis of privileged communication under Minnesota statute. The ruling by the trial court was that the September 15 statements were privileged; however, the September 17 statements were not privileged because they were made at a meeting not intended to be confidential. Gullekson appealed the trial court's ruling.

COURT DECISION

The Minnesota Court of Appeals determined that the trial court did not err in concluding that statements made by Gullekson to treatment staff were not privileged. Gullekson also contended in the court of appeals that he had not been given a *Miranda* warning. The court responded by reporting that there had been no case found providing that incriminating statements made to treatment personnel in a security hospital should be suppressed if not preceded by a *Miranda* warning.

State of New Jersey, Plaintiff-Respondent, v. Benjamin McBride,
Defendant-Appellant
517 A.2d 152 (N.J. Superior Court, Appellate Division, 1986)

Defendant Benjamin McBride appealed convictions of second-degree aggravated assault and two counts of terrorist threats for incidents that occurred with his wife, the victim, on May 10, May 20, and June 30, 1982, and March 15, 1983. The defendant was sentenced to a total of 25 years with 10 years of parole ineligibility.

The May 10, 1982, incident occurred after the couple had been married less than four and a half months. The defendant was angered at that time because his wife had received the "Outstanding Mother of the Year" award from her church in her maiden name. Later that evening, as the couple returned from a political affair in Newark, the wife received a laceration over her eye, bruising and swelling of her hands and knees, and head trauma. After running to the house of a neighbor, she was taken to a nearby hospital, where police were summoned. The following day she was released from the hospital and no arrest was made.

The McBrides attended an election meeting on May 20, 1982, after which, with Mrs. McBride's minister and another woman, they went to the McBride residence for cocktails. The McBrides argued intensely while the guests attempted to intervene. As the couple fled into the street, Benjamin caught his wife and brought her back to the house and allegedly stated, "I missed you last time—I'm going to kill you this time" (p. 155). Later, Benjamin was arrested and released on bail.

The incident that occurred on June 30, 1982, involved Benjamin striking his wife in the head with a metal pipe, banging her head on the asphalt driveway, and choking her, whereupon she blacked out. The victim was then hospitalized in three different institutions for the next five months as a result of this attack. Her consciousness and cognitive functions were impaired, resulting in an organic brain syndrome that caused the symptoms of disturbed mental behavior and "confabulation" (making up stories) as well as retrograde amnesia (the inability to recall events just before the injury).

After Mrs. McBride was released from the hospital on November 24, 1982, she resumed living with her husband Benjamin, allegedly without memory of who had assaulted her on June 30, 1982. In January 1983, she requested to the grand jury that the indictment concerning the May 10 and 20, 1982, incidents be dismissed, because she and her husband had reconciled. Furthermore, she filed a claim with the Violent Crime Compensation Board concerning the June 30 event, asserting that the perpetrator was unknown.

The fourth incident occurred on March 15, 1983, when Benjamin allegedly again threatened to injure his wife. His wife reported having fallen down a staircase a day or two later, bumping her head and having a "flashback" during which she regained her memory of the June 30 incident. Consequently, she brought charges against her husband for the June 30 incident and reactivated her earlier complaints on the May 10 and 20 events. Benjamin was then tried for multiple offenses, and he employed two different attorneys to support his testimony of the four different incidences.

The defendant contended that the trial court erred in preventing his counsel from examining Dr. Saur (i.e., the physician who discharged Benjamin's wife from the hospital on November 24, 1982) concerning Dr. Fox's psychological report. Dr. Saur testified that part of his post-discharge diagnosis and treatment of Mrs. McBride was based upon Dr. Fox's psychological report. The report referred to Mrs. McBride's mental disorder as not caused by the head trauma but by the victim's problems in dealing with reality. The court noted that Dr. Fox's reporting of information to Dr. Saud was protected by the physician-patient privilege. However, the question raised was whether the victim, Mrs. McBride, by signing the criminal complaint, implicitly waived the psychologist-patient privilege, at least insofar as the diagnosis of her mental condition.

COURT DECISION

The New Jersey Appeals Court determined that the victim, by signing the criminal complaint, waived her privilege with regard to the psychologist's diagnosis of her mental condition, which was claimed to be a result of the defendant's conduct. The court also reported that the trial court had erred in refusing to permit the defendant's counsel to cross-examine the state's experts concerning their reliance on the report of the psychologist who had evaluated and treated the victim. Furthermore, it was indicated that the trial judge should have conducted an in camera inspection of the psychological report to determine relevance. However, the appeals court also noted that they could not determine whether the psychologist's report "would or could have affected the outcome of the trial" (p. 160). The case was remanded to the trial judge for further proceedings and the appeals court did not retain jurisdiction.

The New Jersey court case noted that, "although the psychologist-patient privilege affords even greater confidentiality than the physician-patient privilege, it still may be defeated where 'common notions of fairness clearly compel at least limited disclosure of otherwise confidential communications' " (p. 159).

Newell I. Cutter II, Plaintiff and Appellant, v. Robert Brownbridge and Renata Brownbridge—Robert Brownbridge, a Professional Corporation, Defendants and Respondents
228 Cal. Rptr. 545 (Cal. Ct. App. 1986)

This case presents the issue of whether a client's psychotherapist is immune from liability for disclosure of privileged information voluntarily made in a judicial proceeding without first having claimed the psychotherapist-patient privilege. Robert Brownbridge, a licensed clinical social worker who was the defendant in this case, was the psychotherapist for Newell I. Cutter II between 1976 and 1982. From the beginning of the therapeutic relationship, Brownbridge had informed Cutter that all communications and diagnoses would be maintained in confidence.

In August 1982, Brownbridge responded to a request by Cutter's former wife to write a declaration describing his diagnosis of Cutter. The court record did not indicate the process by which the declaration came into existence (i.e., the purpose for requesting the declaration or Brownbridge's rationale for voluntarily providing the information). Later, however, the declaration was filed by Cutter's former wife's attorney as evidence for legal action to suspend Cutter's right to visit his children. It is important to mention that Brownbridge "voluntarily, and not as a result of subpoena or other legal compulsion" (p. 547) composed the written declaration describing his diagnosis and prognosis of Cutter as well as damaging personal details. Subsequent to the written declaration, Cutter maintained that he "suffered humiliation, mortification, shame and severe memory injury and distress and . . . loss of visitation of his children" (p. 547).

In March 1983, Cutter filed a suit against Brownbridge, alleging Brownbridge had "violated his constitutional right of privacy and his common law right of privacy, was a breach of an implied covenant of confidentiality, and constituted intentional infliction of emotional distress" (p. 547). Brownbridge objected on the ground that his declaration was immune from civil liability. He also claimed a conditional privilege based upon his duty to warn others because he perceived Cutter to be dangerous.

COURT DECISION

The California Superior Court indicated that, although Cutter's statements to his psychotherapist are protected by his constitutional right of privacy, an infringement of that right may be constitutionally permitted when the need for disclosure outweighs the right to privacy. Thus a balancing of interests policy must be applied to cases such as this one. In this case, the court determined that Cutter's constitutional right to privacy outweighed the policies underlying the judicial proceedings immunity. The privileged communications statute that exists between psychotherapist and client pertains to a client's constitutional right to privacy. Brownbridge had violated his client's right to privacy and confidentiality by voluntarily publishing material concerning his client without first resorting to a prior judicial determination.

Implications

a. Clients of nonlicensed therapists (i.e., interns, students, assistants) *may not* have "psychotherapist-patient privilege" unless specified by law (as in California, effective January 1, 1989, or in Illinois, if the client perceives the individual to be a professional therapist).

b. Student interns should be protected by malpractice insurance coverage. It is important that students (i.e., counselor trainees) find out whether or not they are covered for malpractice by their school or internship placement site. If not, they may purchase it through professional organizations at a reasonable cost.

c. You should know the judgments of your state regarding limits of confidentiality and privilege. (For example, compare the cases of *Gomez* with *the People v. the City and County of Denver, Colorado.*)

d. If your client utilizes health insurance, he or she may have signed authorization to disclose information. Grand juries investigating insurance fraud may lawfully require psychotherapists to provide requested information as to the identity of their clients, the dates on which they were treated, and the length of each treatment.

e. If a therapist enters psychotherapy as a client and uses third-party payments, he or she may be vulnerable to having this information used against him or her in the future.

f. It is advisable that clear standards and procedures be developed for establishing the parameters of disclosure to law enforcement officials and for resisting pressure from those officials should they insist on more information.

g. At times, the courts interpret the law literally and, at other times, the courts interpret the intent of the law.

h. Sometimes therapists are lower on the hierarchy than medical doctors but in New Jersey the confidentiality is "greater."

i. Generally speaking, you should know the hierarchy of influence on court decisions:

(1) agency policy and procedures
(2) state judicial decisions
(3) other states' judicial decisions

j. Being a client in therapy at any time may be a risk (e.g., going into politics later, the information may be revealed and used against a person or obtaining a security clearance).

k. In doing marital and family therapy, you should know what the state in which you are practicing says about privileged communication with more than two people in the room.

l. In a potential fraud case, *all* of the therapist's cases involving that insurance carrier *may* be subpoenaed.

m. The therapist should get a waiver in writing when a client *first* reveals that he or she understands the therapist is going to talk to supervisor/authorities or the like. Also, if the client wishes to waive confidentiality, this waiver needs to be in writing.

n. If mental status is an issue in a court case, the therapist *may* be ordered by the court to answer questions regarding his or her client.

o. All states have laws mandating reporting of suspected child abuse and many states mandate reporting of elder abuse.

p. If the client is a minor, the psychotherapist may not be able to maintain confidentiality. You should know the ages during which your state considers a person to be a "minor."

q. Your state may have various *exceptions* to confidentiality, such as in California, where a breach of contract opens the door for the psychotherapist to go to a small claims court to collect a fee.

r. While working with insurance companies concerning third-party payments, give only the information requested and only the information that is in agreement with your client having signed a waiver.

s. You protect yourself legally if you only do specifically what is court ordered.

t. The therapist is better protected if he or she is able to obtain written agreements in contract form that delineate what will occur in the sessions to come.

Commentary

Do your clients have a right to *privacy, confidentiality* (within the law), and *privileged communication*? Are you aware of the differences among these terms? Are you aware of how important it is to maintain and understand the limits of confidentiality between you and your client? Do you routinely inform your clients about the limits of confidentiality? Do you hesitate to report when the law requires that you do? Do you know the rules regarding the limits of confidentiality in your state? The following definitions may be helpful for you to distinguish the differences so that you can inform your clients of their rights in regard to these issues.

Confidentiality refers to the idea that, when a person reveals private information and the person receiving the information makes a covert or overt agreement that this information will not be revealed except for the reason for which it was intended, the receiver of the information is held accountable to keep this agreement. Such a situation is considered confidential by the courts when there is a psychotherapist-patient relationship.

Privilege is a legal protection against being coerced to break a promise of confidentiality in legal proceedings (such as in a trial or grand jury inquiry). That is, your clients are accorded a privilege of choosing whether the information that you have about them (such as in their records) can be presented in court. There are exceptions in which a client is not granted privilege.

If you do understand the importance of confidentiality, it will not surprise you that 6.4% of total claims in malpractice suits against psychologists were brought because these psychologists either failed to maintain confidentiality or failed to report abuse when their state outlined the limits (Pope, 1989, p. 25). Miller and Thelen (1987) report that less than 50% of psychologists either are unwilling to report when mandated or fail to inform their client about the limits. These limits may vary from state to state, but in "all states when the welfare of a child is in danger, reporting of the incident to the proper authorities is now mandatory" (p. 707).

We suggest, and others agree, that you inform your clients during the beginning of therapy about the limits of confidentiality. Principle 5 of the APA's *Ethical Principles of Psychologists* (1989) states: "Where appropriate, psychologists inform their client of the legal limits of confidentiality." You can place this information in writing and have your clients sign a form to demonstrate that they knew from the beginning of treatment about their rights or lack of them in regard to confidential information. (See Appendix B for an example of a consent form.) Stromberg et al. (1988) suggest that you put in writing and inform your clients that they lose the right to a confidential relationship:

(1) when they consent to disclosure
(2) when a law requires reporting of an event, such as child abuse
(3) when there is the duty to warn or protect
(4) when reimbursement or other legal rules require disclosure
(5) when they bring a lawsuit . . .
(6) in an emergency.

In cases where *reimbursement* is necessary, you will need to explain to your clients that insurance companies can create a file about them. Insurance companies mandate that therapists give them certain information about clients in order to be reimbursed. Such information can include diagnosis and times and place of appointments, and some companies, such as CHAMPUS, require treatment plans. Your clients need to understand that you have no control over "what they do with it or who may see it" (Stromberg et al., 1988, p. 388). Stromberg et al. (1988) suggest that you give an option to your client to pay you directly so that you do not have to create a record outside of your office. We agree that every client must be aware of his or her options and be fully informed regarding who receives information about them and what it will be.

Conclusions

Here are some recommendations regarding confidentiality:

(1) Do not discuss a case without a valid release unless ordered by a court.

(2) Keep all records under lock and key.

(3) If you have a secretary, make sure he or she is trained to keep material confidential.

(4) Know your state's laws that involve exceptions to confidentiality.

(5) Make sure you discuss the limits of confidentiality with your client.

(6) When providing requested information, send it by certified mail.

(7) In doing marital and family therapy, know what the state in which you are practicing says about privileged communication with more than two people in the room.

(8) If the client is a minor, the psychotherapist may not be able to maintain confidentiality. You should know the age below which your state considers a person to be a "minor."

(9) In situations where the psychotherapist must report by law, the information given should be limited to only what is necessary and related to the issue at hand.

Summary

Establishing and maintaining confidentiality with clients during the therapeutic relationship is an essential ingredient for the client to trust and willingly self-disclose very personal and private information. *Confidentiality*, *privileged communication*, and *privacy* are three important terms that are related yet somewhat different. "Psychotherapist-patient privilege" is granted by state statute and belongs to the client/patient. Nonlicensed therapists' clients may not have privileged communication unless specified by state law. Employing agencies of therapists need to develop and establish clear standards and procedures for breaching confidentiality in cases of emergency. Although some states specify that confidentiality may be breached whenever there is suspected harm to "self or others," other states also include suspected harm to "physical property." Victims of crime may be waiving their privilege of confidentiality and should be informed by the treating therapist. Therapists need to know the parameters of disclosure to law enforcement officials and how to resist pressure from those officials should they insist on more information. Whenever releasing information about a client, the therapist should receive the client's consent in writing. Before speaking to a supervisor/authorities, the therapist should receive a written consent form from the client to waive confidentiality. Even in those instances when the therapist has the legal right to breach confidentiality in cases of suspected harm, it is recommended that the client be informed by the therapist beforehand as a means of possibly retaining the professional relationship. If the client is a *minor* (a term that is defined differently among the states), the therapist may not be able to maintain confidentiality.

Vignette

Therapist Z is seeing a 10-year-old girl who tells him that she hates her father because he beats her mother. The parents contact Dr. Z and want information about how their daughter is doing. They would really like to know some of the things she is talking about, because they would like to be more involved and help their daughter. Dr. Z gives them a general sense of her progress but does not share specifics. He does not discuss this with the girl, because he does not want to chip away at the trust they have built up. What do you think of his practices? How might you deal with the situation differently?

Questions to Consider

(1) In *Sims v. State of Georgia* (1984): Even though this communication was privileged, why couldn't it be utilized in court for such a critical situation?

(2) In *Sims v. State of Georgia* (1984): It is an admirable quality to respect the deceased, but why were previous information/happenings overlooked?

(3) In *Schaffer v. Spicer* (1974): To whose request do you release information? What should you do in the case of releasing the information of a client who is a minor, whose parents are maritally separated and battling for child custody? How does the therapist determine what information to release? Should the therapist consult with someone on this when an attorney requests release?

(4) In *Cutter II v. Brownbridge* (1986): Is it ethical to volunteer this type of information?

(5) In *Cutter II v. Brownbridge* (1986): What reason(s) might you have for not informing your client of having to break confidentiality?

(6) Would you inform your client who is using insurance to pay for her or his counseling that confidentiality may be breached if there is an investigation of possible fraud in billings to insurance companies?

(7) How far would you be willing to go to question the court on the confidentiality issue? Would you be willing to go to an appeal to protect your client? To jail?

(8) A client in the therapist's waiting room overhears a telephone conversation between the secretary and another client. Would this be a breach of confidentiality?

(9) A client in the therapist's waiting room overhears the secretary playing back messages on the office telephone answering machine. Would this be a breach of confidentiality?

(10) What would you include in your *Professional Disclosure Statement* (i.e., a statement informing clients about the therapist's professional background and experiences and about the therapeutic process) concerning the limits of confidentiality?

4

Privacy

Privacy is often discussed in comparison with the terms *confidentiality* and *privileged communication*. Van Hoose and Kottler (1985, p. 48) define *privacy* as "the freedom of clients to determine for themselves the extent and circumstances under which their behavior, beliefs, and opinions are shared with others." Schutz (1982, p. 11) notes that an invasion of privacy "requires that private facts be disclosed to more than a small group of persons, and such disclosure must be offensive to a reasonable person of ordinary sensibilities." Schutz (1982, p. 11) distinguishes "invasion of privacy" from "defamation of character" on two grounds: "[a] even complementary material can be an invasion of privacy; [b] the intrusion into privacy does not require publication of private information—merely the intrusion into the person's private conduct." Hopkins and Anderson (1985, p. 61) mention how a counselor may "be held liable in an action for invasion of privacy if derogatory information is communicated to a third party who has no need or privilege to receive it." These authors also note that, "when a counselor administers a test to a client without first fully informing the client of the criteria to be used, what skills or factors the test is designed to

measure, the uses to which results of the test may be put, or to explain
the results, the counselor runs the risk of invading the client's right to
privacy" (Hopkins & Anderson, 1985, p. 63). A therapist who makes
phone calls to a client's place of work and identifies him- or herself as
a therapist might be providing grounds for an invasion of privacy action.
Or a therapist who uses a picture or the name of a client for commercial
publicity, without the client's consent, may be liable for invasion of
privacy (Woody et al., 1984).

The following court cases make reference to alleged invasion of
privacy. It is worth noting that a therapist may be held liable for invasion
of privacy even years following the termination of the psychotherapeutic relationship. The privacy of a client is to be respected not only while
he or she is engaged in ongoing therapy but for an indefinite period
following termination as well.

Court Cases

(1) *Doe v. Roe* (**1977**)
(2) *Davis v. Monsanto Company* (**1986**)
(3) *Bratt v. International Business Machines Corporation* (**1986**)

Case Reviews

Jane Doe, Plaintiff, v. Joan Roe, and Peter Poe, Defendants
Supreme Court, New York County
400 N.Y.S. 668 (N.Y. Supreme Ct., Nov. 21, 1977)

At the time of this court case, in 1977, the State of New York had not
recognized a common law "right of privacy." In addition no previous
New York case had dealt with the issue of a psychotherapist breaching
a patient's privilege of confidentiality. Consequently, the Supreme
Court of New York County dealt with the right of privacy by making
reference to two other sources: (a) the public policy of the state pro-
claimed by statute and (b) a state regulation that "bars a physician from
disclosing a patient's confidences; and the implied promises of confidentiality which every physician makes to his [or her] patient" (p. 676).
The file for this lawsuit, by prior order of the court, had been sealed
from indiscriminate viewing, and pseudonyms were used for all parties

involved. Jane Doe, a former patient of psychiatrist Dr. Joan Roe, brought an action against the psychiatrist and the psychiatrist's husband, Mr. Peter Poe, alleging that the defendants had invaded her privacy by publishing a book that revealed details of confidential information that had been obtained from psychotherapeutic relationships. Plaintiff Jane Doe sought to recover for compensatory damages and an additional sum of $50,000 for punitive damages as a consequence of the book's publication; $50,000 was the sum she claimed to have already incurred for attorneys' fees regarding this lawsuit.

The two defendants in this case were Dr. Joan Roe, a physician who had practiced psychiatry for more than 50 years, and her husband, Peter Poe, who had been a psychologist for some 25 years. The plaintiff, Jane Doe, and her late, former husband had each been psychoanalytic patients of Dr. Roe for several years. Eight years following Dr. Roe's termination of psychoanalytic treatment with Jane Doe and her former husband, the two defendants coauthored a "book which reported verbatim and extensively the patients' thoughts, feelings, and emotions, their sexual and other fantasies and biographies, their most intimate personal relationships, and the disintegration of their marriage" (p. 671). Dr. Roe's diagnoses of illness suffered by the patients and one of their children were interspersed among footnotes in the book. The book had last been discussed by Dr. Roe with her patient two years before the psychotherapeutic relationship was terminated and was published 10 years later. At the time that Jane Doe's suit had been brought to court, 220 copies of the book had already been sold. Publicity concerning the court case appeared to prompt an increased sale of the defendants' book to their university students and colleagues.

The defendants contended that Jane Doe had consented to the book's publication while she was in therapy. The court viewed this defense as being without substance because the patient was still engaged in psychotherapy and the nature of the illness for which she was being treated was that of her being "unreliable." Furthermore, the consent was never obtained in writing. Thus it was concluded that consent had never been granted by the patient to the defendant.

The defendants argued "not only that there was no unlawful disclosure, the patient's identity having been fully concealed, but that no right of action exists even if the plaintiff is recognizable in this volume" (p. 671). Further, the defendants asserted they had not violated the plaintiff's privacy as under the Civil Rights Law for they did not use the plaintiff's "name, portrait, or picture" in their book (p. 675).

A major contention presented by the defendants was that "the physician's obligation of confidentiality is not absolute and must give way to the general public interest" (p. 677). They claimed that there was a scientific value in the field of psychiatry for publishing their book that outweighed the patient's right to privacy. The court made reference to several other court cases that cited exceptions under which psychotherapists could breach confidentiality: (a) to give warning where a patient clearly presents a danger to others (e.g., *Tarasoff v. Regents of the University of California*, 13 Cal. 3d 177, 118 Cal. Rptr. 129, 131, 529 P.2d 553, at p. 555, 1974), (b) to disclose the existence of a contagious disease (e.g., P.H.L. 2101; *Hofmann v. Blackmon*, 241 So. 2d 752, Fla. App. 1970; *Wojeik v. Aluminum Co. of America*, 18 Misc. 2d 740, 183 N.Y.S. 2d 351), and (c) to report gunshot and other wounds (e.g., PL 265.25). However, the court was emphatic in viewing the defendants' defense as having failed, by stating "in no case . . . has the curiosity of education of the medical profession superseded the duty to confidentiality" (p. 677).

COURT DECISION

The Supreme Court of New York County ruled that plaintiff Jane Doe be awarded $20,000 for compensatory damages from Dr. Joan Roe and Mr. Peter Poe as a result of the published book. It was reported that "she suffered acute embarrassment on learning the extent to which friends, colleagues, employer, students and others, had read or read of the book" (p. 679). Her livelihood was threatened, and she suffered from insomnia and nightmares. "She became reclusive as a consequence of the shame and humiliation induced by the book's publication and her well-being and emotional health were significantly impaired for three years" (p. 679). Although the plaintiff also sought to recover money for punitive damages, the court determined "that the defendants' acts were not willful, malicious or wanton" (p. 679) and, therefore, such an award was not warranted. There were no punitive damages available because the defendants: (a) had sufficiently concealed the identity of the patient and her family, (b) believed that they were rendering a public service by publishing the book, and (c) had no motive to harm. Also, the sum of $50,000 that the plaintiff tried to recover for the costs she had already incurred for attorneys' fees with this case was not granted. Such money would have only been granted if the defendants had acted "in bad faith."

The court recognized that the coauthor of the book, Mr. Poe, was not involved in a physician-patient relationship with the plaintiff and, therefore, had no contractual relationship to her. However, he knew that the book's contents were the patient's production in psychoanalysis. Consequently, he was considered by the court to be a coviolator of the patient's rights and equally held liable for damages. Both coauthors, their heirs, and assignees were permanently prohibited by the court from further distribution and sales of the book.

Howard Davis, Plaintiff, v. Monsanto Company, Defendant
U.S. District Court
627 F. Supp. 418 (S.D. West Virginia, Jan. 14, 1986)

This case was presented to the U.S. district court on January 14, 1986. Both the plaintiff, Howard Davis, and the defendant, Monsanto Company, each moved for summary judgment (that is, disposition without a jury trial) by motions filed on November 4, 1985. Howard Davis brought action against his employer, alleging tortious invasion of privacy and breach of contract. Concerning the motions for summary judgments, the court found the following information undisputed.

Howard Davis was a steelworker employed by Monsanto Company. His position entailed working with potentially dangerous chemicals. In March 1983, he began experiencing marital difficulties. A year later, in March 1984, his wife separated from him and, during that month, he experienced difficulty sleeping, unexpectedly lost 28 pounds in four weeks, and felt nervous. He then voluntarily scheduled an appointment to see mental health counselor, Lyn Lewis, on the morning of March 20, 1984. Lewis subcontracted counseling services for Personal Performance Consultants (PPC), Inc., which provided counseling services to the employees at Monsanto Company as a fringe benefit. At the time of this case, Lewis held a master's degree in counseling and had practiced psychotherapy for some 14 years.

During the initial counseling session on March 20, 1984, at Lewis's office in Charleston, West Virginia, counselor Lewis concluded that Mr. "Davis was dangerous to the point of being suicidal to himself and homicidal toward his wife and others, and that he could easily be provoked into creating a life-threatening situation in the work place and other places" (p. 520). By 2:30 p.m. that same day, several people had been notified concerning Davis's condition. Lewis first contacted Rick

Kinyon, corporate manager of operations of PPC in St. Louis, Missouri, who, in turn, contacted Don Johnson, the personnel supervisor at Monsanto. Johnson then communicated the information to Merle Mahler, Monsanto's personnel superintendent at its Nitro plant. Mahler and Johnson then contacted Lewis to confirm Davis's condition, and she recommended that Mr. Davis be removed from his job and be urged to seek medical treatment.

Mahler, abiding by Lewis's recommendation, contemplated removing Davis from the job. However, before taking such action, he felt that it was first necessary to contact Thomas Collier, the president of Davis's bargaining representative, United Steelworkers of America, Union Local No. 12610. Mahler then conducted a meeting with Johnson, Collier, and Gregory Witt—a union committeeman. The union representative disagreed with counselor Lewis's assessment and the recommendation that Davis be removed from work. Witt arranged a meeting to discuss the situation with Lewis himself and, as of that same day, March 20, 1984, Davis was still permitted to work. However, Davis later took medical disability leave for four weeks and in January 1985 retired at the age of 62.

In December 1984, Howard Davis filed action against Monsanto Company on two counts. The first count alleged a tortious invasion of privacy, and the second count alleged a breach of contract. The court considered the plaintiff and the defendant's motions for summary judgment first upon the tort theory and second on the contract theory.

COURT DECISION

The U.S. district court ruled in favor of the defendant. The court held that "[a] employer's limited disclosure of the information did not constitute the publication necessary to establish cause of action for public disclosure of private facts; [b] disclosures were qualifiedly immune and absolutely privileged; and [c] breach of contract action was barred for failure to resort to grievance process contained in collective bargaining agreement" (p. 418).

The court identified four types of invasion of privacy that were recognized under West Virginia law: "[a] unreasonable intrusion upon the seclusion of another; [b] appropriation of another's name or likeness; [c] unreasonable publicity given to another's private life; and [d] publicity that unreasonably places another in a false light before the public" (pp. 420-421). In this case, Davis complained of the third type (i.e., that Monsanto unreasonably publicized facts about his private life). Responding to Davis's complaint, the court indicated four elements under Section 652D of the Restatement (2d) of Torts (1977) that the plaintiff needed to prove in order to establish a cause of action:

[a] that there was a public disclosure by the Defendant of facts regarding the Plaintiff; [b] that the facts disclosed were private facts; [c] that the disclosure of such facts is highly offensive and objectionable to a reasonable person of reasonable sensibilities; and [d] that the public has no legitimate interest in the facts disclosed. (p. 421)

The court also clarified that a difference exists between the "publication" required in privacy actions of the types outlined by Section 652D and the mere communication to a third party required under libel law: "It is not an invasion of privacy to communicate the private fact to a single person or a small group of persons. The tort of invasion of privacy requires widespread publicity" (p. 421). Thus, with this case, because personnel at Monsanto talked with only two persons outside the management level, such limited disclosure did not constitute the widespread "publication" required to establish a cause of action against the defendant.

The court discussed how the "publication of private facts may also be privileged, either absolutely or qualifiedly" (p. 421). It was recognized that an absolute privilege of a communication of private facts may exist if required by law. However, with this case, the Monsanto Company has qualified privilege because of its responsibility, as an employer in West Virginia, to protect and provide all of its employees with a safe place to work. Additionally, it was understood that a communicator is entitled to a qualified privilege if either (a) "the communication of such information is in furtherance of the communicator's legitimate interest" or (b) "where the communication is for the purpose of another's legitimate interests" (p. 421). Thus, in this case, "Monsanto's divulgence to the Union was in furtherance of its own interests in protecting its plant and employees from danger . . . [and] furthered the Union officials' legitimate interest in protecting its membership from danger and protecting the employment rights of Davis. Accordingly, Monsanto's disclosures were qualifiedly immune" (p. 422). Moreover, Monsanto as an employer was required by law to make the workplace safe, and, therefore, in these circumstances, "Monsanto's disclosures were absolutely privileged" (p. 422).

Davis also unsuccessfully claimed that his contractual rights as a union member had been violated. However, the contract stated that any grievance action brought pursuant to the collective bargaining agreement must adhere to three-step grievance process and be initiated within the six-month statute of limitations. First, Davis had failed to abide by the three-step grievance process as outlined. Second, the incident giving rise to his claim occurred in March 1984, but Davis did not file action until December 1984, that is, nine months later. Thus, in accordance with the statute of limitations, the action was barred.

Robert Bratt et al., Plaintiffs, Appellants, v. International Business Machines Corporation et al., Defendants, Appellees
U.S. Court of Appeals, First Circuit
785 F.2d 352 (argued Dec. 4, 1985; decided March 6, 1986)

Due to bad nerves, headaches, and inability to sleep, an employee consulted a physician retained by the employer. After examination, the physician called the employee's superior and gave the opinion that the employee was paranoid and should be seen by a psychiatrist. When the superior disclosed this information to his boss, the boss wrote a memo summarizing the information and then sent the memo to other personnel.

COURT DECISION

The Massachusetts Supreme Court held that publishing an employer's opinion of unfitness for the job due to mental disorder is defamatory, but the disclosure by an employer of defamatory medical information concerning an employee, which is relevant to the employee's job performance, is conditionally privileged. Summary judgment was granted to the employer.

Implications

a. Consent to publish details of confidential therapy must be obtained in writing.
b. Employers have a responsibility to provide a safe place to work. Thus they may have a "need to know" such factors as the instability or dangerousness of an employee. However, it would be wise for the

therapist to obtain (in writing) a release from the client before contacting the employer.

c. Therapists should disclose information about potential harm from a client only to those who are primarily in danger or to those who are directly involved in preventing harm to self, others (police, paramedics and the like), or physical property. Although duty to warn and protect takes precedence over withholding confidential client information, therapists need to be careful about to whom they reveal such information.

d. Employers, as well as insurance companies (when third-party payments are involved), may have access to information concerning an employee's therapy (*Davis v. Monsanto Company*). It is imperative that clients be informed at the outset of therapy regarding the limits of confidentiality whether or not insurance is covering the cost. Written consent by the client is highly advisable.

e. Whenever conducting psychotherapy with a client or consulting with other professionals concerning a client, therapists need to be aware of others who might be able to overhear or observe the conversation. For example, who else is in the room? Therapists need to consider such factors as the room, privacy, and possible interruptions.

f. It is important that you discuss with the client at the outset of therapy how you should contact the client in cases of emergency, such as when you need to cancel a scheduled therapy session. For example, does the client prefer to be contacted at home or at work? Perhaps the client does not want to be contacted at home or at work because he or she doesn't want anyone else to know that he or she is in therapy. If this is the case, the therapist might suggest to the client that he or she telephone the therapist's office before each appointment for confirmation.

g. Whenever tape-recording (either audio or video) a therapy session, be certain that the client's privacy is respected. Those therapists or counselor trainees who borrow or rent tapes to be returned to the lender after use must be certain to erase all material containing any client information.

Commentary

Privacy

refers to an individual's right to be alone and to decide the time, place, manner and extent of sharing oneself (one's thoughts, behavior or body) with others. The right to privacy is protected under the Constitution of the United States which states that, a person has a right to make decisions about one's own life without interference of others or the government (right to autonomy) and that a citizen has the right to control access to information about oneself if (privacy of disclosure). (Stromberg, 1988, p. 374)

Early in this book, we discussed ways to protect the privacy of your client (informed consent). Other ways (Schutz, 1982) in which you could be found liable for invading the privacy of your client include

1) when you make phone calls to your client's place of work and identify yourself as their therapist.
2) when you send bills and correspondence to a client and identify your relationship to your client in a manner that others might see.
3) when nonessential staff members are present during a client interview.
4) when you discuss your client in a case conference or as part of a class discussion.
5) when the waiting area or treatment rooms do(es) not protect your client's privacy.
6) when support staff or other persons have easy access to your records.
7) even if what you present about your client is complimentary . . . it can still be invading his/her privacy if you do not have their permission. (Schutz, 1982, p. 11)

Therefore, it is imperative you receive written consent from your client to proceed in a manner that could be conceived as invading their privacy.

Recently, Orange County CAMFT (California Association for Marriage and Family Therapists) has stated that employers are demanding greater accountability than traditional insurance companies for an insured's treatment. This has far-reaching implications because it is estimated that, within five years (i.e., 1995), 85% of insurance coverage will be in the form of health maintenance organization (HMO) type of coverage.

Conclusions

An individual has the right to be left alone. Although a breach of privacy tort requires extremely unreasonable conduct on the part of the psychotherapist, the way to protect yourself from malpractice is to get consent to proceed, as follows:

(1) Ask your client about calls at the patient's workplace versus at home in the event you need to telephone.

(2) Ask if you can identify yourself by professional title if spouse, secretary, and so on answers the phone.

(3) Don't identify yourself on the envelope when sending bills or correspondence to your client. Ask your client how to specify the address on the envelope.

(4) Consent to publish details of confidential therapy must be obtained in writing.

(5) Employers have a responsibility to provide a safe place to work. Thus they may have a "need to know" such factors as the instability or danger of an employee. However, it would be wise for the therapist to obtain (in writing) a release form from the client before contacting the employer.

(6) Disclose information about potential harm only to those who are primarily in danger or to those who are directly involved in preventing harm to self or others (police, paramedics, and so on). Although duty to warn and protect takes precedence over withholding confidential client information, therapists need to be careful about to whom they reveal such information.

(7) Concealment of identity and concealment of the motive for service are two general therapeutic principles and are advised.

(8) Employers, as well as insurance companies (when third-party payments are involved), may have access to information concerning an employee's therapy. It is imperative that clients be informed at the outset of therapy regarding the limits of confidentiality whether or not insurance is covering the cost. Written consent from the client is highly advisable.

(9) Whenever conducting psychotherapy with a client or consulting with other professionals concerning a client, therapists need to be aware of who else might be able to hear the conversation. Therapists need to consider such factors as the room, privacy, and possible interruptions.

(10) It is important that you discuss with the client at the outset of therapy how you should contact him or her in cases of emergency, such as when you need to cancel a scheduled therapy session. For example, does the client prefer to be contacted at home or at work? Perhaps the client does not want to be contacted at work because he or she doesn't want anyone to know that he or she is in therapy. If this is the case, the therapist could suggest to the client that he or she telephone the therapist's office before each appointment for confirmation.

(11) Whenever tape-recording (either audio or video) a therapy session, be certain that the client's privacy is respected. Those therapists or counselor trainees who borrow or rent tapes to be returned to the owner after use must be certain to erase all material containing any client information.

Summary

You must be very cautious with regard to your client's privacy. It may not always be obvious when you are invading another's privacy. A colleague (outside of the agency where you work) may unobtrusively ask you about a client; a client's friend, seeing you outside your agency, may want to have you give him or her a message; or you may need to call your client at his or her place of work. All of these incidents (and many more), if not handled appropriately, could lead to an invasion of your clients' privacy. Be sure you have their written permission if you ever need to discuss their cases with someone else, and, if you don't, then silence is the best method to protect your client. Counselor educators need to be especially cautious, whenever sharing their own professional experiences of counseling clients, in teaching or in writing for professional publications, that the full anonymity of the client is maintained. This also includes maintaining full anonymity whenever discussing clients who terminated therapy years before. Therapists also have a professional obligation to respect a client's privacy whenever selecting a setting for conducting the therapy session. For example, counselors employed in a school setting may need to meet with their student clients in various locations on the school premises due to the limited space available. In such instances, the counselor should be certain that it is not possible for other people to hear the conversation between the counselor and the client.

Vignette

On Wednesday, the therapist learns, that unexpectedly, he'll have to leave the state by Thursday for 10 days. He needs to call his clients to reschedule his appointments. He calls one of his clients at home, only to get no answer, so he then calls him at work. The client's secretary answers and takes the message that his appointment has been canceled.

At the next session, the client is angry because his secretary wondered who the doctor was who called. Was this an invasion of privacy? What would you do, if anything, different from what was done in this situation to reach the client?

Questions to Consider

(1) How might you respond to a telephone call in which the person calling identifies himself as the husband of your client and requests that you communicate an important message to his wife later that day during your scheduled therapy appointment?

(2) Might calling the client at home or work to reschedule appointments violate the client's privacy?

(3) What is the procedure for authorizing others to receive information about a person who is at risk of harming self or others?

(4) How responsible is the therapist for seeing that disclosed information is not spread by rumor or procedure to unauthorized individuals?

(5) How do you react if you happen to come in contact with one of your clients in public? Do you acknowledge or ignore him or her?

5

Defamation of Character

In order for a therapist to be liable for defamation of character, he or she must have made, in public, either orally (slander) or in writing (libel), a statement that is "injurious to the reputation of the plaintiff" (Schutz, 1982, p. 10). The therapist's defense against potential libel is that (a) the statement was based on truth, (b) an informed consent permitted the release of information to the indicated party, or (c) it was the legal responsibility of the therapist to release the information (e.g., duty to warn; Schutz, 1982).

Court Case

(1) *Berry v. Moench* **(1958)**

Case Review

Robert J. Berry, *Plaintiff and Appellant, v.* ***Louis G. Moench***, *Defendant and Respondent*
Supreme Court of Utah, 8 Utah 2d, 191, No. 8786 (Nov. 12, 1958)

Mr. Berry sued Dr. Moench for writing a letter that allegedly contained false and derogatory information about him. The Third Judicial District Court of Salt Lake County "entered judgment for the physician and the patient appealed" (p. 814).

Dr. J. S. Hellewell of Evanston, Wyoming, had written to Dr. Moench requesting information about Mr. Berry's mental stability and background. Mr. Berry was engaged to Mary Boothe, who was the daughter of Mr. and Mrs. Williams. Mr. and Mrs. Williams were former patients of Dr. Hellewell. Mr. Berry was a patient of Dr. Hellewell and had gone to Dr. Moench for therapy when having marital difficulties. Mr. Berry had seen Dr. Moench seven years before and had received four electric shock treatments. The doctor had not seen Mr. Berry since the treatments. Dr. Moench wrote the following to Dr. Hellewell, "Since I do not have his authorization, the patient you mentioned in your last letter will remain nameless." "He was treated here in 1949 as an emergency. Our diagnosis was Manic depressive depression in a psychopathic personality." "The patient was attempting to go through school on the G.I. bill. . . . Instead of attending class he would spend most of the days and nights playing cards for money." "During his care here, he purchased a brand new Packard, without even money to buy gasoline." "He was in constant trouble with the authorities during the war." "He did not do well in school and never did really support his wife and children." "My suggestion to the infatuated girl would be to run as fast and as far as she possibly could in any direction away from him" (p. 816).

The plaintiff and Dr. Moench agreed that much of the information that he had written in the letter had been obtained from his former wife, Ethella Berry, the referring doctor (Dr. Miller), and Ethella Berry's sister. The plaintiff also stated that he was in the "top one per cent of his high school class," that he was editor-in-chief of the school paper, and that he had flunked two courses. It was also shown that the plaintiff had had three minor incidents with the law and that he had paid all but $5 toward the purchase of his car. The doctor admitted that he had known that the plaintiff only had $5 left in car payments. The doctor also admitted that other cases with the same diagnosis had been treated successfully and were able to have successful marriages.

COURT DECISION

The court ruled that Dr. Moench had committed libel. *Libel* was defined "as a false and unprivileged publication in writing which assails the honesty, integrity or virtue of another and thereby exposes him to hatred, contempt, or ridicule, or tends to injure him in his occupation" (p. 820). The court did not find Dr. Moench as having malice or having been motivated by spite, hatred, or ill will against the plaintiff. Therefore, they awarded costs to the appellant.

Implications

a. Untrue statements about a client, whether in the form of libel (written) or slander (oral) impair the person's reputation and good name and may be viewed as defamation of character.

b. Defenses against defamation include the following: (i) The statements were true, (ii) the client consented to the disclosure, and (iii) there was an obligation to disclose.

c. If information is not needed for professional or legal reasons, it should not be released.

d. The information provided and the insult to virtue extended in a libel case must be proven to expose the client to hatred, contempt or ridicule, or occupational distress.

Commentary

There are two ways to defame another's character either orally, as in slander, or in written form, as in libel. In order for an oral/written comment to be defaming, it must (a) have been made public, that is, published, or (b) be found to be "injurious to the reputation of the plaintiff" (Schutz, 1982, p. 10).

To avoid being liable you must be able to prove

(1) that what you said or wrote was based on fact,
(2) that there was a consent to release this information, or,
(3) that what you released was because you had "qualified privilege" by the law (e.g., child abuse). (Schutz, 1982, p. 10)

Conclusions

Truth is the best defense against charges of defamation of character. However, we urge each therapist to be careful about what he or she says about anyone.

Summary

When statements are injurious to the reputation of another, they may be viewed as defamation of character. These statements may be written (libel) or oral (slander). The psychotherapist's defenses against defamation are (a) that the statements were true, (b) that an informed consent for release of the information was obtained, or (c) that there was a legal obligation to disclose, such as duty to warn.

Vignette

You have heard rumors from several sources to the effect that a therapist has made it a practice to have sexual relationships with his female clients. A friend of yours calls you regarding his daughter, who is currently seeing this therapist as a client. He asks you if you have any information regarding this therapist and if you would put it in writing so he could show it to his daughter. He tells you he would like his daughter to stop seeing this therapist because she is evolving into such an independent and different person. Would you agree to write the letter? What would you tell the father regarding the therapist? Would you speak to the daughter?

Questions to Consider

(1) In seeking institutionalization of a client, a psychotherapist makes some extremely offensive statements about a client. How vulnerable is the psychotherapist to a defamation suit? What if the statements were made in a criminal trial? What if the statements were made to another psychotherapist in sending information about the client?

(2) How do you prove what is true and what is not, due to the nature of privileged information?

(3) How can one tell when the honesty, integrity, and virtue of another's reputation has been impaired?

(4) What would you do if someone intended to harm you, personally and/or professionally?

6

Failure to Warn and Protect

In Chapter 3, we noted that confidentiality is limited by certain therapist duties in addition to the duties to clients. As a result of the increasing number of court cases in recent years, mental health professionals are becoming more aware of their duties to protect other people from potentially dangerous clients and to protect clients from themselves. Dangerousness to self (i.e., suicide) will be addressed in the next chapter; this chapter will focus on dangerousness to others.

Under what conditions a therapist has a duty to warn a potential victim, law enforcement officials, or another person of a client's dangerousness has been the subject of ever-increasing lawsuits. Unfortunately, the answers provided by the courts over the years appear to be both conflicting and confusing.

The responsibility to protect the public from dangerous actions of v olent clients entails liability for civil damages when the therapists neglect this duty by (a) failing to diagnose or predict dangerous actions of clients, (b) failing to warn potential victims of violent behavior, (c) failing to commit clients who are dangerous, and (d) prematurely discharging dangerous clients from a hospital setting (APA, 1985).

Below are summaries of a variety of legal cases that deal with these four categories of failure to protect.

Court Cases

(1) *Tarasoff v. the Regents of the University of California* **(1975)**
(2) *McIntosh v. Milano* **(1979)**
(3) *Shaw v. Glickman* **(1980)**
(4) *Lipari v. the Bank of Elkorn v. Sears Roebuck & Co. and United States of America* **(1980)**
(5) *Thompson v. County of Alameda* **(1980)**
(6) *Leedy and Leedy v. Hartnett and Lebanon Veterans Administration Hospital* **(1981)**
(7) *Doyle and Doyle v. United States of America* **(1982)**
(8) *Hasenei v. United States of America* **(1982)**
(9) *Cairl et al. v. State of Minnesota et al.* **(1982)**
(10) *Heltsely v. Votteler* **(1982)**
(11) *Davis v. Lhim* **(1983)**
(12) *Chrite v. United States of America* **(1983)**
(13) *Jablonski v. United States of America* **(1983)**
(14) *Hedlund v. the Superior Court of Orange County* **(1983)**
(15) *Brady, McCarthy, and Delahanty v. Hopper* **(1983)**
(16) *White v. United States of America* **(1986)**
(17) *Phillips v. Gibson's Inc., Sentry Insurance and State of Louisiana* **(1986)**

Court Cases

Vitaly Tarasoff et al. Plaintiffs and Appellants, v. the Regents of the University of California et al., Defendants and Respondents
Supreme Court of California In Bank S.F. 23042
(Rehearing Granted March 12, 1975)

The plaintiffs were the parents of Tatiana Tarasoff, who was killed on October 27, 1969, by Prosenjit Poddar. Mr. Poddar was a voluntary outpatient at Cowell Memorial Hospital and under the care of Dr. Lawrence Moore, a psychologist employed at Cowell Hospital at the

University of California at Berkeley. Mr. Poddar had expressed an intent to kill an unnamed girlfriend when she was to return from a trip to Brazil. The girlfriend was easily identifiable as Tatiana Tarasoff. Psychiatrists Dr. Gold and Dr. Yandell had concurred with Dr. Moore's decision to commit Mr. Poddar for observation, but the chief of the department of psychiatry, Dr. Powelson, overruled their decision and directed the staff not to commit Mr. Poddar. Therefore, Mr. Poddar was released. He moved in with Tatiana's brother in an apartment near where Tatiana lived with her parents. Dr. Moore had sent a letter to the chief of police, asking the police department to confine Mr. Poddar. Dr. Moore also "orally notified" (p. 132) campus officers Atkinson and Teel that they should detain Mr. Poddar until they could determine whether Mr. Poddar was rational. When Mr. Poddar assured the campus officers that he would not harm Tatiana, they let him go. Dr. Powelson had asked the police to return the letter written by Dr. Moore, and he directed that copies of the letter and notes taken by Dr. Moore regarding the case be destroyed. The defendants pointed out that Mr. Poddar, after his "encounter with the police," broke off all communications with the hospital staff and did not resume therapy.

The plaintiffs' complaint was not that they did not specifically warn Tatiana but that they did not warn her parents of the danger to the daughter. This case brought out that her parents were "those who reasonably could have been expected to notify her of her peril" (p. 139). When this case was first heard at the Superior Court of Alameda County, the decision was to sustain the defendants' objections, but the plaintiffs appealed the case and thus the case was reheard.

COURT DECISION

The second trial resulted in the judgment of the first trial being reversed and the cause remanded. The fact that three doctors felt Mr. Poddar should be confined for observation suggests that there was evidence Mr. Poddar could be suspected of carrying out his threat. The court concluded that the defendants' "failure to warn Tatiana or those who reasonably could have been expected to notify her of her peril does not fall within the absolute protection afforded by section 820.2 of the Government Code." In other words, they could not be offered immunity just because they worked for a government agency, and they were liable for not warning Tatiana or her parents, who could have notified her of her dangerous situation.

Peggy McIntosh, Administratrix and Prosequendum of the Estate of Kimberly A. McIntosh, Deceased, Plaintiff, v. Michael Milano, M.D., Defendant
Superior Court of New Jersey, Law Division
168 N.J. Super 466, 403 A.2d 500 (June 12, 1979)

Peggy McIntosh, mother of Kimberly A. McIntosh, brought suit against Dr. Michael Milano because he failed to warn the victim, Kimberly, and her parents about the potential harm from Dr. Milano's patient, Lee Morgenstein. Lee Morgenstein entered treatment with Dr. Milano on May 5, 1974, at the age of 15. A school psychologist had referred Lee's parents, regarding treatment of Lee, to Dr. Milano purposively because of Lee's involvement in drugs. Initially, Lee's diagnosis was "an adjustment reaction of adolescence" (p. 503). Lee Morgenstein saw Dr. Milano over a period of two years. During that time, he revealed "fantasies" about using a knife to threaten people who frightened him, "fear of other people, being a hero or an important villain," and his sexual experiences with Ms. McIntosh, who was five years older than he. Dr. Milano began to believe that these fantasies were reality. Dr. Milano did advise that Lee break off the relationship with Ms. McIntosh. It was also revealed that Lee had discussed his possessive feelings toward Ms. McIntosh, how overwhelmed he was about the relationship, and the jealousy he had toward her boyfriend. Lee Morgenstein also was found to have used a B.B. gun and fired a shot at a car (either Ms. McIntosh's or her boyfriend's). It was believed that it was Lee who shot a B.B. gun at Ms. McIntosh's parents' home and hit several windows. Lee also bought a knife, to scare people off, and brought it to therapy to show Dr. Milano. On the day before July 8, 1975, when Ms. McIntosh was killed with a gun, Lee Morgenstein had stolen a prescription pad from Dr. Milano's office and tried to purchase 30 Seconal tablets from a pharmacist. The pharmacist called Dr. Milano, who told the pharmacist not to fill the prescription, to retain the unauthorized prescription, and to send Lee home. Apparently, Lee Morgenstein was despondent over the incident and, the following day, knowing that Ms. McIntosh was going to visit her parents, he forced her to enter his car, took her to a park, and shot her. Lee Morgenstein was convicted of first-degree murder by a jury on March 4, 1976, and sentenced to life imprisonment.

The defense maintained that, because there was no law in New Jersey stating that a therapist has a duty to warn, it should not create one or adopt the *Tarasoff* II rule. The defense argued there is no such duty by a therapist to third parties or potential victims, and that *Tarasoff* II should not be applied, and was wrongly decided in that it (a) imposes an "unworkable" duty on therapists to warn another of a third person's dangerousness when that condition cannot be predicted with sufficient reliability; (b) will interfere with effective treatment by eliminating confidentiality; (c) may deter therapists from treating potentially violent patients in light of possible malpractice claims by third persons; and (d) will result in increased commitments of patients to mental or penal institutions. (pp. 505-506)

Reference was made to several other court cases.

The plaintiff stated that the defendant committed a deviation from standard medical practices by failing to warn. An expert witness testified that he, a psychiatrist, agreed with the plaintiff's view. In addition, the plaintiff, citing various incidents in which Lee engaged in dangerous activities, such as buying a knife to scare people, demonstrated that Lee Morgenstein was to be considered a dangerous individual who could inflict harm on the intended victim.

COURT DECISION

In this trial, the defendant asked for a summary judgment and the court denied him such judgment. "This means no more than that there is a factual question which should be presented to a jury as to whether, based on expert testimony, defendant breached the appropriate duty in this case" (p. 515).

Important to note. This case states,

Experience has shown that for various reasons malpractice cases are not easy cases for plaintiffs to win. Deviations from accepted professional standards are difficult to prove. Concern has been voiced over unwillingness of members of the medical profession to testify against each other even where the most obvious and flagrant cases appeal for reparation.

(See Belli, "Ready for the Plaintiff-Suing the Doctor: A Frustrating Tort," 30 Temp. L.Q. 408, 1957.)

Daniel Shaw v. David R. Glickman, Personal Representative of the Estate of Leonard J. Gallant et al.
Court of Special Appeals of Maryland
45 Md. App. 718, 415 A.2d 625 (June 13, 1980)

The plaintiff, Dr. Daniel Shaw, brought a suit against "a psychiatric team" because they had failed to warn him about the violent nature of Mr. Leonard Billian. The three people involved in this case, Dr. Shaw (the lover), Mr. Billian (the husband), and Mrs. Mary Ann Billian (the wife), were all under the care of the late Dr. Leonard J. Gallant, a psychiatrist, and his psychiatric team, which included a psychiatric nurse known professionally as Patricia Hencke, but privately as Mrs. Gallant, and Mr. Joseph Napora, a psychologist. Mrs. Billian had left her husband during the course of treatment. Dr. Shaw, a dentist, and she were both nude and asleep in the same bed when Mr. Billian entered Dr. Shaw's home at 2:00 a.m. and shot the plaintiff five times. Dr. Shaw survived the incident. The Superior Court of Baltimore City had favored with the defendants and granted them a summary judgment, and this was appealed by Dr. Shaw.

COURT DECISION

The court ruled in favor of the psychiatric team because (a) Mr. Billian had never told the team that he had any hatred or intent to harm Dr. Shaw and (b) Dr. Shaw was seen as assuming the risk of injury when he went to bed with Mrs. Billian. In addition, it was noted that the State of Maryland would have seen the team as violating the statute that "privilege against disclosure belongs to the patient, not the psychiatrist or psychologist" (p. 630). Therefore, the former judgment was affirmed.

Ruth Ann Lipari, and the Bank of Elkorn, Special Coadministrators of the Estate of Dennis F. Lipari, Deceased, and Ruth Ann Lipari, Individually, Plaintiffs, v. Sears, Roebuck and Co., a New York Corporation, and United States of America, Defendant; Sears Roebuck and Co., a New York Corporation, Defendant and Third-Party Plaintiff, v. United States of America, Third-Party Defendant
U.S. District Court, D. Nebraska
497 F. Supp. 185, Civ. No. 77-0-458 (July 17, 1980)

Ruth Ann Lipari brought suit against Sears, Roebuck and Co. for having sold a gun to a mental patient, Ulysses L. Cribbs. On November 26, 1977, Mr. Cribbs, who was a patient at the Veterans Administration (V.A.) hospital, entered an Omaha nightclub and fired shots into the room killing Dennis Lipari and seriously injuring Ruth Ann Lipari. Sears, Roebuck and Co. then filed a third-party suit against the V.A.

hospital for "failure to detain/ commit" Mr. Cribbs. Mrs. Lipari also filed a third-party suit against the V.A. hospital for failure to detain/ commit Mr. Cribbs. Mr. Cribbs had been committed to a mental institution and started day-care treatment at the V.A. hospital on September 23, 1977. In September, while still under the care of the V.A. hospital, he purchased a gun from Sears, Roebuck and Co. On October 17, 1977, Mr. Cribbs, against the advice of his doctor, removed himself from treatment.

COURT DECISION

According to Nebraska law, the "relationship between psychotherapist and patient gives rise to affirmative duty for the benefit of third persons, but such duty arises only when, in accordance with the standards of his profession, the therapist knows or should know that patients' dangerous propensities present an unreasonable risk of harm to others" (p. 185). The court denied the government's motion for a summary judgment and supported the plaintiffs' argument that the defendants had committed negligence by failing to commit.

Clifford K. Thompson, Jr. et al., Plaintiffs and Appellants, v. County of Alameda, Defendant and Respondent
Supreme Court of California, In Bank
27 Cal. 3d 741, 614 P.2d 728, S.F. 24006
July 14, 1980 (Rehearing Denied, Aug. 21, 1980)

Parents of a 5-year-old boy, Jonathan Thompson, filed suit against the County of Alameda for negligence in releasing a juvenile delinquent, James, into the community. After James had been on temporary leave for 24 hours, he went to the Thompson's garage, which was a few doors from his home, and murdered Jonathan Thompson. The plaintiffs felt negligence occurred because (a) the county released a juvenile into the community whom they knew had "latent, extremely dangerous and violent propensities regarding young children and that sexual assaults upon young children and violence connected therewith were a likely result of releasing (him) into the community" (p. 730); (b) the county had selected James's mother as custodian and did not supervise her in her duties; and (c) the county failed to warn the local police, the neighborhood parents, or the juvenile's mother of his propensities to violence.

The defense responded with the following: The county is granted immunity when releasing an individual under the Government Code sections 820.2 and 845.8. Section 845.8 states, "Neither a public entity nor a public employee is liable for: (1) Any injury resulting from determining whether to parole or release a prisoner" (p. 731). Section 820.2 states, "The decision to parole thus comprises the resolution of policy considerations, entrusted by statute to a coordinate branch of government, that compels immunity from judicial reexamination" (p. 731). (2) The county was granted immunity under section 820.2 for selecting James' mother as custodian. Section 820.2 states that the county cannot be held liable for "any injury resulting from determining . . . the terms and conditions of a (prisoner's) release." (3) The county cannot be held liable because Jonathan was not a foreseeable victim because James did not specify whom he intended to kill. Second, a special relationship does not exist between the county and James such as it would between a therapist and his client. If such a relationship does not exist, then duty to warn does not apply. Finally, it was pointed out that "each member of the general public who chances to come into contact with a parolee bear(s) the risk that the rehabilitative effort will fail" (69 Cal. 2d at p. 799, 73 Cal. Rptr. at p. 252, 447 P.2d at p. 364).

COURT DECISION

The Superior Court of Alameda County had dismissed this case and the plaintiffs appealed. However, the Supreme Court of California affirmed the superior court's decision.

Harrison F. Leedy and Gertrude H. Leedy, his wife, Plaintiffs, v. John J. Hartnett, and Lebanon Veterans Administration Hospital, Defendants
U.S. District Court, M.D. Pennsylvania
510 F. Supp. 1125, Civ. No. 80-0201 (April 9, 1981)

Harrison and Gertrude Leedy brought suit against the Lebanon Veterans Hospital for failure to warn the plaintiffs that one of their patients, John J. Hartnett, had a tendency to get violent when drinking. Hartnett was a disabled veteran of the Korean War and was a patient at the hospital from 1956 through March 1978. He was diagnosed as a paranoid schizophrenic and a chronic alcoholic. The hospital personnel were aware of Hartnett's violent outbursts and the aggressive and impulsive behaviors that had occurred during a 10-year period. During the time

Hartnett was being treated at the hospital, he became friends with the Leedys. On September 26, 1977, Hartnett discharged himself from the hospital and informed hospital personnel that he would be staying with the plaintiffs. On March 31, 1978, Hartnett and the Leedys went out to a club to celebrate Hartnett's birthday and, during this occasion, Hartnett drank 24 12-ounce bottles or cans of beer. At 2:00 a.m., they left the club and went back to the Leedys' residence. Later the same night, the Leedys were beaten by Hartnett.

The Leedys charged the hospital with negligence because of their failure to warn them of Hartnett's violent tendencies. The defendants claimed that Hartnett had not specifically indicated that he intended to do harm to the Leedys, and, therefore, they could not be held responsible for his actions toward them. The plaintiffs could not state that Hartnett had ever made any threats toward them. In addition, there was no evidence to suggest that Hartnett had a pattern of violent behavior when he drank. The plaintiffs' position was that, because Hartnett had a tendency to be violent when he drank, this tendency was most likely to come out when he associated with people he knew. The plaintiffs also had an expert witness, Dr. Hostetter, M.D., who testified that the medical staff had a responsibility to warn those who associated with Hartnett of his tendencies to pose a dangerous threat to them.

COURT DECISION

The judgment was for the defendant. The court determined that Leedys were in no greater danger than anyone else who came in contact with Hartnett. The court would not impose liability where an outpatient was not making specific threats at the time of his or her discharge and, therefore, acts of violence were not foreseeable.

Sharon Lee Doyle, Paul J. Doyle, and Isabelle Doyle, Plaintiffs, v. United States of America, Defendant
U.S. District Court, C.D. California
530 F. Supp. 1278
Civ. A. No. 77-3528-RJK (January 28, 1982)

Sharon Lee Doyle, wife of, and Paul and Isabelle Doyle, parents of James Doyle, filed a negligence suit against the U.S. Army for failing to diagnose, discharging prematurely, and failing in their duty to warn potential victims about Carl Russell Carson, who killed security guard James Doyle.

On January 31, 1975, Mr. Carson entered the army at age 19. Mr. Carson went to Fort Polk, Louisiana, for basic training. Mr. Carson told Captain Melvin G. Engstrom that he was not pleased with the army because they were not teaching him quickly enough how to kill people. The captain referred him to the chaplain, to whom Mr. Carson reiterated his desire to commit violent acts. The chaplain recommended Mr. Carson see the army psychiatrist and, before seeing the psychiatrist, Mr. Carson was interviewed by three counselors. All three counselors concluded that Mr. Carson was not an immediate danger to others. The psychiatrist, Dr. Robert W. Johansen, concluded that Mr. Carson's statements were made so that he would be released from the army. However, Dr. Johansen sent Carson to the Neuropsychiatric Ward of the Fort Polk Hospital to be observed for psychotic behavior. Dr. Johansen diagnosed Mr. Carson as having an antisocial disorder but not as being psychotic. Dr. Johansen ordered that 50 milligrams of Thorazine, an antipsychotic drug and tranquilizer, be administered to Mr. Carson four times a day. After remaining on the ward from February 13 to February 18, 1975, Mr. Carson was discharged. Mr. Carson was found to be cooperative, oriented, and adjusted to his environment. Mr. Carson went AWOL (i.e., absent without leave) after he left the hospital and was assigned light duties. During this time, he was found to be cooperative. General Haldane reviewed Carson's medical and administrative files, considered the recommendation of Captain Engstrom, and consulted with legal adviser before he discharged Mr. Carson because he could and did not want to adjust to the army. After his discharge in Louisiana, Mr. Carson went to his residence in Ventura, California, and two days later went to Ventura College, where he shot Mr. Doyle, the security guard, with his rifle. It was discovered later that Mr. Carson had talked about killing his parents and had gone to the college where his father was an instructor. Mr. Doyle had attempted to secure Carson's weapon when Carson fatally shot him.

COURT DECISION

The courts decided to follow Louisiana law even though the killing took place in California. The courts determined that they should follow the laws of the state that had the most significant relationship to the case and where negligence allegedly took place. It should be noted that

Louisiana courts have shown great reluctance to impose liability because of a failure to protect the public from a dangerous individual. In rejecting such claims, the Louisiana courts have focused consideration upon whether defendant had any duty to protect the plaintiff and whether the breach of duty to protect the plaintiff and whether the breach of that duty was the proximate cause of plaintiffs' injuries. (pp. 1285-1286)

Reference was made to the leading Louisiana court case concerning dangerous patients, *Cappell v. Pierson* (15, La.App. 524, 132 So. 391 [2d Cir. 1931]), "which held that the negligent release of an apparently dangerous patient was not the proximate cause of the murder committed by the patient on the day of his release" (p. 1286).

Duty to warn. The court discussed that Louisiana law does not recognize a duty of therapists to warn third parties of a patient's violent intentions and, even if it did, Carson never stated specifically whom he intended to harm. Therefore, even if Louisiana did acknowledge third-party warnings, this case would not warrant such a duty.

Failure to diagnose. The plaintiff argued that, had Dr. Johansen conducted his interviews differently, he would have been able to determine the extent of intent to kill. The court found that, just because a patient makes threats, which is not uncommon among psychiatric patients, this does not in itself prove the patient to be dangerous. The plaintiffs felt that Dr. Johansen did not conduct a proper interview, which would have provided a more correct diagnosis. The court stated that to mandate the boundaries by which a therapist should conduct an interview would violate *Tarasoff's* decision that therapists are entitled to broad discretion as to how they choose to examine a patient. It was noted that Carson had no history of violence and was not violent during observation at Fort Polk Hospital. Therefore, this case did not warrant negligence in this area.

Failure to commit. The plaintiff used AR 40-3, paragraph 6-22(b), which indicates "that psychotic soldiers requiring hospitalization who are ineligible for Veterans Administration care are, upon discharge, to be transferred to the care of their next of kin or to a state hospital." However, the regulations also state that there must be a determination made that the patient needs such care. According to the findings, no such determinations were made because Carson was not seen as violent during his observation time at Fort Polk Hospital or at the time of discharge. The court dismissed the plaintiffs' action.

Walter Hasenei and Thelma Hasenei v. United States of America
Civ. No. K-80-2339, 341 F. Supp. 999
U.S. District Court, D. Maryland (April 8, 1982)

Walter and Thelma Hasenei filed suit against the V.A. Hospital in Harrisburg, Pennsylvania, for negligence in treating John D. Hock, a veteran, who collided with them head-on in a car accident. Mr. and Mrs. Hasenei also brought suit because they concluded that the hospital was negligent when they did not warn the Department of Motor Vehicles about Mr. Hock's inability to drive a car and in not continuing to commit him to hospitalization.

Mr. Hock had a history of being suicidal, alcoholic, violent, and severely depressed. Doctors at the Walter Reed Army Medical Center had seen Mr. Hock on an outpatient basis in 1970 because of his acknowledged desire to join the army and become a helicopter pilot in the hopes of being killed during the Vietnam War. The Walter Reed staff diagnosed him as being an alcoholic and a schizophrenic, paranoid type.

In 1976, Mr. Hock had been drinking heavily and had put a gun to his head. A friend took him to Walter Reed to be admitted for an examination. During his stay, Mr. Hock had a fantasy about killing people in authority, had auditory hallucinations, and stated he feared someday he would lose control and kill somebody. Mr. Hock's mental status examiner found him oriented times three (person, time, and place), as normal, but also found that he lacked certain skills that made him unemployable and unable to plan for his future. Mr. Hock was treated with Thorazine and transferred to the V.A. Hospital in Lebanon, Pennsylvania near his home.

Mr. Hock was discharged two months later from the V.A. Hospital because he did not appear to be mentally incompetent, was motivated for job placement, and was neither suicidal nor homicidal. Mr. Hock was involved in an alcoholics' recovery group. He was placed on outpatient status and required to have a follow-up session in one month. Mr. Hock returned for the follow-up session late and was found to be depressed according to Dr. Jacob Garber, over the recent death of his son, for which he blamed himself. Mr. Hock had told Dr. Garber that he had resumed drinking but not to the amount he was drinking prior to his hospitalization. Mr. Hock stated he had no desire to kill himself because of his belief in reincarnation. Mr. Hock was diagnosed as paranoid schizophrenic in partial remission. Dr. Garber changed his medication from Thorazine (250 mg.) to Mellaril (50 mg.) because Mr. Hock had none of the psychotic features for which Thorazine was prescribed, and depression is one of its side effects. Therefore, Dr. Garber placed him on Mellaril, which is an antidepressant. Mrs. Hock had also been interviewed that day by a social worker, and she had not suggested that her husband was experiencing any suicidal or homicidal thoughts. Mrs. Hock was asked to inform the hospital if her husband's condition changed.

On August 21, 1976, Mr. Hock drove his car, without headlights and on the wrong side of the road, into the Hasenei's car. Mr. Hock's alcohol blood content level was 250 milligrams per liter. Thereupon, the Hasenei's filed suit against the hospital for negligence.

COURT DECISION

The court ruled in favor of the defendant. In the case of duty to warn, the court ruled as such because the therapist could not have foreseen a danger to the plaintiffs. The court ruled that Mr. Hock could not have been committed on August 9, 1976, because, under Pennsylvania law, he would have to have been "severely mentally disabled and in need of immediate treatment and posing a clear threat to others." This was not the case at the time of Mr. Hock's follow-up session. In addition, because Mr. Hock had expressed hostility toward being hospitalized, the courts ruled that the doctor was not negligent in treating him on an outpatient basis. Finally, the court ruled that the hospital could not have acted any differently in preventing Mr. Hock from driving his car. The hospital by law cannot report to the Department of Motor Vehicles, according to the provision of 42 U.S.C. & 4582, because they were treating him for his alcoholic condition. This provision states that

> records of the identity, diagnosis, prognosis or treatment of any patient which are maintained in connection with the performance of any program or activity relating to alcoholism or alcohol abuse education, training, treatment, rehabilitation, or research, which conducted, regulated, or directly or indirectly assisted by any department or agency of the United States shall . . . be confidential and be disclosed only for the purposes and under the circumstances expressly authorized under subsection (b) which states to qualified personnel for the purpose of conducting scientific research, management audits, financial audits, or program evaluation, but such personnel may not identify, directly or indirectly, any individual

patient in any report of such research, audit, or evaluation, or otherwise disclose patient identities in any manner. (p. 1014)

Steven J. Cairl et al., Appellants, v. State of Minnesota et al., Respondents; Mary Ann Connolly etc., Appellant v. State of Minnesota, et al., Defendants and Third-Party Plaintiffs, Respondents, Bruce Hedge, Defendant and Third-Party Plaintiff, Respondent; Ramsey County Welfare Department, Defendant and Third-Party Plaintiff, Respondent, v. Steven J. Cairl et al., Third-Party Defendants, Appellants
Supreme Court of Minnesota
323 N.W. 2D 2O, No. 81-437 (August 13, 1982)

Steven J. Cairl, owner of the fourplex in which Mary Ann Connolly and her two daughters lived, filed suit against the State of Minnesota, the Ramsey County Welfare Department, and Bruce Hedge, the "community reentry facilitator" at the Minnesota Learning Center for failure to warn them about Ms. Connolly's son's dangerous tendencies. Tom Connolly, who had an I.Q. of 57, had been sent home for a Christmas holiday. And although Tom Connolly had been known to set fires, the Learning Center had determined that the fires Mr. Connolly had set while at the center were not sufficient to cause concern. The Learning Center is known for its open-door policy, and part of their treatment is to encourage their youth to make home visits. Bruce Hedge drove Tom Connolly home on December 21, 1977. Bruce Hedge was specifically named because he had private insurance and the plaintiffs claimed that he, therefore, had waived his right to be immune from liability as a government employee. Mary Ann Connolly had been advised that Tom would be coming home. On December 23, 1977, Tom Connolly set fire to the living room couch. Because of this incident, Mary Ann's daughter, Tina Connolly was killed; her daughter, Tamara Connolly was severely burned, and the property of Steven Cairl was destroyed.

COURT DECISION

The ruling of the first trial was that the hospital staff was not held liable by the duty to warn because Tom Connolly had not specifically stated that he would injure the parties who became involved in his dangerous activities and also because his mother was aware of his potential to set fires. In addition, the court did not find Bruce Hedge to have waived his immunity through obtaining private liability insurance because that insurance was intended for his work outside the hospital. The plaintiffs appealed the District Court of Ramsey County's decision. The Supreme Court of Minnesota affirmed the district court's decision.

In the Matter of the Estate of Robert E. Votteler, Deceased, Ramona Heltsely, Appellant v. Helen Votteler, Administrator of the Estate of Robert E. Votteler, Appellee
Supreme Court of Iowa
327 N.W. 2d 759, No. 66985 (December 22, 1982)

Ramona Heltsely brought action against the estate of the deceased psychiatrist, Dr. Robert E. Votteler. Ms. Heltsely claimed that Dr. Votteler was negligent in his duty to warn her of the violent nature of his patient, Lola Hansen. Lola Hansen was known to have suffered severe mental illness over a period of two years. Some of her violent and aggressive activity included threatening her husband, Donald, with a two by four; threatening people who bid against her at an auction; threatening to kill herself; burning her husband with a cigarette; and beating her husband with an iron pipe, for which he had to receive medical treatment. Lola and Donald Hansen became friends of Ms. Heltsely. After Donald left Lola Hansen, he began to socialize with Ms. Heltsely. And, on September 5, 1976, while Lola was still a patient of Dr. Votteler, Lola ran over Ms. Heltsely with her car.

Ms. Heltsely claims that the doctor was negligent in that (a) he did not bring Donald Hansen in to question him about his wife and, therefore, ascertain the full extent of her violent behavior, and (b) he did not warn Donald of Lola's dangerous behavior so that Donald could have warned Ms. Heltsely about Lola's aggressive behavior. Therefore, Dr. Votteler breached his duty to warn. However, Ms. Heltsely did testify that a warning alone from Donald or any individual other than the doctor would not have been taken seriously. The case was originally heard at the District Court of Marshall County, which granted summary judgment for the psychiatrist and the victim. Ms. Heltsely appealed.

COURT DECISION

The supreme court affirmed the district court's decision to grant summary judgment for the psychiatrist. They concluded this case did not fit the limits of *Tarasoff.* The plaintiff assumed that none of Dr. Votteler, Donald Hansen, or the victim was aware of the dangerous nature of Lola Hansen, which was not the case. Second, the victim assumed that, if the doctor had warned Mr. Hansen, he would then have warned the victim. Third, she acknowledged that she would not have taken any warning seriously unless it had been from Dr. Votteler. Finally, because the victim had not specifically stated that she would harm Ms. Heltsely, there was no cause for her to receive a warning from Dr. Votteler. Therefore, the court did not find sufficient evidence to reverse the district court's decision.

Davis v. Lhim
124 Mich. App. 291 (March 1983)

Ruby Davis, administratrix of the estate of Mollie Barnes, deceased, filed suit of negligence against Dr. Yong-Oh-Lhim, a staff psychiatrist at Northville State Mental Hospital, for failure to warn and failure in discharging his patient, John Patterson, who then shot and killed his mother, Mollie Barnes. The Wayne Circuit Court, where the case was originally tried, entered a judgment against the defendant. The plaintiff was awarded $500,000. in damages. Dr. Lhim appealed.

John Patterson had voluntarily committed himself to Northville on six different occasions from 1972 to 1975. Mr. Patterson had been suffering from insomnia, hallucinations, and depression and had been diagnosed as schizophrenic. On September 2, 1975, John Patterson requested of Dr. Lhim that he be released from the state hospital. Dr. Lhim released him into the custody of his mother, Mollie Barnes. At the time of the release, Mollie Barnes was visiting her brother, Clinton Bell. Therefore, Mr. Patterson stayed with his aunt, Ruby Davis, until she felt he was too hard to handle and drove him to the Bells' residence. John Patterson entered the home of Clinton and Exola Bell, found a handgun and began shooting it. His mother, Mollie Barnes, tried to take the gun from him, and he shot and killed her.

COURT DECISION

Points discussed during this case included these: (a) Could Dr. Lhim be given immunity from duty to discharge because he is an employee of a government agency? (b) Could Mollie Barnes be seen as a foreseeable victim? (c) Could the defendants, Ruby Davis, Exola Bell, and Clinton Bell, be awarded damages when they were not directly harmed by the assailant, John Patterson?

Immunity. The court ruled that Dr. Lhim's duty to discharge was not dependent upon his position at the hospital, and, therefore, governmental immunity was not afforded him.

Foreseeable victim. The court concluded that Mrs. Barnes was a foreseeable victim because of evidence of which Dr. Lhim and the hospital staff were aware. On November 12, 1973, a physician at the Detroit General Hospital emergency unit noted the following, "Patterson paces the floor and acts strangely and keeps threatening his mother for money" (p. 306). In addition, the court concluded that not only did this notation conclude that Mrs. Barnes was a foreseeable victim but the fact that John Patterson left the hospital on September 2 without money put him in a foreseeable risk situation in which he could have been determined to commit a dangerous act.

Damages awarded. The courts determined that Ruby Davis and Exola and Clinton Bell were appropriate persons to be awarded damages. All three were closely associated with Mollie Barnes and, therefore, would suffer personally from her death. In addition, Exola Bell was present when her sister-in-law was shot and would suffer emotionally from such an incident.

Warner Chrite, Personal Representative of the Estate of Catherine Chrite, Deceased, Plaintiff, v. United States of America, Defendant
564 F. Supp. 324, Civ. No. 81-73844
U. S. District Court, E.D. Michigan, S.D. (May 26, 1983)

Warner Chrite filed suit against the V.A. hospital for failing to warn his wife, Catherine Chrite, about one of their patients, Henry Oswald and for failing to keep this patient from being released. Mr. Smith (the reason for hospitalization is not clear in the case summary) had been released from the Michigan V.A. hospital. Their reason for his release was the state's law which does not permit a patient to remain under their supervision for more than 60 days. Also, in order for them to have continued his hospitalization, they must have had the court's permission by filing 15 days prior to the release date. On the day of his release, Mr. Smith wrote a note stating, "Was Henry O. Smith Here Yesterday. He is wanted for murder Mother in Law" (p. 346). The hospital staff wrote down the incident but did not warn the mother-in-law, Catherine Chrite, about the threat. After being released, Mr. Smith carried out his threat.

COURT DECISION

The court ruled in favor of the plaintiff. The court determined that the hospital was not negligent for failure to hospitalize the patient because there was no recommendation to keep the patient beyond the 60-day limit. However, the court did find the hospital negligent in its failure to warn Mrs. Chrite about the threatening note. The court ruled that Mr. Smith's written note demonstrated that Mrs. Chrite was a foreseeable victim, and, although Michigan law does not have a specific law regarding the duty to warn, the court made its decision based on the outcome of the *Tarasoff* case.

Meghan Corinne Jablonski (a Minor, by Her Guardian ad Litem, Isobel C. Pahls, Plaintiff-Appellee, v. United States of America, Defendant-Appellant
U.S. Court of Appeals, Ninth Circuit 712 F. 2d 391, No. 81-5786 (Argued and Submitted December 6, 1982; June 14, 1983, as Amended August 8, 1983)

Meghan Jablonski brought a malpractice suit against the Loma Linda V.A. Hospital for the wrongful death of her mother, Melinda Kimball. Ms. Kimball was murdered by a patient, Phillip Jablonski, who was receiving treatment at the hospital when the murder took place. The U.S. District Court for the Central District of California entered judgment for the plaintiff on the grounds that the hospital had committed malpractice by (a) not obtaining past medical records, (b) failure to record and transmit information given by the police, and (c) failure to warn Melinda Kimball about the dangerous nature of Mr. Jablonski. The government (hospital) appealed the judgment.

Phillip Jablonski, on July 7, 1978, had threatened Melinda Kimball's mother, Isobel Pahls, with a knife and attempted to rape her. Shortly after this incident, Mr. Jablonski voluntarily went to the veterans hospital for a psychiatric examination. The police had called the hospital and were informed that he was being treated by Dr. Kopiloff. Dr. Kopiloff could not come to the phone and, therefore, the police spoke to Dr. Berman, head of psychiatric services. The police discussed Mr. Jablonski's prior criminal record, his obscene telephone calls to

Ms. Pahls, and other malicious activity and advised that Mr. Jablonski be placed in an inpatient unit. The police stated that Dr. Berman was to transmit this information to Dr. Kopiloff, but, according to Dr. Kopiloff, no such information was given to him; had it been, he would have hospitalized Mr. Jablonski involuntarily. On July 10, Ms. Kimball drove Mr. Jablonski to see Dr. Kopiloff and informed him about Mr. Jablonski's past history, which included a five-year prison term for raping his wife, and that four days ago he had attempted to rape her mother. Mr. Jablonski informed Dr. Kopiloff that he had been treated previously but refused to give specific information including where he had been treated. Dr. Kopiloff diagnosed Jablonski as having an "antisocial personality" and as "potentially dangerous." Ms. Kimball stated to Dr. Kopiloff that she felt insecure around Jablonski and was warned to leave him while he was undergoing treatment; but she stated that she still loved him.

One of the reasons the court did not rule in favor of the hospital was that the hospital made no attempt to obtain prior medical records. The plaintiffs brought in an expert witness, Dr. Thompson, who testified that it was standard procedure to obtain past medical records and the hospital could have obtained them without the consent of Jablonski because they were located at the Long Beach and Los Angeles V.A. Hospitals. In addition, Jablonski had received extensive medical treatment at the army hospital in El Paso. The El Paso records, which were not obtained, would have shown that Jablonski had on numerous occasions attempted to kill his wife and that he was "demonstrating some masculine identification in beating his wife as his father did frequently to his mother" (p. 393). On July 11 and July 12, Pahls telephoned Dr. Kopiloff and was concerned because Jablonski was not to return to the hospital for a couple of weeks. Dr. Kopiloff asked her to call the police and said that he would see Jablonski on July 14. On July 12, Meghan and Melinda Kimball moved out of Mr. Jablonski's apartment. Ms. Kimball continued to see Jablonski and drove him to his next appointment, where he met with Dr. Kopiloff and Dr. Hazle, Kopiloff's supervisor. Dr. Hazle believed Jablonski was dangerous but did not find reason to commit him on an involuntary basis. Jablonski was given more tests and received a prescription for Valium. During this appointment, Kimball met Dr. Warnell in the hallway and expressed to him her fear "for personal safety" (394). Warnell related this information to Drs. Hazel and Kopiloff but they concluded that Jablonski was not homicidal or suicidal and, therefore, could not be hospitalized involuntarily. Jablonski was to return July 17 for another appointment. However, on July 16, Kimball went to the apartment and Mr. Jablonski was there; soon after he killed her.

The government argued that they had immunity based on 28 U.S.C. § 2680 (a): "That subsection exempts from the waiver of immunity any claim based upon the exercise or performance or the failure to exercise or perform a discretionary function or duty on the part of a federal agency or an employee of the government, whether or not the discretion involved be abused" (p. 395). The court concluded that "discretionary functions" are ones that refer to police choices and that, therefore, the malpractice charges do not fall under this section. The government argued that there was no special patient-therapist relationship because Jablonski was seen as an outpatient. The court found that this was contrary to *Tarasoff* and that such an interpretation did not hold. The government argued that the victim was not specifically targeted by Jablonski. The court found the government liable because, had they obtained prior records, they could have concluded that Kimball would have been targeted as a foreseeable victim.

COURT DECISION

The court affirmed the district court's decision that the government was liable for negligence. This case states that duty to warn does not necessarily entail that an individual give the specific name of a victim and that one could infer from medical data who a foreseeable victim would be.

Bonnie Hedlund et al., Petitioners, v. the Superior Court of Orange County, Respondent; Darryl Jeffrey Wilson, a Minor etc. et al., Parties in Interest
34 Cal. 3d 695, 194 Cal. Rptr. 805
L.A. 31676; Supreme Court of California
September 29, 1983, Rehearing Denied December 15, 1983)

La Nita Wilson, the mother of Darryl Jeffrey Wilson, brought suit against Bonnie Hedlund on behalf of her son, Darryl, who was 8 years old when the trial began. La Nita Wilson and Stephen Wilson, who were not married, had received therapy from Bonnie Hedlund, a psychological assistant. Prior to April 9, 1979, Stephen Wilson had expressed to

Ms. Hedlund his intent to seriously harm La Nita Wilson. However, Ms. Hedlund had not communicated Mr. Wilson's intent to La Nita. On April 9, Stephen Wilson shot Ms. Wilson, who threw herself on her son to prevent him from being harmed.

According to the respondent, Ms. Wilson's son Darryl, age 5 at the time, suffered "serious emotional injuries and psychological trauma" (p. 41). The supreme court ruled that allegations were brought within the three-year statute of limitations required for cases based on professional negligence and that the psychotherapist's duty to warn included Darryl because he was a foreseeable bystander.

The psychotherapists asked the court to dismiss the action and requested a rehearing of the case. Their argument was that a failure to warn a third party did not constitute "professional negligence" but "ordinary negligence." The petitioners claimed that Mr. Wilson made no threat against Darryl, and, therefore, they had no duty to warn him about the threat to La Nita. So the question raised was whether a therapist is professionally negligent if he or she did not warn "an identifiable potential victim that a patient has threatened violence. The therapist may be liable not only to the person against whom the threat is made, but also to persons who may be injured if the threat is carried out" (p. 46).

The respondent stated that Ms. Hedlund did not need to warn Darryl. However, the fact that Ms. Hedlund did not warn La Nita about the danger to her life had obvious consequences for Darryl. Darryl was 5 years old at the time and, therefore, Ms. Hedlund's lack of warning to La Nita failed to protect Darryl, who could be seen as a foreseeable bystander.

COURT DECISION

A rehearing was denied. However, Judge Mosk dissented from the opinion that this was a case of "professional negligence" (malpractice); he concluded that it was one of "simple negligence." He also concluded that he felt the statute of limitations for this case should be one year as was agreed upon in the case *Tresemer V. Barke* (1978, 86 Cal. App. 3d 656, 672, 150 Cal. Rptr. 384, p. 50).

It appears there was a disagreement about the conclusion of this case. But it is clear that it did not suggest that a psychotherapist warn the third party. However, if a third party is determined to be a foreseeable bystander of the party in danger, and the party in danger is not warned, then the psychotherapist is seen as being professionally negligent and, therefore, liable to the third party. There is, however, some dissent among judges as to whether the case can be considered malpractice or one of simple negligence and whether the third party must bring suit one year from the incident or three years. According to this case, because the suit was filed three years from the incident, it was concluded to be within the statute of limitations.

James Scott Brady, Timothy John McCarthy, and Thomas K. Delahanty, Plaintiffs, v. John J. Hopper, Jr., M.D., Defendant
U.S. District Court, D. Colorado 570 F. Supp. 1333, Siv. A No. 830JM-451 (September 14, 1983)

Plaintiffs brought suit against psychiatrist Dr. John J. Hopper for negligence in treating patient John W. Hinckley, Jr. Mr. Hinckley had shot and seriously injured the plaintiffs during his attempt to assassinate the American president on March 30, 1981, in Washington D.C. The defendant, Dr. John J. Hopper, asked for a dismissal of the case.

John Hinckley began treatment with Dr. Hopper in late October 1980. Mr. Hinckley's parents had brought him to Dr. Hopper because they were concerned about his behavior—he had attempted to commit suicide with an overdose of pills. Dr. Hopper had prescribed biofeedback and Valium for Mr. Hinckley as part of his treatment. During the course of treatment, which terminated in March 1981, Mr. Hinckley had never specifically mentioned any intention to kill the president. Dr. Hopper had ascertained that Mr. Hinckley was not seriously ill and, therefore, did not require hospitalization. He requested that Mr. Hinckley's parents remove any financial support from their son. The defendant pointed out that Hinckley had no "history of violence, no previous arrest" (p. 1334) or any previous hospitalizations due to violence. The defense argued that, if Dr. Hopper had breached confidentiality without specific knowledge of a victim, he would have violated Colorado law (Colo. Rev. Stat. 27-10-120 [1] [1973]), and that Dr. Hopper's treatment of the patient concurred with Colorado law (Colo. Rev. Stat. 27-10-101), which supports Dr. Hopper's decision not to hospitalize Mr. Hinckley but to encourage his independence and self-reliance by using the least restrictive means of dealing with his illness.

COURT DECISION

The defendant's motion to dismiss the case was granted. The main issue, according to the court, was what obligation this therapist had to protect the plaintiffs from harm. The conclusion was that a psychotherapist couldn't be held liable to a third party when no specific threat had been indicated. The court did state that the therapist's treatment fell below the standard of care and that a "special relationship" did exist between the patient and the doctor, but this was not the issue at hand. The court concluded that, if they found fault with Dr. Hopper, they would be saying that a therapist holds ultimate responsibility for his or her client, which was not a notion the court could support because human nature is too unpredictable and the field of mental health is presently not an exact science.

Important to note. This case did cite Colorado cases *Sego V. Mains* (41 Colo. App. 1,578 P.2d 1069, 1978); *Leppke v. Segura* (Colo. App., 632 P.2d 1057, 1981). In the *Leppke v. Segura* case, defendants were found liable in a car collision because they jump-started a car of a man who was legally intoxicated. The plaintiffs state that the Colorado appellate courts take a broader view toward third-party liability and focus on the risk-creating situation rather than to the foreseeability of a particular crime. The conclusion is that Colorado courts hold people liable only when threats are given to a specific victim.

Genoa M. White, Appellant, v. United States of America
U.S. Court of Appeals, District of Columbia Circuit
780 F.2d 97, No. 84-5645
(Argued November 18, 1985; Decided January 3, 1986)

Genoa White, wife of patient Dwayne White, had appealed a court decision that did not conclude that her husband's psychotherapist and the hospital to which he had been court ordered were negligent when the husband left the hospital grounds, went to her home, and brutally stabbed her. Mr. Dwayne had been ordered by the courts on February 8, 1969, to be confined to St. Elizabeths hospital. Mr. White, at the age of 18, had attacked police officers and killed one when they were attempting to arrest his father. The hospital had diagnosed Mr. White as an "explosive personality" (p. 99) and concluded that he had a low tolerance for stress. During the 10-year period when he was receiving

treatment at St. Elizabeths, he had shown additional incidents of violence (i.e., assaulting fellow patients and additional police officers)
and, during an authorized leave, had attempted to rob a cab driver. Also,
Mr. White had made additional unauthorized leaves and during one
such leave he had left the hospital to marry Genoa, who was a former
patient at St. Elizabeths. The hospital did not find out about this
marriage until three months later, and some time later staff made notes
of the incident. The hospital had assumed Mr. White was leaving the
hospital grounds to visit his wife. However, they made no special
attempts to tighten his security.

Mr. White was seeing Dr. Lorraine Brown, a clinical psychologist,
weekly. During the course of treatment, Mr. White revealed a fantasy
in which he had shot his wife. According to Dr. Brown, Mr. White
clearly knew the difference between fantasy and reality. In addition,
Dr. Brown pointed out that Mr. White had never assaulted women and
had not been violent for over a year. Therefore, Dr. Brown believed
she had no obligation to warn the plaintiff of possible harm. Dr. Brown
did not discuss this fantasy with hospital staff because the hospital had
a policy known as a "therapist-administrator split": to ensure that the
therapist and patient can develop a trusting relationship, the therapist is
not involved in administrative discussions regarding patient treatment.

Six months after the patient had shared his fantasy, he left the
grounds without authorization and went to his wife's apartment. Prior
to his arrival, his wife had been drinking and had shared with him a
picture of herself in a bathing suit and kimono with a man in boxer
shorts. When the plaintiff turned away from the patient, he took a pair
of scissors and stabbed her 55 times.

COURT DECISION

The U.S. Court of Appeals granted Mrs. White a reversed decision but
remanded the hospital for negligence and not the psychotherapist. The
court ruled that Dr. Brown had followed standard care and could not be
held liable. However, the hospital was negligent because it had not
followed court orders confining Mr. White at all times to hospital
grounds; Mr. White was not to leave their grounds until a court had
decided upon this matter. The hospital personnel in their own words
admitted they had suspected Mr. White was leaving the hospital grounds
to visit his wife but had failed to tighten Mr. White's security.

Carolyn Sue Phillips, Individually and in the Capacity as Natural Tutrix of
the Minor Children, Travis Earl and Tarron Phillips, Plaintiffs-Appellants, v.
William Glen Roy, Gibson's Inc., Sentry Insurance and State of Louisiana,
through the Louisiana Health and Human Resources Administration, Divi-
sion of Mental Health Central Louisiana State Hospital, Defendants-Appellees
Court of Appeal of Louisiana, Second Circuit
494 So. 2d 1342, No. 18045-CA (September 24, 1986)

Carolyn Sue Phillips filed suit against Gibson's and Sentry Insurance
and the Central Louisiana State Hospital for negligence because they
discharged their patient, William Glen Roy. According to the summary
case report, the plaintiff dismissed and settled with Gibson's and Sentry
Insurance prior to trial. The Eighth Judicial District Court, Parish of
Winn, entered judgment for the state hospital, and Mrs. Phillips and her
children appealed that decision.

William Glen Roy, over a 10-year period, had been hospitalized five
times at Central and one time at another institution. He was diagnosed
as being a schizophrenic, paranoid acute, accompanied by aggressive
behavior. Mr. Roy was known to dislike blacks but had never stated
specifically that he intended to harm individuals who were black. He
had made homicidal and suicidal threats but had never carried them out.
His last hospitalization lasted 29 days, during which time he became
cooperative, never threatened anyone, and went home on several occasions and returned. Mrs. Roy requested that he be sent home. The
hospital gave Mr. Roy a supply of antipsychotic drugs and an appointment with a local mental health clinic, which was a routine that followed normal procedures for any patient once released. Mr. Roy got a
job and continued to take his medication until he separated from his
wife. On February 28, 1979, 4 months after he stopped going to the local
mental health clinic and 19 months after he was discharged from the
state hospital, Mr. Roy bought a gun and, while driving, randomly shot
at black people. During this episode, he killed Earl Phillips, the husband
of the plaintiff-appellant.

The plaintiff argued that there was negligence because the hospital
had no follow-up program for Mr. Roy whereby they could monitor
his activities; the hospital failed to notify police about Mr. Roy's violent
nature when he was released; and they did not identify foreseeable
victims to the police.

The court of appeals affirmed the district court decision of entering judgment for the hospital. They based their decision on the fact that the hospital had followed standard care when they released Roy. The patient was not demonstrating behaviors that would permit him to be committed when he was released, and, therefore, they had a duty to release him. Second, they were following their standard procedures when they referred him to a local mental health clinic, and, therefore, they did not need to continue treatment of the patient. It was also noted that they had received information from the local mental health clinic about the progress of Mr. Roy. Finally, the discussion section of the case report pointed out that "the fact that Roy lived a relatively normal life for nineteen months after his discharge supports the reasonableness of the hospital's action at the time he was discharged" (p. 1347).

Implications

a. There is a duty to protect (warn) any intended victim and notify law enforcement in many states. In some states (e.g., Maryland), there is no duty to protect.

b. When there is a duty to warn, if a third party (such as a child) is determined to be a foreseeable bystander of the party in danger, then there is a duty to warn a third-party bystander.

c. In many states, specific threats must be made by the client or acts of violence may not be determined to be foreseeable.

d. When a psychotherapist can infer from data (such as history) who the foreseeable victim will be, there may be a duty to warn without the intended victim being named.

e. There is no assurance of a psychotherapist's immunity just because he or she works for a governmental agency.

f. Therapists should be certain to ask clients during an initial intake session about their prior medical treatment and/or past history of violence.

g. Therapists should have a standard follow-up procedure for all clients especially clients who have been known to be dangerous.

Commentary

Are you aware of whether your state has adopted the *Tarasoff* I rule, which dictates that it is your duty to warn an intended victim, or whether it has adopted the *Tarasoff* II rule, which makes you responsible for assessing foreseeable harm and thus states that you must exercise duty to protect foreseeable victims? Do you use "standard" procedures for assessing and managing potentially dangerous clients? If you do not know the answer to these questions, you may be found liable when you work with a potentially dangerous individual.

State Laws. From the *Tarasoff* case, the Supreme Court of California placed the responsibility to protect the intended victim on the therapist: "To use reasonable care to protect the intended victim.... The discharge of this duty . . . may call for him [or her] to warn the intended victim or others likely to apprise the victim of the danger, to notify the police, or to take whatever other steps are reasonably necessary under the circumstances" (Schwartz, 1985, p. 67).

States vary with regard to measures a counselor/therapist can take when working with a dangerous client and having knowledge of an intended victim. According to Herlihy and Sheeley (1988), 12 of 18 states that have counselor licensure provide some measure to protect counselors when they break confidentiality in order to warn an intended victim. These states include "Alabama, Arkansas, Idaho, Mississippi, Missouri, Montana, Nebraska, North Carolina, Ohio, Oklahoma, Virginia, & West Virginia" (p. 211). However, Herlihy and Sheeley warn therapists to consult legal advisers in the states of Alabama and Arkansas, because these states declare that therapist protections are offered in the states of California, Colorado, Kentucky, and New Hampshire (Herlihy & Sheeley, 1988). States that might "actually prevent a licensed counselor from warning a potential victim" include Idaho, Missouri, Nebraska, North Carolina, Oklahoma, Virginia, West Virginia" (Herlihy & Sheeley, 1988, p. 211), and this could include Maryland.

According to Kermani and Drob (1987), the case of *Brady v. Hopper* should be interpreted as meaning that the duty of therapist is to warn when the serious threat is directed at a specific individual. However, they concluded that *Lipari v. Sears* broadened this duty to include clients "who do not make threats and whose potential victims are unknown to both the treating therapist and the patient himself" (Kermani

& Drob, 1987, p. 284). According to Vandecreek, Knapp, and Herzog (1987, p. 148), "It is probably wise, however, for psychotherapists to assume that they could be subject to the Tarasoff rules."

Assessing and managing the dangerous client. It is your responsibility to have a "standard" method with which to assess and manage a dangerous client. Various professionals (Applebaum, 1985; Herlihy & Sheeley, 1988; Rachlin & Schwartz, 1986; Roth & Meisel, 1977; Woody, 1988) give detailed advice regarding steps to follow when working with a dangerous client. You need to compare and contrast their positions and determine your own procedures.

Roth and Meisel (in Schutz, 1982, p. 61) outlined the specific steps to follow regarding treatment and informing the victim:

1. Ask the patient to warn the victim himself (This has dangerous possibilities of a threatening confrontation escalating into the feared violence. The patient should be so informed.)
2. Get consent from the patient to warn the intended victim.
3. Have a joint session with the patient and intended victim to disclose the threat and explore the factors leading up to it.
4. Have the patient turn in any weapons he possesses.
5. Increase the frequency of therapy sessions.
6. Consider medication as an adjunct.
7. Consider voluntary hospitalization.

Rachlin and Schwartz (1986) make recommendations to therapists on how to avoid malpractice when treating dangerous clients.

1. A therapist can be held liable for failing to obtain the patient's previous medical records. Therefore, if possible, obtain previous medical records and if a patient does not consent for records to be released make note of your recommendations in the chart.
2. The "best defense to allegations of malpractice is careful documentation." Write down your clinical treatment and if in doubt, consult a colleague and make a note in the record.
3. Do not discharge a psychotic person on his [or her] own recognizance.
4. Do not give a prescription to a patient known to be reluctant to take medication. Place patient on one-to-one supervision if this is the [case].
5. Do not use a psychiatrist as an expert witness if he/she is not board certified. (pp. 729-731)

Applebaum (1985, p. 462) suggested a three-stage method for treating potentially dangerous clients:

Stage 1. The process of assessment includes (a) the therapist gathering data relevant to an evaluation of dangerousness and (b) determining dangerousness on the basis of that data.

Stage 2. Selection of a course includes (a) duty to warn a foreseeable victim and (b) duty to protect, which might include hospitalizing the patient (voluntarily or involuntarily); transferring an already hospitalized patient to a more secure ward; maintaining outpatient status for the patient but beginning medication; intensifying individual therapy, family therapy, or other systems-oriented therapy, which might even involve the potential victim.

Stage 3. Implementing the decisions appropriately includes the following: (a) effectively carrying out whatever procedures you've chosen to protect the victims and (b) monitoring the situation on a continuing basis to assess the success or failure of the initial response, the likelihood that the patient will be violent, and the need for further measures to decrease the risk presented by the patient.

Mills, Sullivan, and Eth (1987) point out that, although therapists can protect themselves from liability by warning the police and third parties, this is not always the best method for protecting potential victims. They advise that, in addition to warning, the therapist could use such clinical remedies as reassessment, consultation, changes in medication, or civil commitment (institutionalization).

Kelleher (in Herlihy & Sheeley, 1988, p. 212) has identified possible affirmative duties that have emerged from case precedents. Recommendations for the therapist working with a dangerous client include

(1) intensifying treatment.
(2) attempting to persuade the client to accept voluntary treatment.
(3) attempting to secure involuntary commitment.
(4) warning the potential victim.
(5) warning family or friends who might apprise the victim of the danger, and
(6) notifying the police.

Herlihy and Sheeley (1988, pp. 212-213) have also gathered recommendations from Denkowski and Denkowski (1982), Halleck (1980),

Roth and Meisel (1977), Vandecreek and Knapp (1984), which comprise the following guidelines:

(1) Keeping in mind that the primary objective should be to keep the client in therapy, deal with the aggression as part of the treatment.

(2) To avoid overreacting, remember that clients without a history of violence rarely implement their threats; to be prudent, pursue other options before breaching confidentiality.

(3) Take an informed consent approach by securing the client's permission for disclosure and inviting the client to participate in the process, or by contacting the third party in the presence of the client.

(4) Attempt environmental manipulation such as having the client get rid of lethal weapons.

(5) Be prepared by formulating contingency plans that are derived in consultation with an informed attorney, a local psychiatric hospital, and area law enforcement personnel.

(6) Consult with professional colleagues and attorneys who have expertise and experience in dealing with dangerous clients.

(7) Keep careful records and document all actions taken.

(8) Issue warnings to third parties only as a last resort after actions directly involving the client have been ineffective.

(9) If warning a third party is unavoidable, disclose only the minimum amount necessary to protect the victim or the public, stating the specific threat but reserving any opinion or prediction.

(10) If consideration is given to seeking involuntary commitment of an outpatient client, act in good faith, consult with colleagues, and thoroughly research applicable laws and standards.

Woody (1988, p. 165) gives advice on how to reduce risks when treating dangerous clients, as follows:

(1) Developing a method for assessing dangerousness which includes using the methods associated with one's profession (i.e., social workers taking in-depth personal history, a psychiatrist conducting a mental health exam and a psychologist might administer a psychological test),

(2) Receiving specialized training,

(3) Planning a treatment approach,

(4) Dealing with the Noncompliant Dangerous Client . . .

(a) [the] practitioner recommend that the client and the family seek voluntary admission to a hospital, question police protection or take comparable protective steps

(b) if this protective intervention cannot be obtained then refer client to a professional source with more intervention clout (i.e., medical facility) and

(c) then if the first two steps cannot be obtained the therapist is forced to break confidentiality and get the law involved in the case.

Conclusions

We believe that psychotherapists have a responsibility to protect life.

(1) We urge each of you to know your state law. Most states have a *Tarasoff*-type doctrine whereby you must (a) notify law enforcement of the threat and (b) prove that you made a reasonable effort to communicate the threat to the potential victim.

(2) When no threat was made toward an identifiable victim but you predict that your client is a danger to others, we suggest you consider (a) increasing the frequency of therapeutic contacts, (b) consulting with a colleague, (c) referring for medication, (d) getting your client to voluntarily commit, (e) getting your client to turn over lethal weapons, (f) hospitalizing the client, and (g) advising the client's family and/or law enforcement.

Summary

The psychotherapist's responsibility to protect is determined by individual state's laws. Although most states require therapists to inform their clients' intended victims of harm, some states do not. For example, the state law of Maryland does not include a duty to protect. In fact, a therapist may be sued for breaching confidentiality while attempting to protect a suspected victim in the state of Maryland.

Therapists are encouraged to ask their clients during an initial intake session about any prior medical treatment and/or past history of violence. Any information the therapist receives concerning a client, whether directly from the client or from police or significant others, should be documented in the client's file. Other written documentation that should be kept in the client's file includes any advice given by the therapist to the client, treatment contracts as agreed upon between client and therapist, and the client's response (verbally and behaviorally) to the advice and contracts.

Vignette

You have been seeing a couple named Judy and Frank. It came out in one of your conjoint sessions that Frank had been seeing another woman at work. In an individual session with Judy, she tells you that she is scaring herself with the thoughts she is having about the other woman and about Frank. She feels so betrayed by Frank that she has not been able to get thoughts of doing away with him out of her mind. She even went so far as to purchase a gun and has stored it in her clothes closet. She doesn't see herself as a violent person so she is not too concerned about her thoughts, for she thinks this will all pass. How do you assess whether she is a "dangerous" client? What are the ethical and legal considerations in terms of informing Frank about this situation? How do you go about managing Judy if you do consider her to be a dangerous client? What are the legal and ethical considerations for this case according to your state?

Questions to Consider

(1) When there is a legal duty to warn, it exists only if a therapeutic relationship exists. Under what conditions does such a relationship exist?

(2) How might you determine that a client is dangerous?

(3) Other than civil commitment, are there reasonable ways to therapeutically manage a person who is dangerous to self or others? If yes, what are they?

(4) What is your state law regarding duty to protect?

7

Failure to Take Precautions
Against Suicide

Suicidal statements made by clients create one of the most stressful dilemmas to be dealt with by therapists (Deutsch, 1984; Farber, 1983a, 1983b). "The evaluation and management of suicidal risk is a source of extraordinary stress for most psychologists [and other mental health professionals]" (Pope, 1985, p. 1).

> Case law indicates that therapists have an obligation not only to conduct an adequate examination with regard to suicidal risk (note: therapists are not expected to be infallible, but the examination must meet the relevant legal, ethical, and professional standards), but also, if the client is deemed to be suicidal, to use reasonable care in taking appropriate steps to manage risk. (Pope, 1985, p. 2)

Therapists often find themselves at a loss to know the appropriate course of action when they are dealing with suicidal clients. This is especially true if their values are in conflict with the law. For example, psychiatrists such as R. D. Laing (1967), who argue that suicide is an ultimate right of an individual, have trouble squaring their position with the legal requirement for therapists to report clients who are a danger to themselves. Szasz (1986) challenges the view that mental health professionals have a duty to protect suicidal clients. Szasz argues that suicide is an act of a moral agent who is ultimately responsible, and thus he opposes coercive methods to prevent suicide. Some therapists assume that it is their obligation to do everything possible to keep a client alive; other therapists contend that clients are responsible for their acts. Regardless of your stand on suicide, the key questions are these: Did the therapist know, or should he or she have known, of the risk? Were prudent measures used when preventing the client from suicide? One of the major challenges consists in correctly assessing how dangerous the client is to him- or herself. A therapist can be sued for overreacting or for underreacting to the client's threats.

Court Cases

(1) *Gregory v. Robinson* **(1960)**

(2) *Pietrucha v. Grant Hospital* **(1971)**

(3) *Eady v. Alter* **(1976)**

(4) *Cohen v. State of New York* **(1976)**

(5) *Bellah v. Greenson* **(1977)**

(6) *Johnson v. County of Los Angeles* **(1983)**

Case Reviews

Frank Edwin Gregory, Appellant, v. Paul S. Robinson, Executor of
G. Wilse Robinson, M.D., G. Wilse Robinson, Jr., M.D., and
Paul Hines, M.D., Respondents
338 S.W. 2d 88 Supreme Court of Missouri (1960)

This case involved a suit by a patient for damages for personal injuries filed against physicians who served as partners in operating a mental hospital in Kansas City. Dr. Hines, the hospital psychiatrist on duty at the time of this incident, was accused of negligence in protecting a patient who was being treated for severe depression. Although this particular court case does not involve a suicide, there are several related pieces of information that may be helpful to psychotherapists, especially those working in mental institutions, regarding the topic of taking precautions against suicide.

Mr. Gregory, who was employed at Bendix Aviation Corporation in Kansas City, was admitted to the Neurological Hospital in Kansas City during September 1955 because he was feeling depressed and worried. He was diagnosed as severely depressed and placed with the acutely mentally ill patients on the third floor of the hospital. He received three electroshock treatments as the primary and accepted treatment for his condition. Within a week's stay at the hospital, Mr. Gregory's condition was reported to have improved, although the physicians had not ruled out the possibility of attempted suicide. The hospital staff recognized the need to permit patients

> as much freedom as possible, to treat them as individuals, and to try to "resocialize" them; that therein the physicians knowingly take a calculated risk; that better safeguards could be afforded by strict confinement, but that few patients would be cured; that there is a potential for suicide or for harming others in all acutely depressed mental cases. (p. 90)

Consequently, patients were granted freedom to walk around the different areas of the floor (i.e., their rooms and the accompanying hallways, lounges, and recreation areas). However, the windows were barred and there were only two exit doors (i.e., an elevator door and stairway door), which were locked.

One week after the plaintiff was admitted to the hospital, he leaped from an unbarred window located above a radiator on the stair landing between the second and third floors and suffered injuries. The series of incidents that preceded the patient's jumping from the window are as follows.

Dr. Hines, the psychiatrist in charge, was writing orders at the nurses' station on the third floor of the hospital. The plaintiff approached Dr. Hines and indicated that he was feeling much better, "that he thought it was time to go home . . . [and] asked permission to call his wife to have her come for him" (p. 89). The testimony of Dr. Hines was

> that he explained to Mr. Gregory that he had not yet had enough treatment, that he should have more treatments and stay quite a while longer, and that he could not be permitted to use the phone; that Mr. Gregory seemed

a little unhappy at this, but that he walked on out, apparently without protest. (p. 89)

Mr. Gregory argued in his testimony that Dr. Hines did not answer his "questions."

Shortly after Dr. Hines's talk with Mr. Gregory at the nurses' station, the psychiatrist proceeded to the locked door leading to the stairway, looked in three directions, saw his patient sitting on his bed in his room 15 feet away, unlocked the door, and started entering through the doorway. Unexpectedly, within a few seconds, while Dr. Hines's back was turned, Mr. Gregory pushed Dr. Hines aside and shoved his way through the doorway. Astonished by the experience, Dr. Hines called into the hall for assistance and chased Mr. Gregory down the steps. Mr. Gregory had managed to crawl through the open window on the stairwell landing and was hanging on to the outside windowsill, ready to drop toward the ground two and a half stories below. Dr. Hines noticed his patient's fingers protruding over the windowsill but was unable to rescue him in the limited time available. Mr. Gregory suffered very serious injuries resulting from the fall.

Subsequent to Mr. Gregory's fall from the window, and at the time of court trial, he had reportedly recovered from his mental illness and was employed, although in a position that paid less. Mr. Gregory, as plaintiff, filed a negligence suit against Dr. Hines for having "[a] . . . failed to make a reasonably careful inspection of the area before opening the door; and [b] that defendant 'in passing through said door failed to exercise reasonable care to determine that no patients were therein attempting to follow' him and escape" (p. 91).

COURT DECISION

The Supreme Court of Missouri ruled that Dr. Hines was not negligent by unlocking the barred door leading into the stairway of the third floor, even though he knew that, in patient Mr. Gregory's mental state, there was a possibility he might attempt either to escape or to commit suicide. It is worth noting, however, that this particular court case made reference to several other court cases that indicated that both (a) the time element and (b) having open, unbarred windows accessible to patients residing in a mental hospital are deemed especially important material for possible negligence.

Janina Pietrucha, Individually and as Administratrix of the Estate of Albert Pietrucha, Deceased, Plaintiff-Appellant, v. Grant Hospital, a Corporation, Defendant-Appellee,
U.S. Court of Appeals, Seventh Circuit
447 F.2d 1029 (Illinois, 1971)

This case involved widow Janina Pietrucha, serving as the plaintiff for her 42-year-old deceased husband, Albert Pietrucha. The couple were reported to have been happily married with six children, the oldest of whom was 18 years of age. Janina's husband committed suicide on September 24, 1967, 24 hours after he was admitted to the psychiatric ward of Grant Hospital. The plaintiff filed suit against the hospital for negligence, alleging the hospital failed to exercise ordinary care to safeguard her husband against suicide. "A res ipsa loquitur claim" stated that the "hospital had exclusive control of the decedent and that [the] occurrence was one that would not ordinarily have taken place" (p. 1030). The initial court ruled in favor of the hospital, and the plaintiff appealed.

Background information indicated that the decedent had been treated by psychiatrist Dr. Zaldivar in Loretto Hospital during a two-week confinement period about six months previous to his suicide and at Grant Hospital. Dr. Zaldivar had diagnosed Albert Pietrucha as having "acute" schizophrenia and later discharged him while recommending further psychiatric care.

At the time Albert Pietrucha was admitted to Grant Hospital, about 3:00 p.m., the head of the hospital psychiatric ward and a nurse were forewarned of Albert's "extreme depression, his suicidal tendencies and his recent attempted suicide" (p. 1030). The nurse's log included the forewarning "with a caution to watch closely for any suicide attempt" (p. 1030). Instructions were given to the ward nurses to watch the decedent closely. At about 3:30 a.m., during his first night's visitation, Albert was found hanging from a belt in the men's washroom adjoining his room.

An important question that was addressed during the court proceedings was whether or not the belt used in the suicide belonged to the decedent. A hospital manual of instruction required that certain articles, including belts, be removed from all patients upon admission to the hospital. Differences of opinion were expressed during testimony on the belt. Testimony for the plaintiff reported that the belt was the decedent's and the hospital had failed to remove it from him. The inventoried list of items removed from the patient did not include the belt. However, the hospital's testimony revealed that a nurse had removed the patient's belt during the admission procedures and placed it in a drawer in the nurse's office. Two significant questions subsequent to this incongruency were these:

> If the belt was decedent's and not removed as required by the manual, the jury might have found the hospital was negligent. On the other hand, had the nurse removed the belt and placed it in the drawer, the jury might infer that the hospital was not responsible if during the routine fifteen minute check by the nurse of the rooms in the ward, decedent had not obtained another belt, [but] removed the belt from the drawer. (p. 1031)

The plaintiff moved to call an adverse witness, hospital supervisor Royal, who had allegedly taken the belt from decedent's neck and made a statement to the police at the scene, "This is the man's belt. He should not have had it" (p. 1031). However, according to a certain court rule, because Royal was not an "officer, director or managing agent of the hospital" (p. 1031), the district court refused to honor the plaintiff's motion.

COURT DECISION

The U.S. district court ruled in favor of the defendant by indicating that the hospital was not negligent in respect to the suicidal death of decedent, who had hanged himself with a belt. The plaintiff appealed the judgment and a rehearing was denied. Although the case summary report did not clarify the process of how the decedent obtained the belt, a decisive factor in determining the final court judgment was whether or not the hospital staff had clearly abided by its manual of instruction for admitting the decedent, who had a potential risk of suicide.

Willie Eady, as Administratrix etc., Appellant, v. Jacob B. Alter et al., Respondents
Supreme Court, Appellate Division, Second Department
380 N.Y.S. 2d 737 (New York, 1976)

On April 3, 1975, the Supreme Court of Kings County, New York, dismissed action for plaintiff's claim to recover damages for wrongful death and conscious pain and suffering. The memorandum by the court stated that the action was properly dismissed because no prima facie case was established against the defendant, Unity Hospital. The plaintiff later appealed the supreme court judgment and a new trial was held on March 8, 1986. Unity Hospital was claimed to be liable for failing to properly supervise and restrain a suicidal patient who succeeded in terminating his life.

The plaintiff's decedent was admitted to Unity Hospital on October 18, 1969, for a bronchitis ailment. Four days later, at 11:50 p.m., however, the decedent began behaving in a "very nervous" manner. A disturbance in his room at about 1:30 a.m. on October 23 led to the transferring of the decedent's hospital roommate to another room. The intern's notation in the medical record stated "pt is getting nervous. had shaking all body and tried to jump out from window with the other patient in the same room" (p. 739). Approximately 10 minutes after the reporting of this incident, the patient committed suicide by leaping from the window in his room.

COURT DECISION

The supreme court, appellate division, superseded the original order and reversed the judgment, finding Unity Hospital, the defendant, negligent in failing to provide closer supervision to the patient, who had committed suicide. The court held that the hospital intern's notation that the patient had attempted to jump out the window approximately 10 minutes before the suicide was "admissible to show that patient's state of mind manifested potential to do himself harm and, when considered with testimony that patient had been inadequately restrained following reported incident, was sufficient to make out prima facie case against hospital" (p. 737).

Ellen Fisher Cohen, as Administratrix of the Estate of Alan David Cohen, Deceased, Respondent, v. State of New York, Appellant
Supreme Court, Appellate Division, Third Department
382 N.Y.S. 2d (New York, 1976)

NOTE: This case will be the only case discussed in Chapter 16; see that chapter for the case description.

Melanie Bellah and Robert N. Bellah, Plaintiffs and Appellants, v. Daniel P.
Greenson, M.D., Defendant and Respondent
Court of Appeal, First District, Division
141 Cal. Rptr. 92 (California, 1977)

On April 11, 1975, two years after the suicide death of their daughter,
plaintiffs Melanie and Robert Bellah brought action against defendant
Daniel P. Greenson, a psychiatrist in Berkeley, California, who had
treated their daughter Thomasin (Tammy) Bellah for an unspecified
period of time prior to her death. Tammy had succumbed to a self-inflicted overdose of sleeping pills on April 12, 1973. At the time of
Tammy's death, her parents were temporarily residing in Princeton,
New Jersey, and were unaware of their daughter's suicidal tendencies
because they had not communicated with Tammy for several months.

In the action brought against psychiatrist Daniel Greenson, plaintiffs
Melanie and Robert Bellah filed three allegations against their deceased
daughter's psychiatrist. It was alleged

> [a] that defendant had failed to personally take measures to prevent
> Tammy's suicide; [b] that he had failed to warn others (including plain-
> tiffs) of the seriousness of Tammy's condition and her suicidal proclivity;
> and [c] that he had failed to inform plaintiffs that Tammy was consorting
> with heroin addicts in plaintiff's home. (p. 93)

In addition, "plaintiffs alleged that, as a result of defendant's negligence, they suffered severe mental anguish and pecuniary loss due to
theft from their home" (p. 93).

Defendant Greenson objected to the action filed against him and held
as a defense the statute of limitations. The court judge sustained the
defendant's objection "without leave to amend" (p. 93). On October 1,
1975, the plaintiffs' motion for reconsideration of the judgment was
denied. Two years later, on November 1, 1977, a rehearing resulting
from the plaintiffs' appeal was granted.

COURT DECISION

The court of appeals held that psychiatrist Daniel Greenson was not
liable for negligence relating to the suicide death of the plaintiffs'
daughter or for damages for the plaintiffs' mental anguish and pecuniary
loss due to theft from their home. The court made reference to the case

of *Tarasoff v. Regents of the University of California* (1975), where the supreme court determined that psychotherapists are required to exercise reasonable care to inform the proper authorities and warn the likely victim when suspecting a client might injure another. The *Tarasoff* ruling requires therapists to breach confidential communications only when there is potential risk of violent assault against another person who has been reasonably identified. There was no requirement to breach confidentiality in those situations where risk of harm is self-inflicted harm or mere property damage. Therefore, the current court case declined to further extend the holding of *Tarasoff* and thereby apply liability. The plaintiffs' appeal was dismissed and the original judgment was affirmed.

Dana Renee Johnson et al., Plaintiffs and Appellants, v. County of Los Angeles et al., Defendants and Respondents
143 Cal. App. 3d 298; 191 Cal. Rptr. 704 (May 1983)

Mr. Johnson had been arrested and detained in the Los Angeles County jail for four days as a result of a traffic violation. Two days after he was released, on May 7, 1980, he committed suicide. Mr. Johnson's wife, Dana Renee Johnson, and daughter, Mindy Lyn Johnson, brought a suit against the County of Los Angeles and sheriff's officers alleging the involved parties had violated their duties to (a) confine, (b) medicate, and (c) summon medical care for Mr. Johnson during his confinement. Additionally, they alleged that the sheriff's officers violated their duty to warn them of Mr. Johnson's release from custody. "The trial court sustained the demurrer without leave to amend, and dismissed the complaint" (p. 298). The plaintiffs appealed the trial court's judgment and the court of appeals heard the case.

The facts underlying the appellate court case concern events beginning on May 2, 1980, when Mr. Johnson was arrested by sheriffs for driving on the wrong side of the freeway. Upon his arrest, Mr. Johnson revealed "he was attempting to commit suicide and that 'people' were trying to torture him or kill him, and pleaded that Sheriffs kill him" (p. 304). Mr. Johnson was charged for assault with a deadly weapon and taken to the county jail. Soon afterward, Mr. Johnson's wife, Dana, told sheriffs that her husband "was a paranoid schizophrenic, had been repeatedly hospitalized, and required immediate medication (Thorazine) to correct a chemical imbalance which created [husband's] aberrant conduct" (p. 304). Mrs. Johnson further advised sheriffs that her husband "had suicidal tendencies requiring immediate medical attention, and should not be released" (p. 304). The sheriffs replied that they understood what Mrs. Johnson had said and they promised to hospitalize and medicate her husband. They also told her "not to worry or interfere" (p. 304).

COURT DECISION

The court of appeals reversed judgment of the trial court and ruled that the county had a duty to warn the released prisoner's wife and daughter. The court maintained that "defendants [the county and sheriff's officers] stood in a special relationship to the decedent [Mr. Johnson] and to plaintiffs [wife and daughter of Mr. Johnson] and thus had a duty to warn plaintiffs before releasing decedent" (p. 298). Also, the defendants were held liable for breaching their statutory duty of care to Mr. Johnson pursuant to a government code "by failing to furnish or obtain medical care for decedent [Mr. Johnson] when they knew, or had reason to know, that decedent was in need of immediate medical care, and avers that Decedent's suicide was the proximate result of that breach" (p. 305). The court summary report made reference in part to the relevant Government Code section 845.6:

> Neither a public entity nor a public employee is liable for injury proximately caused by the failure of the employee to furnish or obtain medical care for a prisoner in his custody; but, except as otherwise provided by Sections 855.8 and 856, a public employee, and the public entity where the employee knows or has reason to know that the prisoner is in need of immediate medical care and he fails to take reasonable action to summon such medical care. (p. 305)

However, with regard to the two other complaints filed, the court ruled that the defendants were immune from liability for failure (a) to confine and (b) to medicate Mr. Johnson.

The court case report made reference to several other related court cases, in particular, to the *Tarasoff* (1975) case. With the current case, Mr. Johnson was "not only a foreseeable target of danger, he was the specific and identified potential victim . . . [having] made a specific threat of harm directed at a specific victim—himself" (p. 301). Although this case pertained to a suit that was not filed against psychotherapists, there are several relevant implications that may be used as cautionary guidelines for practice by psychotherapists.

Implications

a. The courts may rely on other judicial decisions in arriving at a decision (*Gregory v. Robinson*, 1960). It is very important to stay up to date on judicial decisions as they pertain to the profession.

b. It is highly advisable that a therapist in private practice belong to a group or consortium of therapists to meet and confer on client case reviews.

c. Different standards apply to an inpatient as opposed to an outpatient.

d. You should know what standards apply. There are three levels to consider:

(1) judicial decisions

(2) policy/procedures of an agency

(3) standards of the community

e. Clear, specific, and objective documentation of treatment and preventive actions taken are good safeguards against liability.

f. We suggest that organizations and institutions offering mental health services have staff training that deals with a review of the legal literature each week and the implications for the unit.

g. Therapists should be very familiar with their employing institutional/organizational manual and policies for dealing with suicidal clients. If such a manual does not exist, we recommend that such a manual be written and adopted by the respective institution/organization as the agreed-upon policy for its employees in handling suicidal clients.

h. At the beginning of the therapeutic relationship, we recommend that therapists ask their clients to identify their "significant others" in case of emergency. We also recommend that therapists receive a written consent form from clients at the beginning of a therapeutic relationship as to whom the therapist may contact in situations in which the client might be contemplating suicide.

i. Construct a written assessment form to be followed for assessing suicide in reference to the client's past, present, and future thoughts and/or behaviors. At the beginning of the therapeutic relationship, it is advisable that therapists do an assessment with regard to the client's past experiences in therapy and any history of suicidal thoughts and/or attempts. At the beginning of such an assessment, the therapist could mention that such a procedure is standard policy for conducting an intake session with every new client. This would help avoid any misunderstandings by the client that he or she is perceived by the therapist as being suicidal. Also, be certain to document the results of your assessment in writing.

j. When dealing with minors, it is advisable that at the beginning of the therapeutic relationship, the therapist create a written contract, designed by both the therapist and the client, concerning the procedures to be followed if the therapist determines that the client is suicidal. In addition, the signature of a parent or legal guardian should be included on the written contract. These procedures may help the client to have more trust in the therapist as well as placing more responsibility on the client in suicidal situations. Such procedures also help to "demystify" the counseling process by informing the client and parent or legal guardian as to what procedures to expect if the therapist suspects the client might attempt suicide.

k. Whenever the client shares any thoughts and/or communicates actions relating to potential suicide, the therapist should document all information acquired from the client as well as the therapist's course of action.

l. Whenever possible, consult with other mental health professionals when dealing with suicidal clients and document your consultation in the client's file.

m. Therapists are advised to have a standard follow-up procedure to be practiced following termination of therapy with a suicidal client.

n. Whenever informing the client's "significant others" about the client's potential for suicide, always inform the client beforehand.

o. A psychotherapist can be held liable for overreacting or for underreacting to a client's threat of suicide.

p. A psychotherapist "should know" the risk of suicide in most cases. Failure to ascertain the potential when the therapist "should have known" may lead to a malpractice suit.

q. When there is a high probability of attempted suicide, the therapist has the responsibility to take steps "to control" the client.

r. Liability occurs most frequently when there is failure to take some action (such as hospitalization), when there is inappropriate hospitalization (open ward versus secure ward), or when the therapist fails to respond to a crisis.

s. A psychotherapist in California has "no duty to warn" if in private practice; however, government agencies have a responsibility to warn before releasing. The statutes for licensed professional counselors in the states of Mississippi, Montana, and Ohio make exceptions relevant to the duty to warn regarding suicidal clients. These three states do not *require* a licensed professional counselor to breach confidentiality and exercise the duty to warn or protect, they only *allow* the counselor to do so (Herlihy & Sheeley, 1988).

Commentary

The law requires you to break confidentiality when you assess a client to be of high risk of committing suicide. However, you can be liable if you do not take prudent measures in dealing with a suicidal client. Do you know when you can be held liable in regard to suicide? Do you have a "standard" method for assessing lethality or for managing a suicidal client? Compare and contrast professional recommendations for working with suicidal clients and compare them with your present standards.

Liability. At this time, "recent reviews have found no successful lawsuit against a psychotherapist or counselor who breached confidentiality to protect the life of a suicidal person" (Vandecreek & Knapp, 1984, p. 51). However, there have been successful lawsuits against psychotherapists who failed to follow standard procedures to protect the life of a patient/client.

When are you most likely to be found liable?

(1) You can be held liable if "you fail to take action to prevent a suicide. A wrongful death action can be taken against you" (Kjervik, 1984, p. 209).

(2) If you are in an *outpatient setting*, you can be held liable if the following occur:

    (a) making a gross error in your professional judgment as to whether or not to confine the patient,

    (b) prescribing potentially suicidal drugs,

    (c) intentionally disclosing essential communication regarding the patient unless there is either a legal duty to disclose or the patient consent exists (Kjervik, 1984),

    (d) failing to commit or hospitalize or hospitalizing inappropriately (for instance, recommending an open-ward facility when a more secure facility is needed or, in contrast, recommending a highly restrictive facility when an open-ward facility would be sufficient), and failing to respond to a crisis or abandoning a patient (Schutz, 1982, p. 73).

(3) If you are in a *hospital setting*, you can be "liable for a client's self-inflicted physical injury, if you have violated a hospital rule or statute or failed to adhere to accepted standards and practices" (Woody, 1988, p. 159).

Legally you are responsible for preventing your client from committing suicide. However, if you have taken recognized steps in trying to prevent suicide, and your client succeeds, you would not be held liable. You are expected to know recognized methods of assessing the potential for suicide and taking prudent measures to prevent it.

Assessment and management. Pope (1985) provides several factors that need to be considered in evaluating the potential for suicide, which include:

(1) Direct verbal warning—according to Pope, a client's verbal warning is one of the best indicators
(2) Past attempts—according to Pope, 80% of completed suicides have attempted suicide in the past
(3) Depression
(4) Hopelessness
(5) Intoxication—between one quarter and one third of all suicides are associated with alcohol
(6) Gender—the suicide rate for men is about three times that for women
(7) Age—risk increases with age with the mid-fifties to sixties having the highest risk
(8) Living alone
(9) Bereavement—50% who complete suicide have experienced maternal loss within the last three years
(10) Race—in the United States, Caucasians have the highest rate
(11) Religion—Protestants have a higher rate than Jews and Catholics
(12) Clinical syndromes—depression, alcoholism, primary mood disorders, and psychoneuroses
(13) Unemployment
(14) Impulsivity—those with poor impulse control
(15) Rigid thinking—rigid, all-or-none thought qualities increase risk
(16) Release from hospitalization—suicide risk is greatest during weekend leaves or after discharge
(17) Indirect statements and behavior signs—statements like "I am going away"

Schutz (1982) gives a nine-step process for managing a suicidal client. These steps go from the most prudent to the least prudent in measure and include the following:

(1) Elicit from the patient, if possible and credible, a promise that he will control his impulses or will call the therapist or a local emergency service.

(2) Make sure that any weapons in the patient's possession are placed in the hands of a third party.

(3) Increase the frequency of therapy sessions.

(4) Contact significant others in the patient's social network (with a consent) and ask them to assist in supporting the patient between sessions or in conjoint sessions.

(5) Utilize a call-in system between sessions to monitor the patient's stability.

(6) Consider using medication as an adjunct to the therapy. Bear in mind, however, that antidepressants may initially increase the risk.

(7) Hospitalize the patient, either on a voluntary basis or, if necessary, through commitment (Schutz, 1982, 68-69)

Kjervik (1984) states that, if you fail to take action that would prevent your client from committing suicide, a wrongful death action suit can be brought against you. A successful wrongful death action suit involves the court finding that you (a) prescribed drugs that could be lethal, (b) made an inappropriate judgment either to hospitalize or not to hospitalize your client, and (c) intentionally disclosed information about your client (confidentiality) when you did not have a legal right to do so.

Conclusions

Pope (1985) gives guidelines for working with suicidal clients, and we suggest you utilize them:

(1) Stay within your areas of competence.

(2) Know your personal limits: Working with this clientele can be draining and demanding.

(3) Know the clinical literature.

(4) Keep a summary of information and guidance handy for quick reference during an emergency.

(5) Become familiar with the legal standards (involving rights to treatment and to refuse treatment, confidentiality, involuntary hospitalization, and so on) as they affect this area of practice.

(6) Know the hospitals that you might use for the voluntary or involuntary hospitalization of suicidal clients and clarify the procedures for each.

(7) Screen all your clients for suicidal risk during the initial contact and remain alert to this issue throughout the course of therapy.

(8) In all instances, but especially if services are provided within the context of a clinic or involve referrals, ensure that clear and appropriate lines of responsibility are elicited and are fully understood by everyone.

(9) Clarify your availability to the client.

(10) Handle your absences—both planned (e.g., vacations) and unplanned (e.g., illness)—by providing your client with information, including the name and telephone number of a therapist he or she can contact whenever you are not available.

(11) Consult with other mental health professionals.

(12) If complex legal questions arise, as they often do in the treatment of suicidal clients, consult with a competent attorney with expertise in this area.

(13) Work with your clients to arrange an environment that will not offer easy access to the instruments the client might use to commit suicide.

(14) Work with your client to arrange an environment that is actively supportive.

(15) Although not denying or minimizing the client's problems and desire to die, also recognize and work with the client's strengths and (though perhaps temporary) desire to remain alive.

(16) Make every effort to communicate and justify realistic hope. (Have the client sign a written, dated contract, agreeing that he or she will not attempt suicide.)

(17) Consider the use of contracts between you and the client.

(18) Explore any fantasies the client may have regarding suicide.

(19) Ensure clear communication and evaluate the probable impact of your intervention.

(20) When considering hospitalization as an option, explore the drawbacks as fully as the benefits and the probable long-term as well as immediate effects of this intervention.

(21) If hospitalization is used, pay particular attention to discharge planning and implementation in light of the increased risk of suicide during the period shortly after discharge.

(22) Be sensitive to negative countertransference and other negative reactions to the client's behavior.

(23) Most important, communicate that you care.

To prevent liability when dealing with a suicidal client, we suggest that you not only properly assess the risk of suicide but have a written contract signed by the client and a witness. This contract provides an agreement between you and your client as to what he or she should do if he or she becomes suicidal. See Appendix B for a sample contract.

Summary

Suicidal statements made by clients may create stress for psychotherapists. It is important that therapists adhere to the written policies of their employing institution/organization, as well as state statutes, when dealing with suicidal clients. A therapist can be sued either for overreacting or for underreacting to a client's threat of suicide. When there is a high probability of attempted suicide, the therapist has the responsibility to take specific steps "to control" the client. Clear, specific, and objective written documentation of treatment and preventive actions taken by the therapist are a good safeguard against liability. Contracts in which the client agrees with the therapist not to attempt suicide should be documented in writing and kept in the client's file. Therapists are strongly encouraged to meet and confer with other therapists for suicidal client case reviews. Whenever informing the client's "significant others" about the client's potential for suicide, therapists are advised to inform the client beforehand.

Vignette

Irving tells you that lately he is very depressed. He wonders about going on and tells you that he sometimes fantasizes what it would be like to end his life. Although he assures you that "he'd never do anything drastic," he does express his concern over his impulses, which are scaring him. What steps would you take to find out how serious a threat Irving is to himself? Would you consult? If you consulted, what would you hope to get from this process?

Questions to Consider

(1) How do you assess the probability and risk of your clients committing suicide?

(2) How might a therapist be sued for breaching the client's confidentiality by informing others that the client is a danger to her- or himself?

(3) What would you do if you were moving to another state and/or geographical location and were required to terminate your therapeutic relationship with a client who was suicidal? What type of referral might you do with your client?

(4) What demographic indicators are there to aid in evaluating suicide potential?

(5) What individual characteristics are important in assessing suicide risk?

(6) Why is it important to know about prior suicide attempts?

(7) What actions might a psychotherapist take before hospitalizing a client?

(8) What are the potential advantages and disadvantages of hospitalizing a client?

8

Sexual Contact with a Client

Overwhelmingly, the courts and health professionals have viewed sex with a client as acting out of the transference and hence as negligence (Pope, Keith-Spiegel, & Tabachnick, 1986; Sell, Gottlieb, & Schoenfeld, 1986). Pope charged that the profession of psychology has so far failed to deal with therapist-patient sex effectively. He points out that APA's current insurance carrier has lost $7,018,165. during the past 10 years due to sexual improprieties. This represents 44.8% of monies paid out for all claims (Pope, 1986, p. 24). According to Sell, Gottlieb, and Schoenfeld (1986, pp. 491), "Despite the existence of this evidence, psychotherapist-client sexual relationships continue to be a major problem affecting the profession."

States are now making laws that a sexual relationship with a patient after termination of treatment is also a liable act. In the state of Florida (Chapter 21U-15-004), the law states that "for purposes of determining the existence of sexual misconduct as defined herein, the psychologist-client relationship is deemed to continue in perpetuity." *Perpetuity* means valid for all time; holding for life or for an unlimited time. California Civil Code section 43.93 states that a patient can now recover damages if the therapist engages in a sexual relationship "within two years following termination of psychotherapy." Also the American Association for Marriage and Family Therapy (AAMFT) *Code of Ethical Principles for Marriage and Family Therapists* (1988) states: "Sexual intimacy with former clients for two years following termination of therapy is prohibited" (Principle 1.2). It would appear that states and professional organizations' codes of ethical principles are playing a more active role in defining what course of action to take regarding such a liability. Many support the contention that, unless the education/supervisory profession models that this behavior is unacceptable, these unethical relationships may continue (Pope, Keith-Spiegel, & Tabachnick, 1986; Sell, Gottlieb, & Schoenfeld, 1986). It should be noted that, at the time of this writing, sexual intimacy with a client is considered a felony in the states of Colorado, Minnesota, and Wisconsin (Pope, 1988).

Court Cases

(1) *Zipkin v. Freeman* **(1968)**

(2) *Roy v. Hartogs* **(1976)**

(3) *Solloway v. Department of Regulation and Board of Medical Examiners* **(1982)**

(4) *Mazza v. Huffaker* **(1983)**

(5) *L. L. v. Medical Protective Company* **(1984)**

Case Reviews

Ada Margaret Zipkin, Respondent, v. Robert F. Freeman, Defendant,
Medical Protective Company, Appellant
Supreme Court of Missouri
(December 31, 1968; Rehearing Denied February 10, 1969)
436 S.W. 2d 753 (Missouri, 1968)

Mrs. Zipkin testified that, while in treatment with Dr. Freeman, they went on overnight trips and that she had been his mistress and had done anything that he asked. She gave him money to buy personal property, stole furniture for his sons, sued her family for inheritance money, and did this because Dr. Freeman told her it was part of her treatment, that this would be a way to get rid of her pent-up hostility toward her family, and also that it would help her to deal with her need to be a man. Dr. Freeman denied the allegations.

COURT DECISION

Dr. Freeman was found liable for malpractice. Dr. Freeman's insurance company refused to pay the damages but the court compelled the insurer to pay, holding that the doctor's actions were the result of mishandling the transference phenomenon. The court ruled that Dr. Freeman was liable for a total of $18,025.47.

Julie Roy, Plaintiff-Respondent, v. Renatus Hartogs, M.D., Defendant-Appellant
Supreme Court, Appellate Term, First Department (Jan. 30, 1976)
381 N.Y.S. 2d 587 (New York, 1976)

Julie Roy, the patient, brought an action suit against her psychiatrist, Renatus Hartogs, M.D., claiming that he had sexual intercourse with her over a 13-month period and that he told her this was part of her prescribed therapy. The plaintiff's counsel had argued that, because of this improper treatment, the plaintiff sought hospitalization on two occasions during 1971. The Civil Court for the City and County of New York awarded the plaintiff $153,679.50 in damages and Dr. Hartogs appealed stating that damages in excess of $25,000. were excessive.

The defendant had to submit new evidence in order to make an appeal. Dr. Hartogs's line of defense was that he was incapable of having sexual intercourse with his client because of his condition, known as hydrocele (21 N.Y. Jur., Evidence 187; 29AM.Jur. 2d, Evidence 439). The defense also stated that the plaintiff's condition was of "long standing, and had begun years before she had become the defendant's patient." Therefore, there was no evidence to suggest that the plaintiff's condition got worse because of the defendant's acts or that she was incapable of continuing the type of work she performed before treatment. Therefore, she may only recover for the aggravation of her condition by the defendant and should not be awarded more than $25,000. in damages.

COURT DECISION

The court stated that, if this were a malpractice case, the defendant would need to be brought before the Board of Ethics, and because it is apparent that the plaintiff can "succeed" (hold a job), the plaintiff is not entitled to punitive damages and the plaintiff should be awarded not more than $25,000.

Michael L. Solloway, M.D., v. Department of Professional Regulation and Board of Medical Examiners, Appellee
District Court of Appeal of Florida, Third District (October 5, 1982)
421 So. 2d 573 No. 81-615, Fla. Dist. Court Appeal (1982)

The Board of Medical Examiners had revoked Dr. Solloway's medical license. They held that the psychiatrist's conduct in engaging in a sexual relationship with his 22-year-old patient before he had properly terminated their professional relationship demonstrated unprofessional conduct. Dr. Solloway appealed because the board used a definition of "unprofessional conduct" from the 1979 statute (458.33 [l] [k] [t]), which states that

> exercising influence within a patient-physician relationship for purposes of engaging a patient in sexual activity. A patient shall be presumed to be incapable of giving free, full, and informed consent to sexual activity with his or her physician and gross or repeated malpractice or the failure to practice medicine with that level of care, skill and treatment which is recognized by a reasonably prudent similar physician as being acceptable under similar conditions and circumstances.

Solloway engaged in such activity in 1977 and, therefore, the court must adhere to the board's 1977 definition of unprofessional conduct. This definition read: "Unprofessional conduct shall include any departure from, or the failure to conform to the standards of acceptable and prevailing medical practice in his area of expertise as determined by the board." The defense stated that the 1977 definition failed to state rules specifically dealing with sexual relationships between psychiatrist and patient and, therefore, it is unclear whether such activity would require revoking a medical license. In other words, the 1977 code does not point out specifically that a sexual relationship is part of unprofessional conduct, and, therefore, because this code was current during the time of the sexual relationship, the board cannot use the 1979 statute as a reason for revocation.

COURT DECISION

The court supported the board's findings stating that a fundamental ethical teaching in the psychiatrist profession precludes sexual activity between a psychiatrist and his or her patient. The court stated that, regardless of which definition was used in the psychiatrist's defense, the act of sexual misconduct is an "obvious" act of unprofessional conduct, and, therefore, specific findings are unnecessary.

Jeffrey P. Mazza v. Robert A. Huffaker and Robert A. Huffaker, M.D., P.A.
Court of Appeals of North Carolina
No. 8115SC1180 300 S.E. 2d 833 (March 15, 1983)

The patient, Jeffrey P. Mazza, filed suit in the Court of Orange County against Robert A. Huffaker, M.D., P.A., for medical malpractice and criminal conversation. A jury had found that the psychiatrist had committed medical malpractice. Jeffrey P. Mazza suffered from manic-depressive psychosis and had been treated by Dr. Huffaker from May, 1971, to July 6, 1979. The plaintiff was taking medication prescribed by Dr. Huffaker. The plaintiff had revealed to Dr. Huffaker that he had been having marital problems. On July 6, 1979, the plaintiff drove to his home and found his wife in bed with Dr. Huffaker.

The court determined that sexual relations between a psychiatrist and the wife of a patient would render previous treatment useless and make a trusting relationship with another therapist very difficult. The court established that a patient can be seriously harmed if the relationship changes from a therapeutic one to a social one and that relationships are not to be terminated too abruptly or great harm may occur from such a disruption. The court awarded the plaintiff $17,000. for compensatory damages (the amount of money paid for services) and $500,000. for medical malpractice. The defendant appealed the court decision.

COURT DECISION

The court of appeals upheld the Superior Court of Orange County's judgment.

L. L., Plaintiff-Appellant, v. the Medical Protective Company,
Defendant-Respondent, Barry Siegel, M.D., and the County of Milwaukee,
Defendants
No. 84-507 Court of Appeals of Wisconsin (December 21, 1984)
362 N.W. 2d 174 (Wis. App. 1984)

L. L., patient, brought suit against her psychiatrist, Dr. Barry Siegel, for engaging in sexual acts with her during the course of treatment.

According to the plaintiff, Dr. Siegel engaged in two acts of fellatio. The Circuit Court of Milwaukee County dismissed the Medical Protective Company from the suit. This company insured Dr. Barry Siegel. The Medical Protective Company claimed that it did not cover malpractice based on sexual, social, and other extratherapeutic contact between the psychiatrist and patient but that its policy covers "professional services rendered or which should have been rendered." The circuit court agreed with the company.

The plaintiff (L. L.) appealed the circuit court's decision and stated that the insurance company should pay for compensatory services.

COURT DECISION

The appeals court reversed the circuit court's decision and stated that, where the meaning of an insurance policy is unclear, it must be construed against the insurer and in favor of coverage. The policy was intended to benefit injured members of the insured. L. L.'s claims against the insurance company for compensatory damages were dismissed and L. L.'s claims against the insurance company for punitive damages were affirmed. L. L. did not challenge the court on this issue. The psychiatrist's performance of sexual acts with his patient constituted "failure to give proper treatment" and the insurance company was reinstated as a defendant and, therefore, must pay compensatory damages.

Implications

a. According to recent statutes, one must not develop a sexual relationship with one's client without risking charges of sexual misconduct. Arguments in defense of a therapist who has sex with clients are not likely to succeed in court.

b. Practitioners who have claimed that the client consented have found that the courts have viewed that the said consent was not voluntary or informed because it was affected by transference.

c. The court is likely to find liability whether the defense contends that sex was part of therapy or the defense contends that sex was separate from therapy.

d. The court is likely to find that psychotherapist-client sex is harmful to the client.

e. The professional relationship between client and therapist may be viewed as perpetual, lasting an unlimited time. In the state of Florida, the therapist-client relationship lasts indefinitely. Therefore, a sexual relationship is *never* legally permitted. On the other hand, some states (e.g., California) have specified a period of time following the termination of the psychotherapeutic relationship; after that time period, the therapist is no longer liable for engaging in a sexual relationship with a former client. As of January 1, 1989, the California law indicates that marriage, family, and child counselors (MFCCs) may not engage in a sexual relationship with a former client until two years have elapsed following termination of the psychotherapeutic relationship.

f. Codes of ethics that are in use during the alleged improprieties may be used in court rather than current statutes. The *AAMFT Code of Ethical Principles for Marriage and Family Therapists* states: "Sexual intimacy with former clients for two years following the termination of therapy is prohibited" (1988, Principle 1.2).

g. Sex between therapist and client destroys trust between them as well as rendering useless any previous treatment.

h. Unless malpractice insurance is specific regarding what it will or will not cover, coverage in favor of the insured is a given.

i. The topic of "sexual contact with clients" is something that therapist training programs need to address in a more structured way.

Commentary

One of the major causes of malpractice suits and ethical and licensing complaints is "sexual intimacies with patients" (Pope, 1987, p. 624). This is cause for great concern because it has such a negative effect on the entire mental health field and such a devastating effect on clients. It has been found that supervisees who have had a sexual relationship with their instructors or supervisors are more likely to have sexual relationships with their clients. It is imperative that we use preventive measures to ensure that such relationships do not occur. Legal institutions are so concerned about this situation that they are mandating that such relationships cannot occur even after termination of treatment. The first step to prevention is awareness, awareness that such an attraction is beginning to occur and that you must take preventive steps.

Kenneth S. Pope (1987) wrote an excellent commentary on this issue of prevention and listed a variety of steps that a therapist could take so that he or she could not only become aware that such countertransference was occurring but could know what to do next to prevent the situation from becoming reality. He advises the therapist to become aware of his or her attraction to the client and then seek professional help. Pope goes on to suggest that the professional treating the therapist do the following: (1) Educate the therapist about what association ethics committees have stated about sexual relationships with clients and what the literature has pointed out about the harm it causes for the client and the therapist as well. In addition, the therapist will need to inform the treated therapist that the law currently states that a therapist should not have a sexual or intimate relationship with a client for perpetuity because transference does not cease, and there is research to support this statement. (2) The treating therapist should insist the treated therapist make an explicit contract in which the therapist agrees to a nonsexual relationship with the client, reevaluate his or her treatment approaches with the client to whom he or she is attracted, and agree to discuss openly with the treating therapist any obsession he or she might have. (3) To deal with the sexual fantasies, Pope suggested the treating therapist use a cognitive-behavioral approach based on covert conditioning. (4) The final phase of treatment would be for the therapist to deal with personal issues that may have affected his or her countertransference (e.g., current marital relationship or family of origin issues). Pope's article gives helpful advice concerning preventive measures for the problem—a legal problem—in which 7% of psychologists engage in sexual relationships with their clients.

The AAMFT *Code of Ethical Principles for Marriage and Family Therapists* states: "Sexual intimacy with clients is prohibited. Sexual intimacy with former clients for two years following the termination of therapy is prohibited" (1988, Principle 1.2).

Sell, Gottlieb, and Schoenfeld (1986) have advocated that the APA ethics code be amended to read "sexual intimacies with clients or with *former* clients are unethical" (p. 507, emphasis added). Not only do we agree with this recommendation, we urge all professional associations to modify their ethics codes to make sexual intimacy with former clients unethical. Furthermore, we believe psychotherapists should avoid *any* dual relationship with a client that might impair the professional relationship.

Summary

Sexual intimacy between a therapist and client destroys the client's trust of the therapist and the therapeutic relationship. State statutes and professional mental health organizations' codes of ethical principles are taking a more active role in specifying the limits of sexual intimacy with a client or former client. Practitioners who present a defense either that sex was a part of therapy or that sex was separate from therapy are likely to be found liable. Also, if the therapist's defense is that the client consented, the court is likely to view said consent as not being voluntary or informed because it was affected by transference. Therapists are cautioned not to use an intervention if they are unwilling to document it in the client's case notes or share it openly with colleagues.

Vignette

A new client you are seeing tells you that her former therapist (whom she names) took advantage of her sexually. She is very distraught and spends much of her session talking about her anger, confusion, and feelings of betrayal. To make matters worse, this is the second time you have heard a similar story about this particular therapist. What are your legal and ethical obligations? What would you say to your client?

Questions to Consider

(1) How can a psychotherapist reduce the risk of a false accusation regarding therapist-client sex?

(2) Would seductive verbal expressions constitute sexual misconduct? What about hugs and/or kissing?

(3) What should a psychotherapist do if he or she sees a movement toward an intimate relationship with a client?

(4) What kind of proof is necessary to prove a sexual relationship is or was in existence between a client and a therapist?

(5) What might you do if your client tells you that he had sex with his former therapist? What might you do if your client, who is a practicing psychotherapist, tells you that she has had sex with some of her clients?

(6) Some therapists take the position that the psychotherapeutic relationship with a client is never terminated completely, in that the client may

return to therapy several months or years later. What is your position concerning the issue of termination?

(7) How do you react to a situation in which a therapist and client are having sex, get married, and get divorced two months later and the client decides to file charges for sexual contact during therapy?

(8) What are some precautions that a therapist can take if he or she finds her- or himself sexually attracted to a client?

(9) Are there any instances in which a sexual relationship between the therapist and client may be beneficial to the client? How does a therapist consider this activity to be helpful to a client?

(10) What reasons might a therapist have for wanting to pursue a social relationship with a client? What are the potential benefits and/or risks for both the therapist and the client in pursuing such a relationship?

9

Injury From Nontraditional Therapy

You should be aware that, if your practice deviates from what is considered standard treatment procedures by most other respected and qualified professionals in your particular discipline (i.e., experimental or nontraditional therapy), you risk being sued. We are not suggesting that there is only one way to treat a particular client's problem, but, as stated by Berman and Cohen-Sandler (1983, p. 6), "Unlike the medical sciences, there is little in mental health treatment that is unequivocally considered standard (except, perhaps, the administration of lithium for manic-depression); in fact, a variety of activities, some viewed as deviant or even radical, may not be unacceptable or 'unreasonable.'" However, using experimental or nontraditional therapy leaves one vulnerable to both a malpractice charge and a charge of unethical conduct. "Generally, suits against innovative therapies have been based on negligence in techniques, assault and batteries (apprehension of and/or harmful or offensive touching without consent), or infliction of emotional duress" (Schutz, 1982, p. 33). If you are using techniques that are not commonly practiced, you will need to have a clear rationale that other professionals in your field will accept and support. It is important to consult colleagues when you are using what

are considered to be nontraditional approaches to treatment. This is
primarily because it is not difficult to prove deviation from average
care. Some examples of what may be considered nontraditional therapeutic techniques might include asking clients to undress, striking a
client, or giving "far-out" homework assignments. Psychotherapeutic
trainees (supervisees) who might be instructed by their supervisors to
try out some unusual techniques on a client need to know how to
respond in such situations.

Court Cases

(1) *Hammer v. Rosen* (1960)
(2) *Solano County Department of Social Services v. Ron B.* (1987)

Case Reviews

Sidney Hammer et al., as Executors of Max Hammer, Deceased et al., Appel-
lants, v. John N. Rosen, Respondent
Court of Appeals of New York, 7 N.Y. 2d 376;
165 N.E. 2d 756; 198 N.Y.S. 2d 65 (March 3, 1960)

In 1955, Alice Hammer and her father, Max Hammer, serving as guardian and ad litem, brought suit against Alice's psychiatrist. Alice sought
damages for malpractice and her father "for breach of contract and for
fraud" (p. 66). The damages recoverable in malpractice were for "personal injuries, including the pain and suffering which naturally flow
from tortious acts" (pp. 67-68). The year in which the malpractice suit
was initiated was the same year in which Alice's seven years of psychiatric treatment for schizophrenia had terminated. Alice was treated by
New York psychiatrist Dr. John N. Rosen. Alice was insane at the time
she initiated the cause of action. Thus, in accordance with "section 60
of the Civil Practice Act" (p. 67), an extension of the time within which
to commence this action was granted.

Dr. Rosen was accused of having beaten his schizophrenic patient
Alice during the course of his treatment. Reportedly, Dr. Rosen treated
his schizophrenic patients by himself acting in a schizophrenic manner
at times. The supreme court, special and trial term, rendered judgment
in favor of defendant Dr. Rosen and an appeal was acknowledged. The

supreme court, appellate division, affirmed, by a divided court opinion, the judgment made by the former court hearing and the plaintiff's appealed. The Court of Appeals of New York heard the case on March 3, 1960 and a prima facie case of malpractice was established, requiring submission of the case to the jury.

Three witnesses testified on Alice's behalf against psychiatrist Dr. Rosen. All three witnesses reported that Dr. Rosen had beaten Alice on a number of occasions during his course of treatment. Defendant Dr. Rosen argued that there was no expert testimony to support the plaintiff's charge of malpractice. The court questioned the very nature of the acts complained of as being improper treatment and malpractice and said that, "if the defendant chooses to justify those acts as proper treatment, he is under the necessity of offering evidence to that effect" (p. 67). In fact, Dr. Rosen had acknowledged in his court brief "that any mode of treatment which involves assaults upon the patient is 'fantastic' " (p. 67).

COURT DECISION

The Court of Appeals of New York reversed judgment made by the former supreme court, appellate division, hearing. Psychiatrist Dr. John N. Rosen was held liable for improper treatment and malpractice. The damages recoverable in this malpractice action were for personal injuries sustained by the patient, including the pain and suffering that naturally occurred from the tortious act.

In re Amber B. and Teela B., Minors
Solano County Department of Social Services, Petitioner and Respondent, v.
Ron B., Objector and Appellant
Court of Appeal, First District, Division 5
236 Cal. Rptr. 623 (California, April 29, 1987)

A petition filed by the Solano County Department of Social Services alleged that Ron B. had sexually molested his 3-year-old daughter, Amber B., and that his one-year-old daughter, Teela B., was at risk of sexual abuse. Consequently, the Solano County Superior Court ordered that the two girls be declared dependent children of the juvenile court and placed in the custody of their mother. In addition, counseling was required for Amber and both parents. "The court did not sustain the allegation identifying Ron as the perpetrator of the abuse" (p. 625), and he was granted supervised visitation. Prior to the hearing, the mother sent a letter to the court stating "that her son had described possible sexual abuse of Amber by an aunt" (p. 625).

Ron B. appealed the ruling, challenging the testimony given by psychologist Dr. Henry Raming. Dr. Raming had been appointed by the court to conduct a psychological evaluation of Amber and to determine whether she had been sexually abused but not to perform therapy. The case was heard again in the court of appeals.

Dr. Raming examined Amber on three occasions and testified at the trial court hearing, on behalf of the Department of Social Services, that Amber had been sexually molested and that she believed she had been molested by her father. Two factors contributed to Dr. Raming's opinion. The first related to Amber's reports of abuse, in which she described a variety of instances of abuse. Dr. Raming supported his opinion by stating that it is

> fairly well documented in the literature . . . that children who have been molested will talk about being abused, but they will do this by consistently giving the . . . same facts of the essence in different words such that they have an event or an experience in their minds and are not merely repeating . . . rote by rote, someone else's words. (p. 625)

The second factor related to Amber's behavior with an anatomically correct female doll in Dr. Raming's office. "During two of Dr. Raming's examinations Amber placed her index finger in the vaginal and anal openings of the doll and pushed and twisted her finger vigorously" (p. 625). Dr. Raming also reported that the behavior portrayed by Amber with the doll

> is fairly consistent with molested children. This is not the usual type of behavior one would see in children who are in a stage of age appropriate sex exploration . . . [W]hen children this age describe or graphically demonstrate anal or vaginal penetration, it's pretty much assumed that the child learned that from experience and not from . . . sex exploration with other children. (p. 625)

Other witnesses who testified on behalf of the Department of Social Services included a police detective and a social worker. Both testimonies supported Amber's reports of abuse and her behavior with an anatomically correct doll. Amber did not testify, and her father, Ron, testified in his own behalf and denied the accusations of any abusive behavior. In particular, Ron challenged Dr. Raming's method for determining that Amber had been abused. He contended that Amber's reports of abuse and behavior with the anatomically correct dolls were interpreted by a new scientific method of proof that had not been shown to satisfy the *Kelly-Frye* test of admissibility.

The *Kelly-Frye* test requires that

> a new scientific method of proof is admissible only upon showing that the procedure has been generally accepted as reliable in the scientific community in which it was developed. . . . The test does not apply to mere expert testimony as distinguished from scientific evidence. When a witness gives his [her] personal opinion on the stand—even if he [she] qualifies as an expert—the jurors may temper their acceptance of his [her] testimony with a healthy skepticism born of their knowledge that all human beings are fallible. (pp. 625-626)

In contrast, "like many laypersons, jurors tend to ascribe an inordinately high degree of certainty to proof derived from an apparently 'scientific' mechanism, instrument, or procedure" (p. 626). Although the *Kelly-Frye* test is mostly "applied to novel devices or processes involving the manipulation of physical evidence, such as lie detectors, experimental systems of blood typing, voiceprints, identification by human bite marks, and microscopic analysis of gunshot residue" (p. 626), the test has also been applied to hypnosis during court proceedings.

A key issue addressed by the court of appeals was the determination of whether Dr. Raming simply gave expert testimony to which the *Kelly-Frye* test would not apply or whether his procedure for detecting child sexual abuse was considered a new scientific method of proof that requires that the test be applied. The court prefaced its concluding judgment by acknowledging the question: "Would a trier of fact ascribe an inordinately high degree of certainty to the technique employed by Dr. Raming for determining the cause of child sexual abuse?" (p. 629). In other words, with this case, the *Kelly-Frye* test needed to be applied.

COURT DECISION

The court of appeals ruled in favor of the appellant, Ron B., and reversed the order of the former superior court ruling that declared that the two daughters become dependent children of the juvenile court. It was reported that "the trial court [had] erred when it failed to require a showing of general acceptance in the relevant scientific community in accordance with [the] *Kelly-Frye*" (p. 629) test. Observing a child's behavior with anatomically correct dolls to detect child sexual abuse was considered to be a new scientific process that required the application of the *Kelly-Frye* test. Any retrial would need to proceed in accordance with *Kelly-Frye*.

Implications

a. Therapists need to have a clear rationale for using nontraditional therapy techniques. If you're experimenting with a certain therapeutic technique or skill intervention, be certain to inform the client beforehand that you are experimenting and explain to the client the rationale for such an intervention. In addition, be certain to document in the client's record whatever you told him or her about your experimenting.

b. Be certain to safeguard the client from any physical and/or emotional harm. For example, if you determine that your client needs to ventilate repressed rage and anger, you might have the client hit a soft pillow.

c. Before using a nontraditional therapy technique, consult with other mental health professionals for validation. You might even consider consulting your professional organization's ethics committee beforehand. As it is not difficult to prove deviation from average care when nontraditional therapy is utilized, it is important to consult with colleagues and to document the consultation.

d. Only scientifically reliable methods may be acceptable as expert testimony in court.

e. Asking a client to perform acts that may result in physical, mental, emotional, or social harm places the therapeutic professional as risk for a malpractice suit.

f. It is recommended that therapists share with their clients some of the potential risks (i.e., physical, mental, emotional, and social) for entering professional counseling as a client. Some of these potential risks may be delineated by contract at the beginning of the therapeutic relationship. In this way, the therapeutic professional may be less vulnerable to a malpractice suit.

g. As a therapist, be especially cautious regarding the physical contact you have with a client. It behooves the therapist to treat clients of both genders with the same amount of physical contact (e.g., regarding touching a client to comfort her or him, shaking hands, hugs). Therapists who initiate hugs with their clients are engaging in risky behavior. Whenever initiating any form of physical contact with a client, it is important for the therapist to be engaging in such behavior only for the client's benefit and not to satisfy the needs of the therapist.

h. Whenever engaging in any physical contact with a client, it is crucial that the therapist discuss with the client the appropriateness of such behavior as perceived by the client and whether or not it is helpful to the client.

i. Any therapist using techniques that are not commonly practiced needs to be able to offer evidence that her or his acts are proper treatment.

j. A client has the right to terminate therapy, *even in the middle of a session*. The therapist should not keep the client in the room, chase the client, or in any way attempt to prevent the client from aborting the therapy session.

Commentary

It is difficult to discern a school of thought or research that is considered nontraditional (i.e., paradoxical intention, psychodrama). Nontraditional therapy is occurring when you are trying an innovative approach to treatment on a client, you have not been trained to use this approach, and there is no research or education regarding this approach.

Nontraditional proper, innovative therapy, or experimental techniques were reviewed in this chapter (also see *Abraham v. Zaslow*, No. 245862, Cal. Suer.Ct. June 30, 1972; *Haammer v. Rosen*, 7 N.Y. 2d 376/165 N.E. 2d 756/198 N.Y.S, 2d 65, 1960; *In re Amber B. and Teela B., Solano Co. Dept. Soc. Serv. v. Ron B.*, 236 Cal. Rptr. 623, Ct.App.Apr. 29, 1987). Schutz (1982, p. 31) states: "A therapist who uses a form of treatment that is innovative for its time must be prepared to justify his decision if a negative outcome ensues." Schutz suggests that obtaining informed consent might act as a shield if innovative therapies are employed. However, we believe that private practice is no place for nontraditional, experimental, or innovative therapies. When an individual comes to you for help, he or she expects the standard treatment procedures in the field.

Conclusions

In the private practice setting, we believe a client expects some traditional form of psychotherapy. We believe that clinicians in private
practice should not experiment on their clients. Such an approach
puts the therapist at risk of being sued for malpractice. We believe
that you would have extreme difficulty in establishing that you were at
or above the standard of care in the services you offered. We are not
opposed to the development of new treatments. We recommend that
such innovation be done in such settings as hospitals or institutions of
higher learning, where there is a need to present a clear rationale to
other professionals. Thus risks, outcomes, side effects, and so on can
all be monitored and evaluated. Furthermore, participants would have
given informed consent if they were to be involved in an experimental
program.

Summary

Therapists need to have a clear rationale for using nontraditional techniques. Furthermore, therapists are encouraged to consult with other
professional colleagues and their professional organization's ethics
committee before using any nontraditional approaches to treatment.
Clients should be informed and given a rationale for the approach by
therapists before any experimental therapeutic technique or skill intervention is used. Safeguards to prevent clients from any physical and/or
emotional harm must be exercised by therapists at all times, and it is
recommended that therapists inform clients of any potential risks (physical, mental, emotional, and/or social) before entering a professional
counseling relationship. Client informed consent is very important for
protecting therapists from any possible liability. Therapists need to
respect the rights of clients to refuse treatment or to terminate therapy
at any time.

Vignette

A practitioner goes to a workshop on body therapies and becomes
convinced that verbal therapy alone is not effective. So, he decides to
get some training in Rolfing. He begins by undergoing his own series

of 12 Rolfing sessions. He also does some reading on bioenergetics and decides to introduce these techniques into his sessions with clients. He does not want to tell them much about the principles of bioenergetics, because he thinks this will get his clients too much in their heads. He begins to use more and more nonverbal techniques and relies less on standard talk therapy under the rationale that "the body does not lie." Are there any legal or ethical issues in this case?

Questions to Consider

(1) If the client refuses to permit the therapist to consult with a colleague, can the therapist discuss the case in a hypothetical way? What documentation would be in order?

(2) Explain how an innovative therapeutic technique might meet the requirements of the *Kelly-Frye* test? If not, where or how does a therapist develop new therapeutic techniques?

(3) What kinds of physical touching in the therapy session are subject to the laws concerning improper treatment and malpractice? What are the potential values and potential harms for physically touching a client?

(4) How might you respond to a client who initiates an affectionate hug with you before and after each therapy session?

(5) In paradoxical procedures, the client may be asked to perform behavior that is the exact opposite of the behavior that is therapeutically desired. How advisable is it to take the risk that the person will perform the undesirable behavior?

10

Diagnosis

Diagnosis is important because it can have a significant influence on the client's life. A psychotherapist's diagnosis may affect whether jobs or promotions are granted, may determine whether a client is awarded freedom from prison or locked wards, and may affect the outcome of a custody hearing (Pope, 1988). Professionals in the mental health field might do well, in their reporting of a diagnosis to a client, to explain that the information is often subject to different interpretations by different diagnosticians. Schutz (1982, p. 25) has identified certain diagnoses that are most vulnerable to legal liability: "Is the patient [a] suicidal? [b] dangerous to others? [c] legally insane? [d] Is the symptom picture due to a medical, rather than mental, illness? Similarly, situations where a given diagnosis results in a tangible loss for the patient—commitment hearings, custody hearings, disability determination—carry increased risk."

Two competent diagnosticians are likely to have different diagnoses, which will direct them to focus on different aspects of a client's life. As noted by Schutz (1982), the literature shows that the reliability and validity of psychotherapists' diagnoses are low. For example, a client might report behavior patterns involving high anxiety. A clinician with a behavioral theoretical orientation might diagnose this anxiety as unhealthy and maladaptive and grounded in unrealistic fears and negative conditioning patterns. However, an existentially oriented clinician might diagnose this anxiety as a healthy response to a challenging situation—indicating that the client is ready for a change in life. The key point is that some insurance companies might dispute your diagnostic classification and your judgments. Therefore, you will need to be able to provide adequate records and the supportive data that led to your specific diagnosis. Some clinicians use the phrase "tentative diagnosis" until they are highly certain that they are correct in their assessments. It is important to mention that a psychotherapist will be considered to have practiced negligently in diagnosis only if the diagnosis is wrong *and* the diagnosis was arrived at negligently (Schutz, 1982). Fink (1983, cited in Schutz, 1982, p. 25) has written that an erroneous diagnosis will be considered

> to be an error in judgment, not negligence, if the diagnostician can show [a] that reasonable doubt exists concerning the nature of the condition involved; [b] that authorities do not agree on the diagnostic procedures to be used and that one of the acceptable procedures was used; and [c] that the diagnostician made a conscientious effort to inform him[her]self of the patient's condition.

Court Cases

(1) *Baker v. United States* **(1964)**
(2) *North American Company for Life and Health Insurance v. Berger* **(1981)**

Case Reviews

Mrs. Kenneth Baker, as Legal Guardian of Kenneth Baker, and Mrs. Kenneth Baker, Individually, Plaintiffs, v. United States of America, Defendant
U.S. District Court
226 F. Supp. 129 (Iowa, 1964)

This case involved Mrs. Kenneth Baker, serving as legal guardian for her 61-year-old husband, who filed suit against the United States. Mr.

Kenneth Baker was a patient under psychiatric care at the V.A. hospital in Iowa City, Iowa, for five days when he attempted suicide by leaping into a 13-foot deep concrete window well on the grounds of the hospital. Plaintiff Mrs. Baker sought to recover damages in the sum of $100,000 for injuries allegedly sustained by her husband from the suicide attempt and for her loss of consortium. Among several acts of negligence, the plaintiff charged that the physician who admitted her husband to the hospital failed to properly diagnose her husband's illness and mental condition. The United States district court reviewed the series of events that related to the patient's suicidal attempt to determine the issue of negligence.

On August 23, 1960, Kenneth Baker was referred by his attending physician, Dr. C. E. Schrock, to the V.A. hospital. Dr. Schrock had Kenneth under his care for approximately 60 days prior to the patient's admittance to the V.A. hospital. A medical certificate completed by Dr. Schrock accompanied the written application for Kenneth's admission to the V.A. hospital and indicated that suicidal content was evident.

Mrs. Baker testified that she conferred with Dr. James A. Kennedy, who was acting chief of the neuropsychiatric service at the V.A. hospital at the time of her husband's admittance. She informed Dr. Kennedy of her husband's suicidal tendency and that she had found a gun her husband had hidden in one of the buildings on the farm premises about three weeks earlier. Subsequently, Dr. Kennedy interviewed the patient for an hour to an hour and a half, reviewed the admitting certificate, and met with the patient's wife and brother. Mrs. Baker was advised by Dr. Kennedy that her husband would be admitted, contingent upon certain financial data being submitted concerning her husband. The requested data were provided the next day, and Dr. Kennedy ordered that Kenneth be placed in an open ward on the tenth floor, based upon the opinion of Dr. Kennedy that the patient did not present a suicidal risk. Kenneth's placement in the open ward permitted him free access to the third floor, for meals; to the recreational area; and to the outside hospital grounds.

On August 27, 1960, the fifth day of Kenneth Baker's residence at the V.A. hospital, he voluntarily went to the grounds immediately outside the hospital building and attempted suicide by leaping 13 feet to the bottom of a concrete window well. "He suffered scalp wounds; fractures of the left clavicle, the 8th, 9th, and 10th ribs; and the left transverse process of the 3rd, 4th and 5th lumbar vertebral bodies. About six hours later the patient suffered an occlusion of the left carotid artery. Thereafter the patient suffered a complete paralysis of his right side" (p. 131). On April 19, 1961, Kenneth was removed from the V.A. hospital and placed in a private nursing home called Restopia, which was where he was still residing three years later, at the time of this court trial.

COURT DECISION

The U.S. district court identified the critical issue of this case as whether or not Dr. Kennedy, the admitting physician of patient Kenneth Baker, was negligent in failing to properly diagnose. The court determined that "Dr. Kennedy exercised the proper standard of care required under the circumstances" (p. 134). The policy of the V.A. hospital is to allow patients as much independence as is deemed appropriate and to foster as much of a normal life as possible. The court recognized that, in the treatment of mental patients, "diagnosis is not an exact science. Diagnosis with absolute precision and certainty is impossible" (p. 132). Therefore, the judgment was in favor of the defendant.

North American Company for Life and Health Insurance, Plaintiff-Appellant, v. Merton B. Berger et al., Defendants, Merton B. Berger, Defendant-Appellee

U.S. Court of Appeals, Fifth Circuit, Unit B
648 F.2d 305 (Alabama, 1981)

North American Company for Life and Health Insurance brought suit against psychiatrist Dr. Merton B. Berger, alleging fraudulent and negligent diagnosis. Dr. Berger served as psychiatric consultant to the Federal Aviation Administration in the Atlanta area from 1968 through 1977. During this time, he diagnosed as "totally disabled" approximately 154 air traffic controllers on the basis of job-related anxiety and depressive neurosis. North American was the designated disability income insurance company for several of these air traffic controllers. Due to the large number of claims filed, North American decided to investigate Dr. Berger and determined that many of his diagnoses of total disability were incorrect. The insurance company then attempted to sue Berger to recover the fees that had been paid to the air traffic controllers.

The U.S. District Court for the Northern District of Georgia ruled in favor of defendant Dr. Berger on the negligence count and the insurance company appealed. The district court ruled that the insurance company could not sue Dr. Berger because North American was not in privity with him. In other words, a psychiatrist can only be subjected to malpractice liability when the injured party is or was the doctor's patient, and North American was not Dr. Berger's patient. There was no contract and no relationship, other than a gratuitous one, between Dr. Berger and North American. Responding to North American's request, Dr. Berger would put in writing information concerning the condition of patients he had examined and his perception of the patients' diagnosis. North American appealed the judgment of the district court and the case was later heard by U.S. Court of Appeals in the Northern District of Alabama.

COURT DECISION

The court of appeals held that the existence of genuine issues of facts precluded summary judgment in favor of psychiatrist Dr. Merton B. Berger. The court also held, because Dr. Berger knew that the insurance company—North American—would rely on his certification and for what purpose, that he "was under duty to exercise reasonable care in performing medical services, making diagnoses, and transmitting them to the insurer" (p. 305). It was recognized by the court that, if Dr. Berger knowingly furnished false information, he could be held liable. However, if a psychiatrist, as in this case, furnished information derived through error, innocently and gratuitously, it does not constitute negligence. North American questioned a rehearing for the case and was denied.

Implications

a. Diagnosis, per se, remains the professional judgment and jurisdiction of the therapist. It is not likely that another therapist would be called upon as an expert witness to challenge the diagnosis of a therapist.

b. Diagnosis is not an exact science. Diagnosis with absolute precision and certainty is impossible.

c. Psychotherapists have a responsibility to exercise reasonable care in performing services and making diagnoses.

d. It seems that the best way to protect yourself as a therapist is through clear and concise documentation and note taking.

e. Malpractice can occur only between the patient and his or her provider.

f. Information derived through error, innocently and gratuitously, does not constitute negligence.

g. Therapists need to be cautious not to report a faulty diagnosis for a client as a means of receiving third-party payments.

h. It is helpful to share your diagnosis with the client.

i. Therapists are encouraged to consult with other mental health professionals to determine the diagnosis for a client, especially in those cases in which diagnosis is difficult. In addition, it is recommended that the therapist document in the client's case record file all consultations for determining the client's diagnosis.

Commentary

This category accounts for 5.4% of the total malpractice claims (Pope, 1989). We know of no cases in which a therapist was found liable solely because of an erroneous diagnosis. However, if a suit was filed against you because of inadequate care or lack of skill, your diagnosis of the client could be proof that you were at fault. In the case of *O'Neil v. State* (New York), an admitting physician was declared negligent because he did not correctly diagnose that a patient, who died from withdrawal of a barbiturate, was a Nembutal addict (Pope, 1989). This stresses the need to take a thorough history of a client, especially a medical and psychiatric history, in order to make an adequate diagnosis for proper treatment.

Appropriate diagnosis for a psychologist includes proper assessment (i.e., clinical testing). Principle 8 of the APA ethical code states,

> In the development, publication, and utilization of psychological assessment techniques, psychologists make every effort to promote the welfare and best interest of the client. They guard against the misuse of assessment results. They respect the client's right to know the results, the interpretations made, and the bases for their conclusions and recommendations. Psychologists make every effort to maintain the security of tests and other assessment techniques within limits of legal mandates. They strive to ensure the appropriate use of assessment techniques by others.

In order to proceed in an ethical and legal manner, the code recommends that psychologists

(1) explain the purpose of testing in language that a client can understand,
(2) report any reservations regarding the validity and reliability or inappropriateness of the norms for the person tested,
(3) not use obsolete techniques, and
(4) be properly trained in using such techniques.

Conclusions

A malpractice suit for faulty diagnosis must prove that (a) the diagnosis was incorrect, (b) it was negligently made, and (c) it resulted in damage to the client. Although it is impossible to diagnose with absolute certainty, care needs to be exercised in reaching a diagnosis. We advise utilizing either the *DSM III-R* (1987) or the *ICD* 9 (1978). Also, in difficult cases, the clinician would be wise to consult with a colleague. Whenever you report a diagnosis to an insurance company or for third-party payment, we recommend you share this diagnosis with the client (if he or she is competent) and consider involving the client in determining the diagnosis.

Summary

Diagnosis is not an exact science, and it can have a significant influence on the client's life. Different competent therapists may give different diagnoses to the same client. Many therapists use a "tentative diagnosis" until they are more certain of their assessment. Therapists will be considered to have practiced negligently in diagnosis only if the diagnosis is wrong *and* the diagnosis was arrived at negligently. Clear and concise documentation and note taking help to protect the therapist from charges of professional negligence. Therapists are cautioned not to report a faulty diagnosis for a client as a means of receiving third-party payments from insurance companies. Whenever therapists have any doubt about assessing a client's diagnosis, it is strongly recommended that they consult with another mental health professional who is competent in diagnosing.

Vignette

You are seeing a woman named Ethel, age 35. She has been referred to you by her place of work, which stipulates that you must inform them of treatment plans and diagnosis. This company has been known to dismiss employees because of various diagnoses. Ethel came to you because of her divorce, which occurred three months ago. In evaluating her case, it came to your attention that she has been depressed for seven years. She has told you that she has tried to commit suicide twice during the seven years but has never told anyone, including her ex-husband. How would you diagnose this case, knowing that her place of work will be receiving the diagnosis? What do you tell Ethel about her diagnosis? Do you inform her about the requirements to inform her place of work? Are there any other ethical considerations regarding this case?

Questions to Consider

(1) Is a treatment plan based on diagnosis of the problem(s)? If yes, what is the significance of the fact that diagnosis with absolute precision and certainty is impossible?

(2) What factors do professional psychotherapists use in forming a diagnosis? What factors do you consider to be most important in forming a diagnosis?

(3) What might be the benefits of sharing a client's diagnosis with her or him? What might be reasons for not sharing a client's diagnosis with her or him? What are some different situations where you would and/or would not share his or her diagnosis with a client?

(4) How might you engage the client in a collaborative process with you as the therapist to determine his or her diagnosis?

(5) Does diagnosis determine your perceptions of a client or do your perceptions determine the diagnosis?

(6) How might a therapist's theoretical orientation for doing psychotherapy influence the diagnosis of a client?

(7) How do you function as a therapist if your theoretical orientation does not adhere to the concept of diagnosis?

(8) Does making diagnosis an "exact science" increase or decrease the liability of clinicians?

(9) Does privacy ever exist between a professional and a corporation? If so, under what circumstances?

(10) What constitutes "total disability"?

(11) What are your reactions to agencies that *require* a diagnosis at the intake session?

(12) What would you do if your views on diagnosis "clashed" with that of your agency?

11

Inadequate Termination or Abandonment

Psychotherapy can be divided into three stages (i.e., beginning, middle, and final). This chapter is concerned with that final stage, which should deal with termination issues. When a therapist abruptly terminates treatment, fails to respond to emergencies, or does not make arrangements for coverage for days not available, the therapist is more likely to be sued for malpractice.

Should a client not be responding to your care and treatment, it would be appropriate to assist him or her in finding another therapist. However, each client has the right to discontinue treatment at any time.

Court Case

(1) *Mary and Crystal v. Gerard Ramsden* (**1980**)

Case Review

Mary and Crystal, Plaintiffs-Appellees, Cross-Appellants, v. Gerard Ramsden,
James Matthew, Edwin Morese, and Patricia Batterman, Defendants-Appellants,
Cross-Appellees
Nos. 78-1954, 78-1955; U.S. Court of Appeals, Seventh Circuit
(Argued January 3, 1979; Decided November 21, 1980;
As Amended November 25, 1980)

Mary, age 17, and Crystal, age 16, were residents of the Goodland
State Camp, "a facility for delinquent female juveniles" (p. 594). Mary
was placed in isolation for attempting to leave the facility without
permission. Crystal was placed in isolation for "cutting a hole in the
security screen of a window in an attempt to escape" (p. 594). The result
of Mary's hearing was that she was to be placed in isolation for 50
days. She remained there only 29 days. Isolation rooms have a bed and
a mattress. The door is thick and has three locks, and there is one
window for observation purposes. Mary received meals in her room and
had no access to telephone, radio, record players, or smoking materials.
Mary and Crystal were isolated from interacting with other residents
while going to the bathroom. They wore pajamas day and night.
    Mary's major complaint was that the psychologist refused to see her
until she was released from the isolation facility. Mary testified that the
room was unusually hot, and, when it was fumigated, she was not
permitted to leave. Crystal testified that, because of the difficulty of
confinement, she had experienced being frightened, had experienced a
period of prolonged crying and anger, and had attempted suicide. She
did not see her psychiatric therapist until after she had been there for
four days. She stated that her room was infested with insects and that
she had to return immediately to confinement shortly after it had been
sprayed with a pesticide.
    Expert witnesses for the plaintiffs testified that isolation was an
ineffective treatment/punishment and that it had adverse effects on
children and adolescents. The court was to decide if cruel or unusual
punishment had occurred in the case of Mary and Crystal and whether
additional pain and suffering had occurred due to the course of treatment. Mary's psychologist testified, and it was in her records that he
had decided not to see her after she had made a request to see him.

COURT DECISION

During the original hearing, the adolescents were not allowed to have witnesses and the court ruled that this was considered cruel and unusual punishment. The court also reported that, although isolating these youths was not in and of itself considered "cruel and unusual punishment," the fact that the psychologist would not see a juvenile after he had been put into isolation was considered so. The court also reported that, during their hearing, they should have the right to provide witnesses on their behalf. The juveniles were given awards for damages.

Implications

a. Asking a client to perform acts that may result in physical, mental, emotional, or social harm places the therapeutic professional at risk for a malpractice suit.

b. Any therapist using techniques that are not commonly practiced needs to be able to offer evidence that his or her acts constitute proper treatment.

c. A person who is put into isolation for punishment has a right to see a psychotherapist upon request. A psychotherapist's failure to see such a person may be ruled by the court as "cruel and unusual punishment."

d. Refusal to see your client in psychotherapy when requested by your client is abandonment.

e. It would be wise to consult with a colleague concerning potential abandonment issues.

Commentary

If you terminate/refer a client inappropriately or without due cause, you can be found liable. Have you ever needed to refer/terminate a client because he or she could no longer pay your fees, he or she needed a specialty treatment for which you had not been trained, or he or she determined that his or her goals had been reached and wanted to terminate prematurely? In each of these situations, you can be found liable if you do not adhere to some principles that demonstrate that you were practicing according to the standard of care.

You can be liable when you

(1) terminate without "due cause" (using the standard of care or some rationale) and your client feels injured because you are terminating too soon,

(2) refer a client without following standard procedures,

(3) do not immediately respond to a call put into your answering phone/service when a client is experiencing a crisis and requests your assistance; and

(4) knew a client was terminating on his or her own too soon and did not use some standard procedure for dealing with his or her termination.

These are instances when you could be found liable, but, had you used some standard procedure, you could have avoided malpractice. These procedures include the following:

(1) Follow-up on your client when you have terminated or referred him or her to another therapist or clinic (Van Hoose & Kottler, 1985).

(2) Assess the appropriateness of the referral.

(3) Give your clients an emergency number when you know you will not be able to get back to them. You can also leave a number for them to call on your answering phone or with the answering service, such as that of a colleague, when you have arranged with your clients in advance that this would be the person to call in case of an emergency.

(4) If you know you will need to refer a client, give him or her advance warning and prepare him or her for the change (Schutz, 1982). If the client does not go to the referral, write to him or her about the risks incurred when he or she does not follow through with the referral.

(5) If your client is going to terminate prematurely, explain to him or her the risks he or she is taking by leaving and what suggestions you have for him or her (Schutz, 1982). Include this information in a follow-up letter to your client.

(6) Chart your rationale and procedure for referring or terminating a client.

(7) Consult a colleague about the case if you have any questions about standard procedure. For example, if you believe you are not qualified to deal with a problem and believe it is appropriate to refer, consult a colleague about the situation and the referral source. Give your client three referral sources. If you believe that this will cause confusion, have him or her call from your office, go over what he or she found out, and assist him or her in the decision-making process.

Conclusions

Termination problems center on abandonment issues and a client's right to discontinue treatment. We recommend you consider the following:

(1) Each client has a right to discontinue treatment. However, each therapist has the responsibility to inform his or her client of the risks of such a decision. This data should be recorded in the therapist's records.

(2) Should the therapist decide to discontinue therapy prior to the final stage, the client should be provided with a written list of referral resources. The reason for making the referral needs to be recorded in the therapist's records.

(3) Failure to respond to emergencies puts the therapist in danger of abandonment charges. It is wise to obtain coverage for emergencies whenever you will be unavailable for many hours or on vacation.

Summary

Mental health professionals need to be sensitive to the fact that, even if they believe it is in the best interest of the client to terminate therapy or be referred out, the client may not understand the benefit of these changes. A therapist needs to prepare his or her client in advance if such a change in treatment is needed. Don't forget to consult with a colleague whenever termination does not follow the usual pattern. Also, remember that your client has the right to terminate at any time.

Vignette

You have been seeing a client named Tim for six months. For the first two months, he was making steady progress and was showing willingness to carry out homework assignments. After that, he became increasingly dependent upon you and appeared to be doing less and less in his personal life. In fact, from your perspective, it appeared that Tim was reverting to old, dysfunctional patterns. You have consistently encouraged him to function independently of you, but to no avail. You are finding yourself becoming increasingly annoyed and impatient with him. You have even explored the idea with him of terminating therapy.

He replied to your proposal, "You are just like my mother, going to abandon me when I need you the most." Do you see any ethical or legal ramifications of either continuing or terminating treatment with him? If you felt certain that he was no longer benefiting from the relationship, would you be inclined to terminate or refer, regardless of Tim's reaction? What do you need to do in this situation to avoid charges of malpractice? How would you respond if he brought suit against you for abandonment?

Questions to Consider

(1) If your client terminates therapy, must you resume therapy if the client later changes his or her mind and wants to continue treatment?

(2) If your client becomes upset during therapy and runs out of the room, should you let him or her go or follow? What if he or she falls and is seriously injured while you are giving chase?

(3) What do you do when a client refuses to transfer to another therapist when you have determined that such a change is in his or her best interest?

(4) On the average, how many therapy sessions should focus on termination issues?

(5) A client is moving several hundred miles away. He or she wants to have some referral sources in case he or she wishes to continue therapy. How many sources should you give? How do you determine which sources to give?

(6) Would it be appropriate for a therapist not to see any clients in emergency situations and to inform all new clients that, in the event emergency treatment is needed, the client can go to the local mental health facility for care?

(7) What type of follow-up might you do (if any) should your client decide to abruptly terminate the therapeutic relationship without any forewarning?

(8) What might you do when a client you have been doing therapy with for several months reveals that, due to limited finances, he or she must immediately terminate therapy? What might you do if this occurs at a time when your client is in crisis?

12

Releasing or Obtaining Information and Informed Consent to Treat

The psychotherapist, when seeing a new client, should make it a practice to secure any previous mental health records in a prompt manner. If the client has been in therapy before, the therapist should request that the client sign a consent to obtain information from the previous therapist. If the client refuses, this should be documented in the records. Also, you need to honor all valid requests for information in a prompt manner. Whenever records are requested, they should be sent within two weeks if possible. We believe that it is unwise to take more than 30 days to transmit information. According to Schutz (1982, p. 180), "Raw psychological data in which the user is identified are released only with the written consent of the user or his or her legal representative" and the person to whom the information/data are released is seen as a qualified person in his or her field.

Court Cases

(1) *Underwood v. United States of America* (**1966**)
(2) *Merchants National Bank and Trust Co. of Fargo v. United States of America* (**1967**)

(3) *Stowers v. Wolodzko* (1971)

(4) *Jablonski v. United States* (1983)

(5) *Dymek v. Nyquist* (1984)

(6) *Peck v. the Counseling Service of Addison County* (1985)

Case Reviews

Frank J. Underwood, as Administrator of the Estate of Shirley Underwood Dunn, Deceased, Appellant, v. United States of America, Appellee
U.S. Court of Appeals, Fifth Circuit
356 F.2d 92 (Alabama, 1966)

The father and a personnel representative of a woman who was murdered by her former husband brought action against the United States, claiming negligence. Two areas of negligence were noted:

(a) by allowing Edward F. Dunn, an airman in the United States Air Force stationed at Maxwell Air Force Base, Alabama, who was in an emotionally and mentally disturbed state of being . . . to obtain a .45 caliber automatic pistol that was used by Airman Dunn to kill Shirley Underwood Dunn; and (b) by allowing Edward F. Dunn . . . to return to duty, the performance of which gave him access to a dangerous . . . 45 caliber automatic pistol." (p. 94)

The United States denied that it owed any responsibility to Mrs. Dunn or that it was negligent of any duty. The district court rendered its decision in favor of the defendant, the United States, and the plaintiff appealed.

The evidence related to this case indicated that the Dunns were married on October 1, 1955, and separated on July 7, 1962. At that time, the couple's three children were ages 6, 4, and 2. On the evening of July 24, 1962, Mrs. Dunn swore out a warrant before the police charging her husband had committed assault and battery upon her. Airman Dunn was arrested the following day, and, on July 31, 1962, Mrs. Dunn acquired a decree of divorce.

On the morning of August 8, 1962, Sergeant Harold E. Thomas, the noncommissioned officer in charge of security and law enforcement in the Air University at Maxwell Field, brought First Class Airman Dunn with him to the office of Colonel Endicott. Colonel Endicott determined that Dunn was " 'under great emotional strain . . . he was crying part of the time, and he was worrying about his children' . . . and instructed Sergeant Thomas 'to take him over to the hospital so he could be admitted.' " (p. 95). Dunn was directed to the psychiatric clinic and left with the noncommissioned officer in charge of the clinic, Sergeant Gerald Grover. The admitting physician and psychiatrist, Dr. Friedman, recommended that Sergeant Grover contact Mrs. Dunn to assist in making an evaluation of Airman Dunn's condition.

A day or so after Airman Dunn's admission to the psychiatric clinic, his former wife was contacted and met with Sergeant Grover. She revealed to Sergeant Grover "that Dunn had previously committed assaults upon her, that she had been hit, that he tried to attack her with a crow bar, and that he had threatened her" (p. 95). Mrs. Dunn discussed how she feared her former husband and described how he had persisted in annoying her by such acts as following her around in his car. Sergeant Grover believed that Airman Dunn "had the potential of possibly inflicting harm on someone, himself, or her" (p. 95) and later shared this thought with Dr. Friedman. He also told Dr. Friedman about the information learned from the conversation with Mrs. Dunn. Dr. Friedman advised Sergeant Grover not to make a written note of this, " 'that he would convey this information to the physician who would be picking up the case, since Dr. Friedman was leaving the area shortly' " (p. 96). Dr. Friedman was in the process of being transferred from Maxwell Air Force Base; therefore, on August 10, 1962, he referred patient Dunn, and all accompanying medical records, to psychiatrist Dr. Edwin Arthur Larson for care. However, Dr. Larson was not informed in any manner of Sergeant Grover's conversation with Mrs. Dunn or of the threats made on her life until after the homicide.

While in the psychiatric clinic, patient Dunn was medicated with a tranquilizer, Thorazine (250 mgs.), on the day of admission (August 8), which was reduced the following day (to 25 mgs. four times a day), and discontinued on August 15, the day of his discharge from the hospital. His diagnosis was "maladjustment, situational acute, moderate, improved, manifested by anxiety, depression. Stress: 3274 Moderate, separation from wife and children; Predisposition Unknown" (p. 96). At that time, Dunn returned to duty in the status of outpatient and was not restricted in any way.

On September 4, 1962, Airman Dunn secured a .45 caliber automatic pistol with bullets from the weapons cabinet behind the air police desk. He commented to the acting desk sergeant that he had to pick up a

prisoner. The desk sergeant permitted Dunn to take the pistol and ammunition, even though another officer, Sergeant Finley, was the only
person designated to authorize the release of firearms. The same day,
Sergeant Finley had observed Dunn to be nervous and shaken up,
turning as " 'white as a sheet' " (p. 97) after he had received a telephone
call. The pistol was used by Dunn to shoot and kill his former wife.

COURT DECISION

Although the U.S. district court rendered a decision in favor of the
defendant, the United States, the court of appeals reversed the judgment. The court of appeals held that psychiatrist Dr. Friedman was
negligent for not communicating information he had concerning Airman Dunn's threats to his former wife. Psychiatrist Dr. Larson was not
held liable for negligence in releasing Airman Dunn to duty without
recommending any restrictions. The court recognized that Dr. Larson
had not been informed of any threats that Airman Dunn had made
toward his former wife until after she had been murdered. Damages
awarded to the appellant were measured by the pecuniary injuries to the
three minor children resulting from their mother's death. The court of
appeals also reported that the district court had erred in excluding the
bill for Mrs. Dunn's funeral expenses as indicated by the Alabama
statute.

The Merchants National Bank and Trust Company of Fargo, a Corporation,
as Administrator and Personal Representative of the Estate of Eloise A.
Newgard, Deceased, Plaintiff, v. United States of America, Defendant
U.S. District Court
272 F. Supp. 409 (North Dakota, 1967)

This suit was brought on behalf of three North Dakota minor children,
all having the last name of Newgard: Elizabeth, born September 16,
1955, Ann Marie, born April 13, 1958, and Robert William, born
December 28, 1960, whose mother was shot and killed by the children's
father. William Bry Newgard, the father of the three children and
husband of Eloise A. Newgard, was a mental patient on leave of absence
from a V.A. hospital at the time he murdered his wife. The children
sought to recover compensatory damages for the wrongful death of their
mother.

The chronology of events depicting Mr. Newgard's psychosis was observed in the early morning of January 17, 1965, when his wife Eloise, in a state of panic, telephoned Fargo physician Dr. Mark V. Traynor to come see her husband immediately at their apartment. Dr. Traynor, responding to the call, considered Newgard to be completely psychotic, as evidenced by his glassy-eyed appearance and "senseless talk about horses, cattle 'and God most of the time' " (p. 411). Eloise had also telephoned her pastor, Reverend Richard C. Faust, to come to the apartment. Both Eloise and her husband had taught Sunday school in his church. However, Mr. Newgard had been dismissed from his teaching responsibility after the pastor had heard several complaints from the church members who attended Mr. Newgard's class.

While the pastor and physician were at the apartment, Mr. Newgard, clothed in only boxer shorts and a T-shirt, shouting that he was "the reincarnation of Jesus Christ . . . , proceeded to pull his shorts down, exposing himself, and saying he was 'going to repopulate the world' " (p. 411). He then accused his wife of "unfaithfulness and threatened to kill her" (p. 411). Reverend Faust reported that Newgard said the "God of Fire" would repopulate the world (pp. 411-412).

Later in the morning of January 17, 1965, Reverend Faust managed literally to walk Mr. Newgard through the streets of Fargo to St. Luke's Hospital. The same day, upon admission to the Neuropsychiatric Institute of the hospital, psychiatrist Dr. Albert C. Kohlmeyer examined Newgard and reported that the patient was "a schizophrenic, chronic, with acute exacerbation, paranoid type" (p. 412). Two days later, Newgard was committed to the state hospital at Jamestown, North Dakota, where he resided for two months.

On March 23, 1965, Newgard was transferred to the V.A. hospital at Fort Meade, South Dakota, and placed under the direct supervision of psychiatrist Dr. Leonard S. Linnell. Newgard was also treated weekly with psychotherapy and examinations by a clinical psychologist, Dr. Jesse H. Craft, and administered tranquilizers. Dr. Truman M. Cheney, a vocational and counseling psychologist, met with Newgard to test the patient's vocational aptitude. Consistent with the hospital policy, Newgard was assigned various jobs around the hospital.

Sometime early in July, 1965, Eloise Newgard telephoned the V.A. hospital after she had heard that Dr. Linnell and the authorities were planning to discharge her husband. She spoke with Dr. Curt L. Rosenbaum. Dr. Rosenbaum later reported that he made a written report of the telephone call; however, at the time of the court proceedings, no such report was located in the files.

On July 18, 1965, Dr. Linnell released Newgard from the V.A. hospital. Dr. Cheney had made arrangements for Newgard to have a work leave at the ranch owned by Mr. and Mrs. Clarence A. Davis. The Davises had never before employed a patient from the V.A. hospital to work on their ranch. Dr. Cheney informed Mr. Davis that Newgard had had " 'a mental disturbance, a nervous breakdown' and that Newgard wanted hard work to forget some of his troubles and for rehabilitation purposes" (p. 413). Mr. Davis did not receive any instructions of what to do if Newgard happened to leave the ranch. It was Mr. Davis's belief that he had just hired another farmhand and that Newgard was quite free to come and go as he desired. Mr. Davis had not been informed "that Newgard was under hospital surveillance, that he could not leave South Dakota, or even that he was a mental patient" (p. 414).

Newgard had once hold Mrs. Davis that "he resented the fact that his wife had him committed" (p. 414) and that he was angry toward his wife "because she had served those divorce papers on him" (p. 414). On the evening of Friday, July 31, 1965, after receiving his wages from Mr. Davis, Newgard got possession of a car and drove to his mother-in-law's home in Detroit Lakes, Minnesota. He first attempted to run over his wife Eloise with the car he was driving. After failing in that, he got out of the car and shot and killed his wife.

The plaintiff alleged that the government, through the V.A. hospital, "undertook the custody, care and treatment of Newgard, knowing him to be an insane and incompetent person with homicidal tendencies, and that the Government's inexcusable negligence was the proximate cause of Eloise A. Newgard's death" (p. 415). The government contended in defense that the United States is exempt from liability according to a law stating there is a discretionary function or duty on the part of a federal agency. The defense further argued that Newgard's release to work on the ranch was consistent with the exercise of due care in accordance with a V.A. regulation.

COURT DECISION

Before determining the amount to be paid to the plaintiff to recover damages, the U.S. district court addressed the issue of what law to apply to this multistate case. The decedent and her children resided in North Dakota, her husband was a patient at a South Dakota hospital, and the murder occurred in Minnesota. The court applied "the most significant relationship" or the "most significant contacts" rule for multistate torts. It was determined that the very real relationships with the parties involved in this litigation were with the state of North Dakota. Accordingly, North Dakota law was applied while ruling in favor of the plaintiff to recover the sum of $200,000 from the defendant as compensatory damages. Under North Dakota law, several factors were considered in arriving at damages: "decedent's age, health, condition in life, habits of industry and sobriety, mental and physical capacity, disposition to frugality and customary earnings and use made of them" (p. 411). In addition, consideration was given to include periodic pay raises in the decedent's financial earning potential with her job as a registered nurse, had she lived. Damages concerning the pecuniary value for loss of services that decedent's children would probably have received (e.g., the expense of educating the children) and the declining value of the dollar were also taken into account.

The court was of the opinion that several of the defendant's agents were negligent. Dr. Linnell was considered to have been tortiously negligent through subprofessional conduct and both Dr. Linnell and Dr. Cheney were considered to have demonstrated gross negligence. Mr. and Mrs. Davis, the ranch owners, should have been informed by Dr. Linnell or Dr. Cheney that Mr. Newgard was mentally ill and given specific instructions about what to do if the patient left the ranch. In addition, Dr. Craft was negligent in not placing a letter in Newgard's file that was received while Newgard was on the Davis ranch, which contained delusional references about selling some cattle. Dr. Curt L. Rosenbaum, chief of staff at the hospital, who had spoken to Eloise Newgard shortly before her husband's release, was negligent for not documenting the telephone call and pursuing the matter further.

Ethel K. Stowers, Plaintiff and Appellee, v. Joseph Wolodzko, Defendant and Appellant
Supreme Court of Michigan
386 Mich. 119; 191 N.W. 2d 355 (November 9, 1971)

Ethel K. Stowers, plaintiff, was a patient of psychiatrist Dr. Joseph Wolodzko. She filed for damages that she claimed were a result of her treatment during a 23-day commitment at a private inpatient facility, Ardmore Acres. Mrs. Stowers stated that, without her knowledge or consent and at the insistence of her husband, who called the hospital, she was forced to enter an ambulance and be under the care of Dr. Wolodzko. Mrs. Stowers also stated that she was not allowed to call relatives or a lawyer while she was at the Ardmore Acres.

The defense stated that, when she arrived at the hospital, Dr. Wolodzko and Dr. Anthony Smyk signed a sworn statement that they had found Mrs. Stowers mentally ill and then filed for a certificate with a probate court for temporary hospitalization until a hearing regarding her sanity could be held. The defense noted that a judge did order that Mr. Stowers be committed until a determination could be made regarding her sanity.

The Circuit Court of Wayne County granted Mrs. Stowers $40,000. in damages but stated that the case could be appealed if damages were in excess of $30,000. Dr. Wolodzko appealed the decision.

COURT DECISION

The court ruled in favor of Mrs. Stowers and granted her the original damages of $40,000. The court determined

(1) that the doctor could not be held liable up to the time the plaintiff was hospitalized (M.C.L.A. 330.21, M.S.A. 14.811)—based on the fact that the doctor was following acceptable emergency procedure prior to her hospitalization;

(2) that the doctors were incurring a risk when they administered treatment because the court had not determined at the time that the patient was "mentally insane"—therefore, the doctor was liable for assault and battery; and

(3) because the doctor did not permit Mrs. Stowers to make a telephone call to a lawyer or her relatives during her hospitalization, he was held liable for false imprisonment (32 C.J.S. False Imprisonment 1, p. 621)—according to the law, patients are to be allowed to make telephone calls if the call is intended to obtain their release.

Jablonski v. United States of America
9th U.S. Cir. Ct. Appl (June 14,1983)

NOTE: This case was the thirteenth case discussed in Chapter 6; see that chapter for the case description.

Dymek v. Nyquist
No. 83-1651 (Ill.App.Ct., September 18, 1984)

A father had been awarded custody of his 9-year-old son. His former wife took the child to a psychiatrist, who provided psychotherapy for the boy for one year without the father's knowledge and consent. The psychiatrist allegedly knew the mother was not the custodial parent and that there was no court permission for treatment.

COURT DECISION

The court held the psychiatrist had no authority to subject the child to psychotherapy.

Charles and Margaret Peck v. the Counseling Service of Addison County, Inc.
Supreme Court of Vermont
499 A.2d 422 (Vermont, 1985)

NOTE: This case was the second case discussed in Chapter 2; see that chapter for the case description.

Implications

   a. If a client is referred to a new therapist, significant information needs to be discussed between the two therapists, such as the client's propensity for doing harm to self, others, or physical property.
   b. Communications from other psychotherapists need to be brought to the attention of new therapists becoming involved with a client and such information placed in the client's file. Also, all telephone calls regarding clients should be clearly documented.
   c. It is very important during an initial "intake session" for therapists to inquire whether or not the client has previously been a client in counseling. If a client has participated as a client in therapy, the therapist is encouraged to obtain the client's written consent to contact the former therapist, in a timely manner, requesting a written report concerning the client.

d. If a client reveals to you that he or she is currently seeing another therapist, it is important that you do not continue seeing the client until he or she has terminated the other professional relationship or there has been an agreement and a rationale for the client seeing you and another therapist concurrently, for example, a client may be seeing one therapist for individual treatment and another therapist for group therapy. Continuing to see a client while he or she is seeing another therapist creates the risk of the different therapists working at "cross-purposes" with a client. Whenever two different therapists are seeing the same client, they need to have a good working relationship to best meet the needs of the client.

e. When putting a patient with a potentially dangerous history under the care of another person, the caretaker(s) should be notified about the patient's history, for the sake of not only their own lives but others' as well. When a mentally ill patient goes to work for an employer, psychotherapists have a responsibility to notify the employer about the client's potential risk to self, others, and/or physical property.

f. Whenever the therapeutic relationship is terminated as a result of either the therapist or the client moving to another geographical location, the therapist is responsible to forward information to the new therapist. It is also important that the therapist have the client sign a consent form before such information is released.

g. Information obtained concerning abusiveness or harm to self, others, and/or physical property should be documented promptly.

h. It is crucial for therapists to be familiar with their respective state laws concerning potential harm to self, others, or physical property. Some states define the law as pertaining only to a serious threat of physical violence against a reasonably identifiable victim or victims (e.g., California, Colorado), while the Kentucky statute requires mental health professionals to warn the potential victim(s) and to notify the police, even in those instances when no particular victim is identifiable. The New Hampshire statute "is unique in that it requires psychologists to warn or protect when there is 'a serious threat of substantial damage to real property,' as well as to persons" (Herlihy & Sheeley, 1988, p. 208). Herlihy and Sheeley (1988, pp. 210-211) suggest that "a literal interpretation of statutes that extend privileged communication without including an exception for cases of clear and imminent danger to others might actually prevent therapists from warning potential victims." Knapp and Vandecreek (1982) refer to a Maryland case, *Shaw v. Glickman* (1980), where "the court noted that because Maryland's privileged communication statute does not allow for breaches of confidentiality when the lives of others are threatened, the psychotherapists could not have warned the victim even if they had known about the threat" (Herlihy & Sheeley, 1988, pp. 210-211).

i. Whenever obtaining or transferring information concerning a client, it is important that the therapist abide by the documented procedures of his or her agency. It behooves mental health institutions/organizations to have a written policy concerning the transferring or obtaining of client information. Institutional procedures (or lack of) are more likely to be held liable than the individual clinicians who follow these procedures.

j. Clients can recover damages for being treated without consent, even if the treatment was competent and not negligent.

k. Psychotherapists should not see children when the parent who brings in the child does not have legal custody (unless ordered by the court or unless consent is obtained from the parent who has legal custody).

Commentary

Informed consent involves not only the *permission to treat* but *permission to transfer or obtain information*. In this section, we will examine both of these issues. They also have been included in Chapter 3, Confidentiality, but, because they stand out as liability issues, we will go into detail here to emphasize their importance.

How often do you inform your clients of the kind of treatment you offer, the potential risks, their rights as clients, or the estimated length of treatment? Hopefully, you take time to go over these questions and others with your clients in addition to receiving verbal or written agreements from them or their legal guardians that they understand what treatment is about and, after being informed, agree to commit to treatment. If you have not discussed these issues with your clients and have assumed that, because they come to you voluntarily, this means they have consented to treatment, you could possibly be liable for tort. A psychotherapist needs to obtain an informed consent from his or her client for permission to treat the client and permission to obtain or release information regarding the client's treatment from or to other professionals. Professional organizations and other professionals in the field have suggested the following guidelines in getting a client's permission to treat.

CONSENT TO TREAT

The National Association of Social Worker's *NASW Standards for the Practice of Clinical Social Work* (1989) gives specific instructions as to what a contract to treat should contain, as follows: (a) agreement about fees; insurance; length, frequency, and location of sessions; appointments missed or canceled without adequate notice; vacation coverage during an absence; and collateral contracts (this information may be provided on a standardized form; (b) agreement regarding goals of treatment; and (c) informing the client of his or her rights.

You need to get consent from your clients in order to give them treatment or you can be held liable for tort. There is a financial award given for damages in a tort (civil wrong) case. A tort includes such issues as assault, battery, false imprisonment, intentional infliction of mental distress, and abandonment (Bray, Shepherd, & Hays, 1985).

If the client is a child (note that the age of a minor varies in different states), a prisoner, senile, comatose, a participant in research involving deception, or incapable of understanding or comprehending necessary treatment (as in the case of psychotic disorders), consent must be obtained from his or her guardian or parent. In addition, Woody (1988, p. 377) stated that the "committed patient must be given all information at the professional's disposal that the patient requires to make a reasonable, intelligent decision regarding choice of treatment."

Some specific issues involving minors in California are as follows:

(1) A psychotherapist *must* obtain parental consent to treat a minor child (Cal. Civil Code 25.8). Treatment without consent constitutes battery upon the child, and the professional may be sued for damages or disciplined for unprofessional conduct.

(2) There are certain statutory exceptions to the requirement of parental consent. Statutes (Cal. Civil Code 25.9) provide that a minor may obtain mental health treatment without parental consent when
  (a) he or she is at least 12 years old,
  (b) he or she is mature enough to participate intelligently in treatment,
  (c) he or she presents a danger of serious physical or mental harm to him- or herself or others without such treatment—or he or she is the alleged victim of incest or child abuse, and
  (d) therapy is related to drug or alcohol problems.

(3) Although minors can consent to their own treatment, the statute contains a preference for the involvement of parents unless the psychotherapist believes it would be inappropriate.

The main method of obtaining informed consent has been verbal, however, currently, many (Handelsman & Galvin, 1988) are proposing that the therapist get a written consent from the client to treat. See Appendix B for an example of a consent form.

OBTAIN A CONSENT TO RELEASE OR OBTAIN INFORMATION

We would like you to consider the following questions: How often do you ask a client for a release to obtain information when he or she has been to a prior therapist, his or her children have seen a school counselor, or your client was referred to you from another source? If these procedures are not routine in your practice, you may need to reconsider and make it a matter of practice. Therapists have lost cases because they did not get prior information regarding their clients that would have helped them proceed in a more effective method of treatment. In addition, you may be asked to release information about your client or your records concerning that client. Do you know what an appropriate consent needs to contain so that you can legally release your records, and do you release your records in a timely manner? Did you know you are still legally responsible for your client, for a certain period of time, even though he or she is going to another therapist or clinic? It is imperative that you know what to do when it comes to releasing or obtaining information about your clients.

In this chapter, we have learned about the need to transfer or obtain information (*Merchants National Bank v. U.S.*, 272 F.Supp. 409, North Dakota, 1967; *Underwood v. U.S.*, 356 F.2d 92, 5th Cir., 1966; *Jablonski v. U.S.*, 9th U.S. Cir. Ct. Appl. June 14, 1983). When seeing a new client, it would be wise to make it a practice to secure any previous mental health records in a prompt manner. On the flip side, you need to honor any valid request from a therapist for your information about a client. Don't be lax in honoring that request, for, if the client were to commit suicide, we believe you are likely to be liable because of your failure to transmit this information. By *valid request*, we mean a signed release, as discussed earlier in this chapter.

The American Association for Counseling and Development (1988) states, in its *Ethical Standards*, that, "if an individual is already in a counseling relationship with another professional person, the member does not enter into a counseling relationship without first contacting and receiving the approval of that other professional" (Section B.3). "If the member discovers that the client is in another counseling relationship after their counseling relationship begins, the member must gain the consent of the other professional or terminate the relationship, unless the client elects to terminate the other relationship." This requires the therapist to get permission to release or receive information about the client in the form of a legally sound consent form.

Format. It is important to know what an adequate release form should contain before releasing any information to any source about your client. Criteria for a consent form were discussed by the Privacy Protection Commission (which had no legally binding power but summarized many experts' views), which recommended that such a consent form be (Stromberg, 1988, p. 392):

(a) in written format;

(b) signed by the individual . . . or by someone authorized in fact to act in his [her] behalf;

(c) clear as to the fact that the medical care provider is among those either specifically named or generally designated by the individual as being authorized to disclose information about him [her];

(d) specific as to the nature of the information of the individual is authorizing to be disclosed;

(e) specific as to the institutions or other persons to whom the individual is authorizing information to be disclosed;

(f) specific as to the purpose(s) for which the information may be used by any of the parties named in (e) both at the time of the disclosure and at any time in the future;

(g) specific as to its expiration date, which should be for a reasonable period of time not to exceed one year, except where an authorization is presented in connection with (a life insurance policy).

According to Woody (1988), there are three elements that a form must contain. His suggestions add one more to the recommendations made by the Privacy Protection Commission. His list includes the following:

1) the form should indicate the specific material that is to be released,
2) the reason why the information is to be released and
3) the receiver of the information should be named (Woody, 1988, p. 136)

It is important that you examine a consent form to see if it has the necessary legal elements. If you find it is missing some of these elements, you should return the release form and request that it meet the required criteria.

Informing appropriate parties. These consent forms include the word *inform* because it is your duty to advise your client, even if he or she has signed a consent form, about the request to release information regarding him or her and the material that will be released. You should ask if he or she has any concerns or wishes about the consent to release (Stromberg, 1988). In this way, you have informed your client that he or she gave consent and, because he or she was fully informed, this procedure keeps you from being liable.

If your client has a guardian or conservator, you need to make sure that the individual signs the consent form. You may want to have minors sign consent forms, even though, legally, they are not entitled to sign, because it demonstrates that you have made the effort to inform them of what is happening in an effort to protect their rights.

In regard to what you should *not* do when it comes to informed consent: (1) If your client asks you to falsify records, do not agree to such an arrangement. If the client specifically requests it, you may, however, limit the information that is given. You may want to make a note that the client made such a request and give the rationale for agreeing to the request. (2) You should not release records that you obtained from another practitioner (Woody, 1988, p. 137). Inform the person questioning your records that he or she needs to get permission from the other practitioner for his or her records. Remember that the original record keeper has the right to the records.

Conclusions

Informed consent. We agree with Bray, Shepherd, and Hays (1985), Woody et al. (1984), and Schutz (1982) that it is the responsibility of the clinician to obtain informed consent. Specifically, the client must be informed of the following:

(1) the risks of such treatment or no treatment
(2) the possible consequences of treatment
(3) other alternatives for treating the presenting problem
(4) the benefits of treatment
(5) a complete explanation of the treatment (which could include procedures such as interpretation, confrontation, guided imagery, and touching)
(6) when confidentiality cannot be adhered to (limits of confidentiality; e.g., if a client uses insurance to pay for therapy, he or she foregoes client privileged communication)
(7) that he or she is free to withdraw his or her consent for treatment and terminate treatment
(8) frequency, duration, and the probable length of treatment
(9) any particular agency procedure and/or policies (e.g., maximum number of sessions client may be seen)
(10) the role of the person who is providing therapy and his or her professional qualifications (e.g., a Professional Disclosure Statement)
(11) therapist expectations of the client's role during the therapeutic relationship
(12) a statement that any questions about the procedures will be answered at any time
(13) a statement indicating that you are required to inform potential victims of any threats made

Consent to release/obtain information. When dealing with consent to release or obtain information, you should consider the following:

(1) It is advisable to routinely request a release when you have a client who has seen another therapist.
(2) If you are asked for information, make sure you have a valid written release.
(3) You need to send information in a prompt manner. (We suggest within two weeks.)
(4) The release form should indicate the specific material to be released and state how long the release is valid.
(5) We agree with Woody (1988) that a practitioner should not release records obtained from another service provider.
(6) It is advisable that clear standards and procedures be developed for establishing the parameters of disclosure to law enforcement officials and resisting pressure from those officials should they insist on more information.

(7) The therapist should get a waiver in writing when the client first reveals that he or she understands that the therapist is going to talk to supervisor/authorities and so on. Also, if the client wishes to waive confidentiality, this waiver needs to be in writing.

(8) All current state laws mandate reporting suspected child abuse. State laws may also mandate reporting suspected adult/elder abuse.

(9) While working with insurance companies concerning third-party payments, give only the information requested and information that is in agreement with your client having signed a waiver.

(10) You protect yourself legally if you only do specifically what is court ordered. Report information to the court only when subpoenaed and release information only to judiciary services.

(11) Always date the receipt of information pertaining to a client. Sometimes there may be a lengthy time period between the postmark date and when you actually receive the information.

(12) Information transferred should be in written form. If you give information by phone, follow with written data.

Summary

Whenever obtaining or transferring client information, it is important that the therapist adhere to his or her agency's policies and procedures. Any information that is released or received concerning the client should be documented by the therapist in the client's record. When seeing new clients, psychotherapists should ask whether or not they have been in therapy before and request any previous mental health records. Information obtained concerning abusiveness and harm to self, others, and/or physical property should be documented promptly, within 24 hours.

If a client is referred to a new therapist, the original therapist has a responsibility to review the client's file with the new therapist. It is also important that the therapist have the client sign a consent form before releasing such information. However, some states may require reporting to protect others or property without the client's consent. It is crucial for therapists to be familiar with their respective state laws concerning potential harm to self, others, or physical property because differences exist among the state statutes. Any written client information that is transferred to another therapist and/or institution needs to include the client's mental status, diagnosis, type of treatment, and potential risk to self, others, and/or physical property.

Whenever a dangerous client transfers to another therapist, the first therapist is responsible for forwarding such information to the new therapist. When a potentially dangerous client is put under the care of another person, the caretaker(s) should be notified of the client's history.

Vignette A: Consent to Treat

You are seeing a family of three including a daughter aged 13. This daughter, Sally, is concurrently seeing a counselor at her school. In private, the daughter tells you she is thinking of committing suicide. You see the need for her to get a psychiatric evaluation. In addition, her parents have asked you to keep them informed of all that Sally is telling you in your private sessions with her. How many of the above issues involve informed consent? What are your legal and ethical responsibilities regarding minors, especially in family therapy? If there is informed consent, whose signatures need to be on the release forms?

Vignette B: Consent to Treat

A mother brought her 8-year-old child in for therapy. After the sixth session, the mail carrier delivers a letter from the father's attorney indicating that the father has sole legal custody and that you are treating this child without his informed consent. He demands that therapy be terminated immediately. Also, the father provides you with a signed release from him with instructions that you are to send photocopies of all records to the father's attorney. What might you do?

Vignette C: Transfer of Records

You have been referred a client from his previous therapist. In the initial interview, you discover that this client had been hospitalized during treatment with the other therapist. The client also tells you that he asked to be referred to another therapist but hesitates to tell you why. Would you obtain previous records and, if so, how soon after the initial session would you ask for those records? Whose client is he: yours or the previous therapist's and for how long?

Questions to Consider

(1) What components are necessary for "informed consent"?

(2) What exceptions are there to "informed consent"?

(3) What might you do if your client refuses to sign a release to obtain information about prior treatment?

(4) In honoring another's request for information, how do you protect yourself if no release has been given by the client?

(5) How soon must a therapist respond to a client's signed release to forward written case notes to another therapist? How is *promptly* defined?

13

Illegal Detainment

Mental health hospitals have been scrutinized by legal authorities for a variety of reasons. There are concerns about intrusions on guaranteed legal rights, inescapable physical and emotional side effects resulting from hospitalization, and the potential abuse and neglect that may occur to patients. Whenever assessing the state's rationale for mental health activities, two key issues need to be balanced in determining what is best for patients and for society. One is the theory of *parens patriae*, whereby the state "acts out of its duty to provide protection and care for those unable to be self-sufficient" (Woody et al., p. 299). Second, it is the police power of the government that permits "the state to intervene in the lives of residents who appear to present a risk of danger to others" (Woody et al., 1984, p. 299). When decisions made by hospital personnel affect the patient's rights, the court is likely to assess whether or not the Fourteenth Amendment's equal protection clause or the Eighth Amendment's prohibition against cruel and unusual punishment have been violated (Woody et al., 1984). The "quid pro quo" argument suggests that the state must provide the involuntarily hospitalized patient some type of benefit (usually determined by adequate treatment) that outweighs the losses to a patient resulting from the confinement. If one is held illegally, the injury is deprivation of liberty. "Illegal detainment" may also be described as "confined against will" (AACD, 1988a) or "false imprisonment" (APA, 1989).

Court Cases

(1) *Lake v. Cameron* (**1966**)
(2) *Rouse v. Cameron* (**1966**)
(3) *Whitree v. State of New York* (**1968**)
(4) *O'Connor v. Donaldson* (**1975**)

Case Reviews

Catherine Lake, Appellant, v. Dale C. Cameron, Superintendent,
St. Elizabeths Hospital, Appellee
U.S. Court of Appeals
364 F.2d 657 (District of Columbia, 1966)

Catherine Lake petitioned for release while she was confined as an insane person in St. Elizabeths Hospital in the District of Columbia. The district court dismissed her request and she appealed. The U.S. court of appeals remanded the case to the district court for further proceedings. During the course of these court proceedings, Congress enacted the 1964 Hospitalization of the Mentally Ill Act, which was a change in the applicable statutory law.

The facts surrounding this case indicate that, on September 29, 1962, when Catherine Lake was 60 years old, a police officer discovered her wandering aimlessly about the streets and escorted her to the D.C. General Hospital. Twelve days later, Catherine filed a petition for a writ of verbal habeas corpus in the district court. The court judged her to be "of unsound mind" (p. 658) and ruled her transfer to St. Elizabeths Hospital, a large facility with approximately 8,000 patients. It was determined that the indigent woman was suffering from a mental illness with the diagnosis of "chronic brain syndrome associated with cerebral arteriosclerosis" (p. 659). She was reported to be dangerous to herself and in need of care and supervision that could not be provided by her family. While she was held at St. Elizabeths Hospital for observation in connection with pending commitment proceedings, she was permitted to amend her petition seeking release by naming the superintendent of the hospital as the defendant. On November 2, 1962, her petition was dismissed without a hearing being held or the requirement of a return.

At both the district court commitment hearing and the habeas corpus hearing on remand, Catherine Lake testified that she felt competent to be at liberty. More specifically, she requested an immediate unconditional release from St. Elizabeths Hospital. There was no indication of a desire to consider suitable alternative institutions. Her major habeas corpus contention was that of total confinement in a mental institution. However, as evidenced by the later court proceedings, two related issues appeared to be not only the fact of confinement but also the place of confinement.

At the court of appeals hearing, appellant Catherine Lake made reference to the new District of Columbia Hospitalization of the Mentally Ill Act, which was a statutory law that came into effect after the hearing in the district court. The new law indicated that, if the court or jury ascertains that a

> person is mentally ill and, because of that illness, is likely to injure him[her]self or other persons if allowed to remain at liberty, the court may order his[her] hospitalization for an indeterminate period, *or order any other alternative course of treatment which the court believes will be in the best interest of the person* or of the public. (p. 659, emphasis added)

In light of the new law, Mrs. Lake contended in both written and oral argument that the court of appeals was required to remand to the district court for a consideration of suitable alternatives. Her counsel communicated clearly that Mrs. Lake's real complaint was that she was totally confined in a mental institution and that "she would rather be in another institution or hospital, if available, or at home, even though under some form of restraint" (p. 659).

COURT DECISION

The court of appeals held that the proceedings initiated by Mrs. Lake would be remanded to the district court for inquiry into alternative courses of treatment. The record portrayed Mrs. Lake to be a person who was somewhat senile, had poor memory, had wandered away on a few occasions, and was unable to care for herself at all times. The suggestion was made that the district court consider [for example], whether the appellant and the public would be sufficiently protected if she were required to carry an identification card on her person so that the police or others could take her home if she should wander, or whether she should be required to accept public health nursing care, community mental health and day care services, or whether available welfare payments might finance adequate private care. (p. 661)

It was recognized that Mrs. Lake's mental condition did not warrant that full-time involuntary confinement be considered as one of the permissible alternatives. The government, while seeking to provide some sort of custodial care, could not compel Mrs. Lake to accept its help at the price of her freedom. She had a right to be treated with the least restrictive alternative. As evidenced by the court ruling, a change in the applicable statutory law after Mrs. Lake was first committed to the hospital was deemed appropriate for consideration of the case. It was further clarified that "to require in a habeas corpus proceeding that the court consider an intervening statute applicable to the situation is not to require a new commitment proceeding, nor does it open one already concluded" (p. 662).

Charles C. Rouse, Appellant, v. Dale C. Cameron, Superintendent,
St. Elizabeths Hospital, Appellee
U.S. Court of Appeals
373 F.2d 451 (District of Columbia Circuit, 1966)

Although no legal guidelines were established for subsequent court proceedings, this case recognized that involuntarily committed mental patients who are being acquitted of an offense by reason of insanity have a right to adequate treatment, despite knowledge of the offense. The purpose of involuntary hospitalization was also discussed as being for treatment and not for punishment. Failure of hospitals to provide suitable and adequate treatment cannot be justified by lack of staff or facilities. The issue of providing adequate treatment entails the requirement for hospitals to conduct initial and periodic inquiries regarding patients' needs and conditions while documenting such action. Relating to this case was the 1964 Hospitalization of the Mentally Ill Act, which requires hospitals to "keep records detailing psychiatric care and treatment and make them available to the patient's attorney" (p. 455).

Charles C. Rouse was arrested on a street corner in the District of Columbia at 1:45 a.m. by a police officer for possessing a dangerous weapon. He was carrying a suitcase containing "a .45 caliber Colt automatic pistol loaded with seven rounds of ammunition. He also had 100 rounds of .45 caliber bullets, 500 rounds of .22 caliber ammunition, two electric drills, a hacksaw and hacksaw blades" (p. 464). The municipal court found Rouse not guilty, by reason of insanity, of carrying a dangerous weapon. Such an act by a sane person is considered a misdemeanor for which the maximum punishment is one year of imprisonment.

On November 9, 1962, Rouse was involuntarily committed to the John Howard Pavilion, which is an area of maximum security confinement at St. Elizabeths Hospital. At this governmental mental institution, he received both individual and group psychotherapy for his personality disorder of overt antisocial behavior. At the time of this U.S. court of appeals hearing, Rouse had already spent three years at St. Elizabeths Hospital. Although Rouse had voluntarily left group therapy several months before this court hearing, he had not received any psychiatric treatment for the past 18 months. Also, there had not been any inquiry by psychiatric staff concerning the suitability of group therapy for his particular illness. Prior to this court hearing, on two different occasions, Rouse had been unsuccessful seeking release from the hospital, claiming that he had not received adequate psychiatric treatment and that he was sane and unlawfully detained. Issues arose during the court proceedings as to whether Rouse had dangerous propensities that were related to his abnormal mental condition.

COURT DECISION

The U.S. court of appeals discharged Rouse's writ of habeas corpus and dismissed the appellant's petition, with leave to renew after a reasonable time. The court was of the opinion that Rouse needed to take advantage, first, of the opportunities for greater freedom in the hospital before being released into society. Testimony revealed that Rouse prematurely terminated membership in the hospital's group psychotherapy because he said that he did not want to experience the discomfort that he believed was necessary for him to change. Also, Rouse was reported to have not accepted the increasing privileges and responsibilities granted him in the hospital, and he had denied himself the benefits of occupational and recreational therapy.

Although this court case did not establish any new legal guidelines, it paid particular attention to several already existing laws that are pertinent to mental health professionals. First, involuntary hospitalization is for the sole purpose of treatment, and patients cannot be punished during such confinement, despite knowledge that the patient is being acquitted of a governmental law offense by reason of insanity. Second, all mental patients are entitled to complete and adequate treatment. Failure to provide suitable and adequate psychiatric treatment is not excusable because of limited staff or facilities. Third, one who is involuntarily committed and in custody for violating the law is entitled to relief in habeas corpus. In other words, mental patients have a right to obtain a writ of habeas corpus as a protection against illegal imprisonment. Fourth, a mental hospital patient may not be confined for dangerous propensities unless they are related to or arise out of an abnormal mental condition. In other words, the dangerous propensities, standing alone, do not warrant continued confinement in a governmental mental institution.

Victor J. Whitree, Claimant, v. State of New York, Defendant
Court of Claims of New York
290 N.Y.S. 2d 486 (May 14, 1968)

NOTE: This case was the first case discussed in Chapter 2; see that chapter for the case description.

O'Connor v. Donaldson
Certiorari to the U.S. Court of Appeals for the Fifth Circuit
422 U.S. 563 (1975)

In January 1957, at the age of 49, Kenneth Donaldson was civilly committed to confinement as a mental patient in the Florida State Hospital in Chattahoochee, suffering from "paranoid schizophrenia." The patient's commitment was initiated by his father, who believed that his son was suffering from "delusions." Donaldson was confined at the Florida State Hospital against his will for almost 15 years. On a number of occasions during his confinement, he unsuccessfully petitioned the state and federal courts for his release, "claiming that he was dangerous to no one, that he was not mentally ill, and that, at any rate, the hospital was not providing treatment for his supposed illness" (p. 565).

Finally, in February 1971, at the age of 64, Donaldson brought this lawsuit before the U.S. District Court for the Northern District of

Florida, alleging that the hospital's superintendent, Dr. J. B. O'Connor, and other members of the hospital staff at Florida State Hospital in Chattahoochee, named as defendants, "had intentionally and maliciously deprived him of his constitutional right to liberty" (p. 565). Dr. O'Connor had already retired as superintendent before Donaldson filed this suit. A few months following O'Connor's retirement, and a few months before the court trial, Donaldson had secured his release from the hospital and a judicial restoration of his competency, with the support of hospital staff. Also, he had secured a responsible job in hotel administration immediately upon his release. Although Donaldson's original lawsuit was filed as a class action on behalf of himself and all of his fellow patients residing in the same department of the hospital, he later amended the complaint following his release from the hospital and after the district court had dismissed the action as a class suit. The amended complaint repeated Donaldson's claim for compensatory and punitive damages.

During the four-day U.S. district court trial, the evidence demonstrated that Donaldson's hospital confinement "was a simple regime of enforced custodial care, not a program designed to alleviate or cure his supposed illness" (p. 569). Therefore, this case did not involve involuntary treatment but simply involuntary confinement. Hospital staff witnesses testified that there were substantial periods of time when Donaldson "was simply kept in a large room that housed 60 patients, many of whom were under criminal commitment" (p. 569). Several requests made by Donaldson to Dr. O'Connor for ground privileges, for occupational training, and to discuss his case with him or other staff members were repeatedly denied.

Donaldson had initiated several requests for release during his 15 years of confinement. In fact, several of his requests were supported by responsible persons who were willing to provide him the necessary care upon release. For example, in 1963, a representative from "Helping Hands, Inc.," a halfway house for mental patients that was conceded to be a "good clinic," wrote to Dr. O'Connor requesting release of Donaldson to its care. This occurred at a time when Donaldson was 55 years old and his parents were considered too elderly and infirm to assume responsibility for him. However, O'Connor never informed Donaldson's parents about the "Helping Hands" offer. In addition, there were four separate occasions between 1964 and 1968 when John Lembcke, one of Donaldson's college classmates and a longtime family friend, asked O'Connor to release Donaldson to his care. All the requests made by Lembcke were denied by O'Connor.

Dr. O'Connor's principal defense at trial was that he had acted in "good faith" pursuant to state law, which he believed to be valid. The law authorized "indefinite custodial confinement of the 'sick,' even if they were not given treatment and their release could harm no one" (p. 570). O'Connor maintained that he was, therefore, immune from liability for monetary damages. The statute to which Dr. O'Connor was referring did not clearly provide a "right to treatment" for involuntarily committed patients, neither did it provide a "judicial procedure whereby one still incompetent could secure his[her] release on the ground that [s]he was no longer dangerous to him[her]self or others" (pp. 566-567). However, that particular Florida statutory law had already been repealed at the time of these court proceedings. The revamped statutory law specifies the right of mental patients to receive individual medical treatment. In addition, there is no constitutional basis for confining a mental patient involuntarily, or against the patient's will, if the patient is not dangerous to him- or herself and is capable of surviving safely in freedom by him- or herself or with the assistance of willing and responsible family members or friends. Consequently, the hospital staff had the power to initiate the statutory procedure to release a patient, such as Donaldson, who was not dangerous to himself or others, even if he remained mentally ill and lawfully committed. The only requirement was the submission of a judicial restatement of the patient's "mental capacity."

Donaldson argued that, throughout the period of his hospitalization, he was not dangerous to himself or others. He asserted further that, if he were mentally ill, or if the hospital staff believed that he was mentally ill, they withheld from him the treatment necessary to improve his mental condition. The defendants claimed that Donaldson's detainment was legal and proper, or, if it was not legal and proper, it was the result of a mistake without malicious intent. Evidence revealed that Donaldson had repeatedly refused treatment that was offered him while in the hospital, "claiming that he was not mentally ill and needed no treatment" (p. 578). There was also some evidence that Donaldson, who was a Christian Scientist, at times refused to take his medication. This information was acknowledged as supporting Dr. O'Connor's "good faith" defense. The court indicated that it is universally recognized by behavioral specialists "that an uncooperative patient cannot benefit

from therapy and that the first step in effective treatment is acknowledgment by the patient that he[she] is suffering from an abnormal
condition" (p. 569).

COURT DECISION

The jury of the U.S. District Court for Northern Florida returned a
verdict for Kenneth Donaldson against Dr. O'Connor and a codefen-
dant. Donaldson was awarded compensatory damages of $38,500., in-
cluding $10,000 in punitive damages. Punitive damages were awarded
on the grounds that O'Connor had maliciously confined Donaldson to
cause a deprivation of his constitutional rights to freedom. The Court
of Appeals for the Fifth Circuit subsequently, on broad Fourteenth
Amendment grounds, affirmed the judgment of the district court and
held that

> a State cannot constitutionally confine . . . a nondangerous individual who
> is capable of surviving safely in freedom by himself or with the help of
> willing and responsible family members or friends, and since the jury
> found, upon ample evidence that petitioner did so confine respondent, it
> properly concluded that petitioner had violated respondent's right to
> liberty. (p. 563)

The issue of the Fourteenth Amendment initiated constitutional questions of whether persons involuntarily civilly committed to state hospitals are guaranteed a right to treatment. The court's opinion was that
"regardless of the grounds for involuntary civil commitment, a person
confined against his will at a state mental institution has 'a constitutional right to receive such individual treatment as will give him a reasonable opportunity to be cured or to improve his mental condition' "
(p. 572). "Conversely, the court's opinion implied that it is constitutionally permissible for a State to confine a mentally ill person against his
will in order to treat his illness, regardless of whether his illness renders
him dangerous to himself or others" (pp. 572-573). The jury had determined that Donaldson was dangerous neither to himself nor to others.
They also found that, even if Donaldson were mentally ill, he had not
received treatment. Furthermore, as indicated in a footnote of the court
summary report, the jury quite likely surmised "that O'Connor knew
not only that Donaldson was harmless to himself and others, but also

that he was not mentally ill" (p. 573). Circumstantially, regardless of the "treatment" Donaldson had received, O'Connor was at fault.

Implications

a. Therapists should inform clients of their rights regarding detainment before detaining them.

b. It is recommended that, at the beginning of the therapeutic relationship, therapists collect information from clients regarding their significant others and those to be notified in case of emergency. In addition, it is beneficial to have clients sign a consent form for releasing information in case of emergencies.

c. Mental health professionals who are not psychiatrists are encouraged to establish a good working relationship with a psychiatrist. This will enable therapists to consult and obtain additional (i.e., medical) treatment pertaining to clients that may lie outside their area of competency or certification.

d. Patients have a right to be treated in "the least restrictive alternative." Therapists need to know what resources are available in the community as alternatives to institutionalizing a client. Also, therapists are encouraged to investigate these resources to determine their therapeutic value.

e. Therapists need to familiarize themselves with institutions that may be appropriate for admitting their clients. It is important that therapists find the appropriate institution to meet the particular needs of each individual client.

f. After admitting a client to an institution for inpatient treatment, be certain to follow-up with the client to communicate caring and to determine whether the client is receiving proper and adequate treatment.

g. Once a patient is institutionalized to receive psychological and/or medical treatment, he or she cannot be punished during such confinement. *All* patients have the right to receive proper and adequate treatment when institutionalized, regardless of what crime they have committed. The sole purpose of involuntary hospitalization is for treatment, *not* punishment.

h. An insufficient number of staff members at an institution will not hold up in court as grounds for an institutionalized patient receiving inadequate treatment or no treatment at all.

i. Patients may not be confined in an institution for dangerous acts unless the acts are related to or arise from an abnormal mental condition.

j. When working in an inpatient facility, therapists need to document all relevant information regarding any attempts to treat patients. The patient's participation (or lack of), as well as the therapist's participation in the practice of psychotherapeutic activity, should be thoroughly documented in a timely fashion.

k. When working in an inpatient facility, it seems to be crucial to document, on a *daily* basis, the patient's behavior, affect and mood and the treatment (both medical and psychological) received.

l. Ongoing psychiatric and psychosocial examinations concerning inpatients' mental status on a monthly basis are a good rule of thumb for those who are being held against their will in a treatment facility. It is also important to document *all* such examinations in a patient's record file.

m. Every human being is entitled to a legal representative, if and when requested.

n. Whenever involuntarily hospitalizing a patient, it is advisable to consult with several professional colleagues on staff to determine length and type of treatment.

o. Before admitting a client who is receiving individual psychotherapy to group therapy, it is important that the therapist evaluate the appropriateness before the client attends the group or shortly thereafter.

Commentary and Conclusion

A major area of litigation involves the charge of illegal detainment or wrongful commitment. Schutz (1982) points out that "false imprisonment is an intentional tort requiring actual imprisonment or commitment without probable cause" (p. 26). Schwitzgebel and Schwitzgebel (1960) offer a number of guidelines for therapists who have the legal right to commit a patient:

1. Carefully evaluate your client. (If you fail to directly examine the patient you are open for possible error.)
2. Your client needs to be seen alone [by the psychotherapist].
3. Evaluate the extent that drugs may account for the patient's actions.

4. Rule out physical conditions which might account for the behavior through a physical examination.
5. Make accurate verbatim quotes.
6. Your report should differentiate observation from reported data.
7. Make sure there is no conflict of interest (i.e., avoid any dual relationships).
8. The facility used must be able to provide the treatment needed in the least restrictive setting.
9. Follow due process and adhere to all legal requirements.
10. Investigate to determine if a patient's stories are true rather than assume they are the symptoms of a mental illness.
11. Obtain a history and evaluate current mental status. (Schwitzgebel & Schwitzgebel, 1980, pp. 279-284)

We find the above guidelines offered by Schwitzgebel and Schwitzgebel (1980) to be comprehensive and suggest they be followed.

Summary

Therapists need to be very familiar with community resources before hospitalizing their clients. It is advisable to consult with professional colleagues before involuntarily hospitalizing a client to determine length and type of treatment. Also, clients should be informed of their rights regarding detainment before they are detained. Patients have a right to be treated in the "least restrictive alternative" and may not be confined in an institution because of dangerous acts unless the acts are related to or arise from an abnormal mental condition. Once a patient is institutionalized to receive psychological and/or medical treatment, he or she cannot be punished for a crime that has been committed. The main purpose of involuntary hospitalization is treatment and not punishment. Legally, an insufficient number of staff members or lack of facilities to provide adequate treatment will not hold up in court as a basis for providing inadequate treatment or no treatment at all. Mental health staff personnel need to conduct initial and periodic inquiries regarding patients' needs and conditions as a part of treatment. It is important to conduct ongoing psychiatric and psychosocial examinations concerning an inpatient's mental status *and* to document all examinations in the patient's record. Furthermore, any attempts to treat the patient, including any uncooperative responses by patients, need to be documented.

Vignette

You work for an inpatient facility. You get a call from an irate husband who tells you he needs for you to come get his wife. He explains that his wife has become irrational and confused and will not listen to anything he says to her. He tells you that you must pick her up right now. He states that he would prefer not to let her know that you are coming to get her and asks you to come dressed in a way that would not reveal your status. He adds that if you do not come now he believes she might kill herself. What is your immediate reaction to this case. Would you go immediately to the home? Are you aware of what your state laws say regarding commitment and illegal detainment? If you should have a chance to talk to her and she tells you that she is "perfectly sane" and it is her husband who is out to get her, how do you handle this situation?

Questions to Consider

(1) How does one determine what "adequate treatment" is?
(2) If a psychotherapist asks a patient to voluntarily commit him- or herself to a mental hospital because "it would be more convenient" for the therapist, would this represent a violation of the concept to be treated in "the least restrictive alternative"?
(3) How do you determine whether or not a client's dangerous propensities are related to a mental condition?
(4) How might you become familiarized with your community resources and the quality of services provided?
(5) What is the difference between "involuntary treatment" and "involuntary confinement"?

14

Wrongful Release

Several forms of due process protection have changed the traditional discretionary decision on the part of hospital administrators or treatment personnel to release a psychotherapy patient from a civil commitment. Several states now provide for mandatory periodic review to assess the status of each patient. For example, an Arizona statute requires that reexaminations of each hospitalized patient by "appropriate professional persons, including a physician" be conducted every 90 days (Woody et al., 1984, p. 321). A hospital is required to discharge a patient when the patient is deemed to be no longer in need of care and treatment.

"Another form of periodic review is the requirement that commitment continue only for specified periods of time, after which the hospital must either release the patient or seek a renewed court order of commitment" (Woody et al., 1984, p. 322). Although the hospital may not keep the patient any longer without a renewed contract, it has the discretion of releasing the patient prior to the expiration of the commitment period (Woody et al., 1984). It is likely that the court will translate this into "no longer dangerous to self or others." The determination will be based on the findings and recommendations of the professional psychotherapists who are directly involved in the care and treatment while the patient is hospitalized. As this is a basic part of their employment, the courts will probably not insulate this aspect of their professional service from liability (i.e., the standards for the medical malpractice should be expected to be applied in any action for negligent release of a patient from a mental hospital).

Court Cases

(1) *Semler v. Psychiatric Institute of Washington* **(1976)**
(2) *Durflinger v. Artiles* **(1981)**

Case Reviews

Helen Semler, Administratrix of the Estate of Natalia Semler, Deceased, Appellee, v. Psychiatric Institute of Washington, D.C. et al., Defendants, v. Paul Folliard, Appellant
Helen Semler, Administratrix of the Estate of Natalia Semler, Deceased, Appellee, v. Psychiatric Institute of Washington, D.C., Inc. et al., Appellants, v. Paul Folliard, Third-Party Defendant
Nos. 74-2345, 74-2346
U.S. Court of Appeals, Fourth Circuit. (Argued November 10, 1975; Decided February 27, 1976; Certiorari Denied October 4, 1976)

As documented in the court summary report, at the time of this lawsuit, in 1975, there had not been another Virginia case similar to this claim. Mrs. Helen Semler filed a negligence action against defendants Psychiatric Institute of Washington, D.C., Psychiatric Institute of America, Professional Associates of the Psychiatric Institute of Washington, D.C., and Ralph W. Wadeson, Jr., M.D. Mrs. Semler sought to recover damages for the death of her daughter, Natalia, who had been killed by John Steven Gilreath, a Virginia probationer and patient at the institute. "The original defendants filed a third party complaint against Paul Folliard [who was employed by the Institute and served as], Gilreath's probation officer, seeking indemnification or contribution from him if they should be found liable" (p. 123). The court referred to the original defendants and the third-party defendant collectively as "the appellants."

John Steven Gilreath, the patient in this case, was indicted in Fairfax County, Virginia, for abducting a young girl in October 1971. "The presentence report informed the judge that on three previous occasions Gilreath had molested other young girls" (p. 124). Pending trial, Gilreath entered the Psychiatric Institute of Washington, D.C., for treatment. His doctor, Ralph W. Wadeson, Jr., stated he did not consider John to be a danger to himself or others as long as he was in a supervised, structured way of life, such as that provided at the Psychiatric Institute. The state judge issued Gilreath a 20-year sentence but suspended it on the condition that Gilreath continue to be treated and confined at the institute.

A few months later, the state court judge allowed Gilreath to visit his family for Thanksgiving and Christmas. This consent was granted in response to a request made by Paul Folliard, Gilreath's probation officer, and upon Dr. Wadeson's recommendation. Subsequently, the judge permitted Gilreath to have additional passes based upon Dr. Wadeson's recommendation and, in early 1973, he authorized probation officer Folliard to award Gilreath weekend passes at his discretion.

In May 1973, Dr. Wadeson recommended that Gilreath be transferred to "day-care" status, and this was approved by the court. Without court approval, in July 1973, Folliard gave Gilreath a three-day and later a fourteen-day pass to investigate the possibility of living and working in Ohio. Tentative arrangements had been made by Gilreath to work for his uncle and attend therapy sessions at a nearby hospital. Dr. Wadeson had been consulted by Folliard concerning Gilreath's possible transfer and felt that such a change would be beneficial to the patient. However, Folliard had not submitted either of these passes to the judge for approval.

On August 29, 1973, Dr. Wadeson discharged Gilreath from the institute, based upon the assumption that Gilreath would be accepted for probation in Ohio. However, the Ohio authorities rejected Gilreath's application for transfer of probation. On September 19, Gilreath followed the advice of Folliard by returning to Virginia, where he met with Dr. Wadeson, who recommended that he receive additional therapy. Rather than restoring Gilreath to day-care status, Dr. Wadeson enrolled him in a therapy group that met two nights a week. As an outpatient of the institute, Gilreath lived, first, at home with his parents and, later, alone while working as a bricklayer's helper. Consequently, no one monitored his medication; neither was he under constant supervision.

Furthermore, he lacked daily psychiatric supervision to assist him during times of mental stress.

Gilreath informed his probation officer about his new arrangement as an outpatient, but Folliard did not report the information to the judge. Folliard was promoted in late September and a new probation officer was assigned to Gilreath around October 1, 1973. On October 29, 1973, some six weeks after his return to Virginia, Gilreath killed Natalia Semler, the plantiff's daughter.

COURT DECISION

The U.S. District Court for the Eastern District of Virginia, sitting without a jury, awarded plaintiff Mrs. Helen Semler $25,000. against the psychiatrists at the institute and required probation officer Paul Folliard to contribute one-half of the judgment. Folliard appealed the judgment, the case was heard by the court of appeals, and the judgment of the district court was affirmed. The court of appeals held that the Psychiatric Institute had breached the state's court order imposing a duty to protect the public by retaining probationer Gilreath until he was released by a court order; his sentence had been suspended on the ground that he receive treatment at and remain confined in the institute. In addition, probation officer Folliard was held liable for approving the transfer of probationer Gilreath from day-care to outpatient status without the state judge's approval. It was reported that the probation officer knew that his own authority was limited to granting passes and that only the state judge reserved the authority to change the probationer's status. The transfer of status was believed to be the proximate cause of Gilreath killing the young girl.

The appellants contended that "the transfer [of Gilreath] from day care to out-patient status was simply a normal progression of treatment that required no additional judicial approval" (p. 125). However, the district judge recognized significant differences between Gilreath's day care and outpatient care. While addressing the issue of "consequent injury," and having heard expert psychiatric testimony, the district judge determined "it was less likely that Gilreath would have killed the plaintiff's daughter had he remained on day care" (p. 126).

Probation officer Folliard contended that "he was improperly joined as a third party defendant and that he [was] . . . immune from liability because he was performing a discretionary duty (p. 127). The court of appeals affirmed the district court's judgment rejecting Folliard's

defenses. The court made reference to Virginia law and ruled that
Folliard was performing a "ministerial act" and consequently was not
entitled to immunity. A *ministerial act* is defined by Virginia law as
"one which a person performs in a given state of facts, in a prescribed
manner, in obedience to the mandate of legal authorities without regard
to, or the exercise of, his own judgment upon the propriety of the act
being done" (p. 127). Thus, although Folliard's issuance of passes to
Gilreath was considered to be discretionary, the act of granting approval
for Gilreath's change of status from that of day care to outpatient was
deemed "ministerial." The probation officer was responsible to abide
by the mandate of the court order by submitting any questions for
Gilreath's change of status to the state judge.

Irvin L. Durflinger, Individually and as Next of Kin of
Raymond Durflinger, and Ronald Durflinger, Plaintiffs, v.
Benjamin Artiles et al., Defendants
Civ. A. No. 75-63-C6
U.S. District Court, D. Kansas (June 12, 1981)

Mr. Irvin Durflinger filed suit against a hospital and doctors for prematurely discharging his son Bradley. Bradley Durflinger had a history of
bed-wetting and being a loner and runaway. In 1973, Bradley, with a
hatchet in one hand and a meat fork in the other, waited for his maternal
grandparents to come home in Hutchinson, Kansas. He explained that
he was waiting to "knock them off and take the Toyota" (p. 324).
Bradley was admitted to Larned State Hospital because of his assault
on his grandparents. For involuntary commitment, a probate court must
rule that an individual is mentally ill. Bradley was found by the Reno
County Probate Court to be mentally ill and to the "extent he is in need
of care or treatment and is or probably will become dangerous to himself
or the person or property of others if not given care or treatment"
(p. 324). After being at Larned, it was decided that he should be
transferred to a hospital in Salem, Oregon. Both his parents and the
treatment team at Larned were expecting the transfer. However, Dr.
Benjamin Artiles, clinical director, who had never seen Bradley, sent a
note to the leader of the treatment team, Dr. Francisco Izaguirre. The
note stated,

I do not understand why we should assume the responsibilities & expenses of a transfer all the way to Oregon of someone [sic] who is 19, physically healthy and suffers from a character disorder and who furthermore is not motivated for treatment.

It rather looks to me that we should discharge this patient. (Pl.Ex. 10, p. 324)

Dr. Artiles stated he knew that Bradley had been diagnosed as a "sociopath with anti-social features" (p. 324), which meant he could be a danger to the community. After being discharged, Bradley went to his home and, with a loaded gun, waited for his family to return. He shot and killed his mother and his brother Corwin. He later testified that he needed the family car in order to leave.

The defendants disagreed on the reason for allowing the discharge. Dr. Artiles stated it was because the patient showed no motivation for therapy and the treatment team stated it was because Bradley was "doing so well" (p. 325). However, the hospital records show that Bradley refused to partake in vocational rehabilitation. The defendants pointed out that it was the family who aggravated Bradley to commit such a violent act. The court concluded that was reason for not discharging the patient to the custody of his parents.

The defendants argued against Dr. O'Connor serving as an expert witness for the plaintiffs. Dr. O'Connor discussed what was standard care in procedures to discharge. The defense argued that Dr. O'Connor was not qualified to testify because he was not a medical doctor and that he practiced in Kansas and would not be knowledgeable about standard of care practices in Oregon. The case *Riggs v. Gouldner* (150 Kan. 727, 96 P.2d 694, 1939) was cited to establish the rules for being an expert witness. This case established that, if the witness's training was to use the same methods for treating and diagnosing, it did not matter if the therapist came from a different school of medicine. The court further pointed out that "an expert may acquire knowledge of the applicable standard in the same manner that he acquires his other expert knowledge—through practical experience, formal training, reading, and study" (p. 329). With this knowledge, an expert witness can claim to understand what constitutes standard care procedures. Therefore, O'Connor was accepted as an expert witness.

Dr. O'Connor discussed six elements that need to be examined to determine the lethality of a patient and that these elements must be examined before one determines if a person is to be discharged. The first element is the patient's *admitting complaint.* According to O'Connor, lethality was high because of the incident with the grandparents. The second element is the *patient's history.* According to O'Connor, Bradley's history of stealing, being AWOL (i.e., absent without leave), lying, and running away made him a moderate risk. The third element is related to the patient's *diagnosis.* Bradley was diagnosed as a passive-aggressive with antisocial features, which placed him at high risk. The fourth element to be considered is the patient's *test results.* Bradley had taken an MMPI (Minnesota Multiphasic Personality Inventory), which showed him to be high on the manic scale and low on the depression scale. O'Connor felt that Bradley's hospitalization would tend to reverse these scores, thus making him a moderate risk. In addition, O'Connor pointed out that the records showed an intent to give the patient an incomplete-sentence test, but this order was never carried out. O'Connor felt this was not a quality test. The fifth element is *ward behavior.* According to O'Connor, there was nothing to indicate that Bradley had improved his behavior, which put him at risk. Finally, there is the element of the *"effectiveness and appropriateness" of treatment.* O'Connor testified that the standard of care for discharge would have been to give the patient a mental status exam, an MMPI, and other tests and to have a discharge plan. In addition, the plan would have to have provided the patient with a structured environment.

COURT DECISION

The court denied the defendants' motion for a retrial and granted the plaintiffs $67,300. in damages. One of the doctors had settled out of court for $25,000. The court determined that the hospital and doctors had indeed committed negligence in discharging the patient. The court determined that they had not met the standard of care when they did not conduct further testing of the patient, and they did not have a discharge plan. Further, they had released Bradley without considering the consequences.

Implications

a. It is important that extreme changes in patient care be monitored in a supportive and evaluative fashion.

b. If an individual is confined in a hospital by court order, any proposed changes to the patient's status need court approval before implementation.

c. It is advisable to check first with the client whether there might be someone whom he or she would prefer the therapist or administrative personnel to notify before being released.

d. Be certain to tell the client first whenever you intend to notify her or his significant other(s) concerning her or his release.

e. When dealing with court mandated cases, it is advised that the therapist not make any definitions about termination or changing patient status until having sought legal counsel.

f. Professional psychotherapists who recommend patients for release from hospitalization because they are no longer dangerous will most likely be held accountable by the courts.

g. All client consent should be obtained in writing.

Commentary

As you have read, you are at risk if you fail to hospitalize a client who needs hospitalization or if you hospitalize someone who does not need hospitalization. Furthermore, you are at risk if you discharge a patient who is still a danger to self or others. When a patient is no longer in need of care and treatment, discharge from the hospital is necessary. The legal system will most likely interpret this to mean "no longer a danger." Before discharging a patient, it would be most appropriate to directly evaluate the patient, review all records, and have a discharge plan.

Conclusions

We recommend the following before releasing any patient from a hospital setting:

(1) Evaluate the patient face to face.
(2) Review all records to determine how other staff members view this patient.
(3) You are at risk if you discharge a patient who is still a danger to self and others.

(4) Have a discharge plan.

(5) Determine whether anyone needs to be notified of the patient's release.

(6) If an individual is confined in a hospital by court order, any changes in the patient's status need court approval before implementation.

(7) It is advisable to check first with the client to see if there is someone whom he or she would prefer to be notified by the therapist or administrative personnel before he or she is released.

(8) Be certain to tell the client first whenever you intend to notify his or her significant other(s) concerning his or her release.

(9) When dealing with court mandated cases, it is advised that the therapist not make any definitions about termination or changing patient status until having sought legal consultation.

(10) All consent of client, by the client, should be obtained in writing.

Summary

In contrast to the potential malpractice suits for illegal detainment/ wrongful commitment of a patient discussed in Chapter 13, this chapter addressed the opposite dilemma, that is, the issue of wrongful release of a patient from an inpatient mental health treatment facility. Therapists who recommend patients' release from hospitalization because they are no longer believed to be dangerous will most likely be held accountable by the courts for any subsequent wrongful actions of the patient. It is strongly recommended that reexamination of each hospitalized patient be conducted at specified periods of time and be documented in the patient's record. The determination to release a patient prior to the expiration of the contracted commitment period should not be done without first consulting all staff who are directly involved in the care and treatment of the patient. In addition, it is advisable to check with the client about significant others to be notified before initiating a release and to inform the significant others about the plans for release. It is also helpful to solicit emotional support for the client from the client's significant others while arranging for a release. Whenever the courts are involved in involuntarily committing an individual to a mental institution for treatment, therapists should not change the patient's status (e.g., from inpatient to outpatient or from individual treatment to group treatment) without first seeking legal counsel. Any changes in the patient's status need court approval before implementation.

Vignette

You are a therapist who has a client in an inpatient facility. The time has come for your client to leave the facility. During the last session, he tells you for the first time that he intends to kill his wife and children when he leaves the hospital. He has told you he does not want you to tell his wife and children that he is going to do this. How will you handle this case? What must you legally and ethically do? What rights does this client have? Will you consult anyone regarding this case? If so, who? Are you aware of your state's requirements regarding wrongful release?

Questions to Consider

(1) If professional staff disagree on a patient's "potential danger," what are ways of dealing with this dilemma?

(2) How accurate are psychotherapists in predicting dangerousness?

(3) How do you determine the "standards of the community"?

(4) When working as a mental health professional for an inpatient treatment facility, what is your responsibility in learning its regulations and/or procedures and getting it to protect you and the client?

(5) How do you determine whether or not the client is competent to issue his or her own informed consent while serving as a client in therapy?

(6) How do you determine who will be notified concerning a client's release if the client has no close relatives or close friends?

(7) What are the potential consequences of seeking judicial approval for every decision about a court ordered client?

15

Undue Influence

Suits in which a third party alleges that the therapist is exercising undue influence over a patient and is thus abusing the relationship are most likely to occur when (a) the client bestows a lavish gift on a therapist or leaves an estate to the therapist; (b) when a client's spouse, following a separation/divorce, charges the therapist with alienation of affection; or (c) when a parent alleges that a therapist suggested a course of action to a minor against a parent's wishes (Schwitzgebel & Schwitzgebel, 1980). In addition, undue influence is more likely to occur when the therapist uses a more directive, problem-solving type of therapy.

Court Cases

(1) *Patterson v. Jensen et al.* (**1945**)
(2) *Flemming v. Hall* (**1965**)
(3) *H. Jon Geis v. Landau* (**1983**)

Case Reviews

In re Faulks' Will; Patterson v. Jensen et al.
Supreme Court of Wisconsin
246 Wis. 319, 17 N.W. 2d 423 (Jan 16, 1945)
(Rehearing Denied May 1, 1945)

Will Jensen had lived with Mary and George Faulks from the age of 11.
He attempted to stop the probate of Mary Faulks's will (George Faulks
had been deceased since 1934) because he objected to Dr. Patterson
(Mary Faulks's personal doctor) being named as the principal beneficiary. Mary Faulks, who died in December 1942, had no children but
had mothered Will Jensen, who came to her from an orphans' home. In
1935, Mary Faulks's will did not name Dr. Patterson as a beneficiary.
In 1941, Mrs. Faulks made another will in which Dr. Patterson was
named as a beneficiary for the amount of $11,000. Will Jensen did not
object to the 1941 will. However, in 1942, Mrs. Faulks made a final will
in which she named Dr. Patterson as the primary beneficiary, and it was
this will that was contested by Mr. Jensen.

Dr. Patterson had met Mary Faulks in 1937 and in 1940 became her
regular physician. In 1940, Dr. Patterson borrowed $8,600. from Mary
Faulks for a home and in return gave her a promissory note for $4,000.
Mary Faulks, in the same year, gave further gifts of money to Dr.
Patterson, which included $1,100. for an airplane hanger, $2,500. for
partial payment for a second airplane, and a paid family vacation to
Yellowstone Park—and Mrs. Faulks went along on the trip. Dr. Patterson had stated that, in return for the gift of $1,100., he would take care
of Mrs. Faulks's medical needs for the rest of her life.

On January 10, 1942, when Mrs. Faulks became ill and had to be
hospitalized, Will Jensen and his wife paid her a visit. They argued with
her over the attention she was giving Dr. Patterson. They had objected
to Dr. Patterson taking her on plane trips when he knew she had a weak
heart. She asked them to leave, and they did not see her again nor did
they attend her funeral in December 1942.

Jensen's lawyers argued that, based on the evidence that Mary Faulks
had continued to do whatever Dr. Patterson asked of her including
taking plane trips when it was not in her best interest, she was a "person
unquestionably susceptible to undue influence." They further argued
that Dr. Patterson was in a position to influence her unduly and did so

to procure improper favors. The defense pointed out that Mary Faulks
insisted that she go up in Dr. Patterson's plane even against his advice
and that the money she gave him was to be reimbursed not only
financially but with the promise that Dr. Patterson would give her free
medical care for the rest of her life. The defense also noted that no one
had contested the 1941 will, which named Dr. Patterson as a beneficiary.

COURT DECISION

For the contestant to prove undue influence, it must be established
by "clear, convincing, and satisfactory evidence which means something more than a mere preponderance of evidence." The court determined that Mary Faulks was not mentally impaired when she had her
last will drafted, and there was no clear evidence of her concealing the
contents. In addition, the court found that, although Dr. Patterson had
the ability to have undue influence over Mrs. Faulks, there is no
evidence that "at any time or any place" that he "suggested the making
of the will or suggested its contents," and, therefore, there is no clear-
cut evidence to suggest that Dr. Patterson became the primary beneficiary because of undue influence. Influence gained by kindness and
affection was not regarded as undue "if no imposition or fraud be
practiced, even though it induced the testator (Mrs. Faulks) to make an
unequal and unjust disposition" (In *Mackall v. Mackall*, 135 U.S. 176,
172,10 S.Ct. 705,707,34 L. Ed. 84, the Supreme Court of the United
States).

*In the Matter of the Estate of Albert F. Wood, Deceased, May A. Flemming
and National Bank of Detroit, Proponents and Appellees, v. Countessa Wood
Hall, Contestant and Appellant*
374 Mich. 278, No. 32 Jan. Term. 1964, 132 N.W. 2d 35
Supreme Court of Michigan (January 4, 1965)

Contestant, Countess Wood Hall, attacked the validity of the Albert F.
Wood's will on the ground that he was unduly influenced by the
proponent May A. Flemming. Albert Wood (who died at the age of 91)
was the uncle of the Countess. Albert Wood lived and worked on the
upper floor of a four-story Wood Building (owned by Albert Wood) in
which Miss Flemming had worked for over 30 years. Although no
evidence was brought forth that there was a personal relationship

between Miss Flemming and Mr. Wood, the contestant pointed out that Mr. Wood had given Miss Flemming power of attorney over his estate and had opened a joint savings account with Miss Flemming. Mr. Wood's will gave payments of $300. per month to Miss Flemming, left his property (including the Wood Building) to Miss Flemming, and included a later letter giving a $100,000. U.S. treasury note to Miss Flemming.

COURT DECISION

The court upheld the will based on two findings: (a) that there was no proof of a confidential relationship between Miss Flemming and Mr. Wood and (b) that Mr. Wood was found to have sought independent legal advice and not the advice of Miss Flemming when drawing up his final will and the attached letter. The second finding was given more weight than the first.

H. Jon Geis, P.C., Plaintiff, v. Betsy Landau, Defendant
Civil Court of the City of New York, New York County
458 N.Y.S. 2d 2000, 117 Misc., 2d 396 (January 11, 1983)

Psychotherapist Dr. Jon Geis sued his former client, Betsy Landau, for unpaid fees for psychotherapeutic services. Betsy Landau had seen Dr. Geis from fall 1969 to fall 1977. During the time she was seeing Dr. Geis, she was going through a divorce and had told him it was difficult to pay for his services. When Mrs. Landau had terminated therapy, she had an outstanding bill of $8,000. She told the court that she had paid $4,500 of her bill, that Dr. Geis had told her not to worry about the bill, and that he would defer payment. However, the defendant stated that the plaintiff had never discussed the fact that she was "getting in over her head." Mrs. Landau also stated that even though she knew the doctor felt he was doing her a favor by delaying payment, she was feeling "strangled" by him because the bill was increasing as therapy continued.

   Dr. Geis is a clinical psychologist who was educated at Columbia University and practices therapy in New York City. Dr. Geis maintains that, even though the defendant paid him $4,500., she still owed him $8,000. when she terminated treatment in September 1977. Dr. Geis had written a letter to the defendant stating, "Before you panic about the enclosed (bill) think it all over realistically. While it is important to try to be as conscientious as possible re your responsibilities to your therapist, that therapist, while trying to live his own life responsibly re himself and his patients, has no intention of letting you fall into the abyss." In a note written at a later date, Dr. Geis wrote "not to worry about the bill." Dr. Geis also stated that he decided it was unwise to refer the patient to a low-cost clinic. According to the court, Dr. Geis "made a unilateral decision that only he could help the defendant." Dr. Geis also stated he knew that Mrs. Landau could not receive funds from her former husband but he considered her to be an "ethical person" and felt she would pay her bill.

COURT DECISION

The court determined that Dr. Geis and Mrs. Landau had a "confidential relationship," and, therefore, it would "carefully scrutinize transactions between such parties to prevent any abuse of confidence or betrayal of trust." The judge, David B. Saxe, stated that, because of this relationship, Dr. Geis had exercised excessive power over his client, who was dependent upon him for resolutions to her problems. The judge stated that he had doubts that there was no other alternative (low-cost clinic) available to Mrs. Landau that would have been able to assist her with further treatment. The judge stated that his decision to grant judgment to the defendant (Mrs. Landau) did not mean that a therapist can never "extend credit to a patient," but, when a therapist knows that the client has no means by which to pay the account, such credit is not considered fair.

Implications

a. Influence gained by kindness and affection is not likely to be regarded by the court as undue. However, when a psychotherapist utilizes the power of the therapeutic relationship for the purpose of some financial gain for the psychotherapist, the court is likely to find that undue influence was exercised.

b. When a psychotherapist treats a client who is unable to pay the full charges, he or she may have difficulty collecting the balance as the court is likely to find that a psychotherapist has an obligation to the client not to let the client expose him- or herself to a lawsuit by the therapist.

   c. Accepting gifts from clients, being involved in conflict of interest when a couple divorces, and giving advice to a minor against his or her parents' wishes are all possible situations for third-party suits.

   d. The client is not to serve you, the therapist; you are to serve the client.

   e. Undue influence may exist when a therapist spends personal, that is, nonprofessional, time with a client.

   f. Undue influence is decreased when no confidential relationship exists and when more than one professional has influenced the client.

Commentary

Has a client ever wanted to give you a gift or put you in his or her will? Have you ever dealt with a client who, during the course of treatment, separates from or divorces his or her spouse? Have you dealt with a minor's course of action that deviates from his or her parents' wishes? If you find yourself in these situations, you will need to be careful what direction or course of action you take. According to Schutz (1982), these are the types of situations that fall under the category of "undue influence." Schutz (1982) suggests that the simplest method of avoiding malpractice is to "steadfastly refuse to act in any way that directly or solely benefits" oneself (p. 46).

   In the case of a client wanting to give you a gift, it may be hard to refuse a gift after it has been bought. Thus it would be wise to announce in the beginning of treatment that you can accept only what was originally contracted for as a fee for service. If your client hints at putting you in his or her will, you would be wise to tell the client it is unacceptable for you to be placed in the will. It is also wise to include spouses in treatment when a relationship is being discussed. Studies have shown that seeing only one client can affect the relationship (Olsen, 1976). A similar situation arises when seeing minors. You would be wise to consult with the parents so that they can understand the direction of treatment. They are the legal guardians of the minor and must provide consent for treatment, so it is important that they understand what they are consenting to when they sign an agreement. However, it appears that there are no suits concerning parent-child undue influence but that spouses filed complaints when the therapist became involved personally with their client/spouse (Schutz, 1982).

According to Schutz (1982), cases of this kind may increase because therapy has gone from being mainly nondirective to being more directive in its orientation.

> This action is most likely to arise (1) when family members protest because a patient bestows a lavish gift on the therapist or leaves his estate to the therapist, (2) when a patient's spouse, following a move for a separation or divorce, accuses the therapist of alienation of affection; or (3) when a parent accuses a therapist of suggesting certain courses of action to a minor, against the parent's wishes. (p. 45)

Schutz (1982) suggests that the simplest method of avoiding malpractice is to "steadfastly refuse to act in any way that directly or solely benefits" oneself (p. 46). Schutz (1982) also points out that he knows of no cases in which a suit was based on parent-child undue influence and that spouse accusation occurred when a personal relationship ensued between the therapist and the client-spouse.

Conclusions

To avoid being charged with undue influence, psychotherapists should consider the following:

(1) Do not encourage or accept gifts from clients.
(2) Know the law of your state. Telling a client to divorce a spouse is risky because some states have laws pertaining to alienation of affection.
(3) Do not become involved in any dual relationship with a client.
(4) Influence gained by kindness and affection is not likely to be regarded by the court as undue. However, when a psychotherapist utilizes the power of the therapeutic relationship for the purpose of personal financial gain, the court is likely to find that undue influence was exercised.
(5) The inequity of payment between the client and therapist may imply, when the client doesn't pay, that the therapist has undue influence. When a psychotherapist treats a client who is unable to pay the full charges, he or she may have difficulty collecting the balance as the court is likely to find that the psychologist has an obligation to the client not to let the client expose him- or herself to a lawsuit by the therapist.

(6) Giving advice to a minor against his or her parents' wishes may cause a third-party suit.
(7) The client is not to serve you, the therapist; you are to serve the client.
(8) Undue influence may exist when a therapist spends personal, that is, nonprofessional, time with a client.
(9) Undue influence is decreased when no confidential relationship exists and when more than one professional has influenced the client.

Summary

Undue influence over a client may range from obvious situations, such as telling a client to mortgage his or her home to continue treatment (and he or she does), or asking a client to include you in his or her will (and the client does), to the not so obvious situations where you might tell a client to get out of his or her marriage (and the client does), or you accept from them a gift you considered small (when, in fact, it is a large contribution according to the client's expenses). You need to be cautious when the issue is money and the money goes beyond the fee for service. You may find that, after therapy is terminated, your client will regret the financial decision and take you to court. It is best to consult reputable colleagues regarding any financial, sexual, social, or political favors you may request of or advise your client to make that go beyond the accepted "standard of care." Whenever a psychotherapist utilizes the power of the therapeutic relationship for the purpose of personal gain, the court is likely to find that undue influence was exercised. Psychotherapists should not abuse the therapeutic relationship. Remember, you are there to serve your client.

Vignette

You have been seeing a lawyer for a year as a client in therapy. You have come to find out that he is a very honest and sincere lawyer and that he specializes in real estate cases. You have just found out that one of your real estate properties is in jeopardy and could be declining in value. You feel desperate to contact a lawyer regarding this problem and have considered contacting him to represent you. You know that this lawyer would be more than happy to help you out and that he has good knowledge of the situation. In fact, he has stated several times in treatment, "Please ask me, you have been so good to me." Would you be inclined to take this lawyer up on his offer? What could you do about this situation that would not be illegal or unethical?

Questions to Consider

(1) What are some problems in a psychotherapist borrowing money from a client?

(2) Are there any problems in a psychotherapist taking a large sum of money from a client in payment for any future psychotherapy the client might need?

(3) If a client cannot afford to pay for counseling services, what do you do?

(4) If a client in treatment has been promptly paying for his or her counseling and then, after a period of time, can't afford to pay, what is the therapist's obligation—legally, morally? Would you be willing to see a client for sessions without receiving prompt payment for your services, and, if so, how many?

(5) What constitutes excessive power over a client?

(6) If you deeply believe in the client-therapist relationship, and this becomes very meaningful to the two people involved, and your client wants to show appreciation, what sort of appreciation do you consider to be acceptable and what sort not acceptable?

16

Negligent Supervision

Counselor supervisors are more frequently becoming named as defendants in malpractice suits due to the increased number of professional and intern counselors under their command (Snider, 1985). Slovenko (1980) predicted that litigation involving supervisors is certain to be the "suit of the future." When one undertakes to supervise the work of another therapist, one also assumes a legal liability not only for one's own behavior but for the acts of the supervisee. It is very important that supervisors become familiar with each therapy case of every supervisee (Cormier & Bernard, 1982) and that any major decision the supervisee/therapist makes be reviewed and modified (if needed) by the supervisor. "In the eyes of the law supervisors are accountable for the actions of the welfare of their client" (Cormier & Bernard, 1982, p. 489). The most important legal doctrine referring to supervisors' responsibilities to the clients is that of "respondeat superior," also known as the doctrine of vicarious liability (Cohen, 1979; Cormier & Bernard, 1982). According to this doctrine, a supervisor who is in a position of authority or responsibility is responsible for the acts of her or his trainees or assistants (Cormier & Bernard, 1982).

Court Case

(1) **Cohen v. State of New York** (1976)

Case Review

Ellen Fisher Cohen, as Administratrix of the Estate of Alan David Cohen,
Deceased, Respondent, v. State of New York, Appellant
(Claim No. 57074) Supreme Court, Appellate Division,
Third Department 382 N.Y.S. 2d (April 15, 1976)

Ellen Fisher Cohen filed suit against the State of New York to recover
for the death of her former husband, 23-year-old Alan David Cohen. At
the time of this court trial, Ellen had remarried. Alan committed suicide on April 22, 1971, the same day he was released from his inpatient
voluntary stay at the Downstate Medical Center psychiatric department
for a condition diagnosed as paranoid schizophrenia. He had spent four
months living in "Ward 52, which consisted of 32 beds, with an open
door, and a program organized around the concept of a therapeutic
community" (p. 129).

In January 1971, Alan Cohen voluntarily admitted himself to the
State University of New York, Downtown Medical Center psychiatric
department, to be treated for paranoid schizophrenia. Prior to this
admission, Alan had been an outpatient at the psychiatric ward of the
Kings County Hospital. The psychiatric department at Downtown Medical Center had an open-door policy with a program emphasis on a
therapeutic community. A statement was written on Alan's admission
record that he had shown suicidal potential.

The court of claims rendered judgment for the claimant, Ellen Cohen,
on the grounds that her former husband, who had suicidal propensities,
had not been actively supervised by a qualified psychiatrist. She was
awarded $150,000., and the state appealed that the award of damages
was grossly excessive.

The defendant in this case reported "an established hierarchy to
provide medical care which in Alan's case was: Dr. Bjork (attending
doctor); then Dr. Rosenberg, a third year resident; and then Dr. Sverd,
a first year resident and treating physician" (p. 130). The court found
that Dr. Sverd, who served as Alan's treating physician, was not a

qualified psychiatrist. Therefore, the court issue was whether or not the defendant's doctors made a careful examination of Alan and then exercised reasonable medical care in determining that he should not be restricted to the ward on April 22, 1971. "The determinative factual issue [was] whether or not a qualified psychiatrist was actively supervising the care of the decedent" (p. 130). Although the court record established that the hospital's practice was for patients to be discussed at team meetings held about three times a week, it was not established that any evaluation of Alan's propensities to suicide was made by a qualified psychiatrist during his stay. There was nothing in the hospital records to support a finding that Dr. Bjork ever made a medical judgment based upon the nurse's notes or a personal interview with Alan. Furthermore, the medical record did not contain any comments by Dr. Bjork or any other qualified psychiatrist regarding suicidal propensities of the decedent. Not only did the hospital fail to have a qualified psychiatrist supervise the suicidal patient, there was also a lack of proper medical notes. The court recognized the fault herein as "not with Doctors Bjork, Rosenberg or Sverd as individuals, but rather with the lack of policies requiring more direct management of a patient's treatment by a qualified psychiatrist" (p. 130).

COURT DECISION

The supreme court, appellate division, ruled that evidence supported the finding that the decedent, who had suicidal propensities, had not been actively supervised by a qualified psychiatrist. Although Dr. Sverd had made an error of judgment in releasing Alan, the case concerned more than a mere error in judgment. There were "many errors of judgment made by a doctor not qualified in an unsupervised status to make a judgment; made by those in [a] supervisory capacity; and, all made without careful examination" (p. 129). As reported in the court summary report, "The rule of law is well established that a doctor is not liable for a mere error of judgment provided [she]he does what [she]he thinks is best after a careful examination" (p. 129). The presiding judge also reported that the decedent had not been treated or supervised "with ordinary and reasonable care and diligence, or with that medical judgment and skill required by the acceptable standards of the community" (p. 129). However, it was determined that the decision made by the court of claims to award claimant Ellen Cohen $150,000. for damages was grossly excessive. The amount of the reward was reduced to $35,000., with appropriate interest and costs. At the time of his death, Alan was a third-year medical student at the Downstate Medical University of the State of New York. However, "The court found that the claimant had not sustained her burden of proof that the decedent would have been accepted back into medical school and successfully pursued his career as a doctor" (p. 130). The presiding judge for the supreme court, appellate division, reported that Alan's "condition would have always been somewhat fragile and that his work would have to be in fields not subject to the pressures of executive or professional life" (p. 131).

Implications

a. Supervisors are legally liable for all professional actions of their supervisees.

b. Supervisors need to provide active, direct, ongoing supervision with all supervisees.

c. Supervisors need to meet directly with their supervisees' clients for examination purposes and for conducting any form of psychological assessment and/or evaluation. It is very important that mental health agencies/hospitals have a written policy requiring more direct management of a patient's treatment by an appropriately credentialed therapist (e.g., licensed psychiatrist, licensed psychologist). Before permitting a supervisee to use any major interventions and/or initiate any major actions with a client, the client needs to be examined *personally* by the qualified supervisor.

d. Supervisors are strongly encouraged to keep updated supervisory case notes. A file folder that includes summaries of all supervisory sessions and is kept in the employing agency's confidential file is helpful. *All* supervisory communications with supervisees regarding clients should be documented as well as all details concerning a client's medical and psychological treatment.

Commentary

Suits against supervisors are on the rise even though they currently account for only 9% of total malpractice claims filled against psychologists (Pope, 1989). One reason for such an increase is that supervisors do not realize that their supervisee's clients are seen by the law as primarily their (the supervisors') responsibility. Are you supervising more clients than you could possibly maintain with a full understanding of all their cases? Do you supervise in a manner that assures you the maximum ability to know how your supervisees are proceeding with treatment? Have you screened your supervisees to know what level of competency they have attained or whether they understand legal and ethical issues? Are you checking that your supervisees' records are up to date and hold an accurate account of treatment procedures? If you are answering the above questions in the negative, then you may find yourself in a weak position if any of your supervisees' cases become court cases. You need to be adhering to what professional organizations and other professionals are advising about the process of supervision.

> The most important legal doctrine that applies to supervisor's responsi-
> bilities to client is that of respondeat superior, also referred to as the
> doctrine of vicarious liability (Cohen, 1979). According to Cormier
> (1979) someone in a position of authority or responsibility, such as a
> supervisor, is responsible for acts of his or her trainees or assistants. Stated
> another way, supervisors are ultimately legally responsible for the welfare
> of clients counseled by their supervisees. (p. 488)

APA's ethical standards suggest that supervisors provide clients informed choice about supervision and supervisees' clients' confidentiality and provide supervisees' protection from physical or mental harm, as well as their clients, and due process. Due process, according to Cormier and Bernard (1982), refers to supervisors working with their supervisees in a manner that the following occurs: They explain objectives/goals of supervision to supervisees, train them in standard assessment and evaluation procedures, and explain to their supervisees what their (the supervisors') expectation and goals are for supervision and in what manner they will evaluate their (the supervisees') performance. The supervisor is expected to explain these procedures to the supervisee in the beginning of their relationship as well as explaining due process and protection from physical and mental harm. In addition, Cormier and Bernard (1982, p. 486) advise that supervisors are to be careful about "imposing their theoretical bias on supervisees, to refrain from promoting supervisee dependence, and to allow counselors the right to make their own mistakes. It is important, however, that while supervisors protect counselor autonomy, they take steps to ensure client well-being."

According to Schutz (1982), "One of the major difficulties in psychotherapy supervision is monitoring and maintaining the distinction between errors in treatment and truly destructive behavior (p. 48). To avoid such an error, and thus avoid malpractice, we have put together a list of suggestions; we have also incorporated ideas from Woody (1988) and Schutz (1982), as follows:

(1) A standard assessment needs to be made regarding the supervisee as to what clientele he or she can treat.

(2) Do not take on an overload of supervisees or cases.

(3) Document the supervision.

(4) Be familiar with every case.

(5) Avoid dual relationships, such as supervising colleagues or someone with whom you have a personal relationship.

(6) Use live or video supervision.

(7) Give written and verbal evaluation to the supervisee.

(8) Have the supervisee evaluate your performance in writing, using a standard instrument.

(9) Make sure records are accurate and up to date and sign off supervisees' records.

(10) Be able to use a variety of supervision models.

(11) Get further training in supervision. The American Association for Marriage and Family Therapy has a supervision certificate.

(12) Do not sign insurance forms for clients you have not supervised.

(13) Keep regular supervision hours, weekly. Do not supervise during lunchtime.

(14) Make sure you are covered by your or the agency's malpractice insurance.

Conclusions

Supervisors are responsible for client well-being. Supervisors are also responsible for the acts of their supervisees. With this in mind, we advise the following:

(1) Assess what types of cases your supervisees can treat.

(2) Review *all* cases assigned to supervisees.

(3) Make sure clients know the status of the supervisee (i.e., intern, assistant, and so on).

(4) Document all supervision in written records.

(5) Use live as well as taped supervision for which you must obtain client consent.

(6) Make sure supervisees keep records in an appropriate manner.

(7) Use written evaluations for supervisees.

(8) Keep a regular (weekly) time to supervise an intern/supervisee. As a supervisor, you need to provide active, ongoing supervision with all supervisees.

(9) Know the legal rules regarding supervision. There are different licensure requirements for different professions (e.g., psychologist, social worker, and marriage, family, and child counselor).

(10) As a supervisor, you are legally liable for all professional actions of your supervisees.

(11) As a supervisor, you need to meet directly with your supervisees' clients for examination purposes and for conducting any form of psychological assessment and/or evaluation. It is very important that mental health agencies/hospitals have a written policy requiring the direct management of a patient's treatment by an appropriately credentialed therapist (e.g., licensed psychiatrist or licensed psychologist). Before permitting a supervisee to use any major interventions and/or initiate any major actions with a client, the client needs to be examined personally by the qualified supervisor.

(12) As a supervisor, you are strongly encouraged to keep updated supervisory case notes. A file folder that includes summaries of all supervisory sessions, kept in the employing agencies's confidential files, is helpful. All supervisory communications with supervisees regarding clients should be documented as well as all important details concerning a client's medical and psychological treatment.

(13) When you sign insurance forms for clients treated by a supervisee, make sure this information is furnished to the insurance company.

Summary

If you are in a supervisory role, it has never been more apparent that this role has the same amount of legal implications as does your own practice. The supervisor is ultimately responsible for the client's welfare. That is, a competent supervisor will treat all of his or her supervisee's cases as if they were his or her own. This may require all of us in a supervisory role to observe firsthand every case a supervisee is treating (video or live), review with supervisee all records and sign them, and not take for granted that the supervisee is qualified to handle all of the cases referred to him or her. Furthermore, evidence of super vision needs to be documented. Perhaps those of us in a supervisory role will think twice about supervising if we cannot follow every case treated by the supervisee.

Vignette

You are currently supervising 10 students who are each seeing five clients weekly. One of your supervisees would like to take you to dinner and discuss one of his cases. This student tells you that he is becoming attracted to one of his clients and that he would like to terminate treatment and refer her so that he could date her. He mentions that he does not want to take up regular supervision time talking about his case because he has too many other issues pertaining to his other cases to discuss. What are the ethical and legal considerations found within this vignette?

Questions to Consider

(1) What do you believe constitutes "adequate counselor supervision"?

(2) What type and amount of training do you believe is needed to qualify a psychotherapist to serve as a supervisor?

(3) How often should a supervisor meet with his or her supervisees and how long should each supervisory session last?

(4) When might you, as a supervisor, determine a need to meet personally with your supervisee's client?

(5) Is it possible for a supervisor with a different theoretical orientation from that of supervisee to provide adequate supervision?

(6) How would you describe your supervisory relationship with your supervisees? What would you discuss as your responsibilities as a supervisor and his or her responsibilities as a supervisee?

(7) What would you do, as a supervisor, if you heard that one of your supervisees was dating one of his or her clients?

(8) As a supervisor, how do you ensure that interns/supervisees will maintain confidentiality?

(9) If a psychological assistant, intern, or other supervisee violates a client's privacy, can the supervisor be held liable if he or she was not involved in or aware of the breach?

PART III

17

Ethical Issues

This chapter deals with the topic of professional ethics and definitions of related terms. Our main purpose is to provide you with a general understanding of the concept of professional ethics within the mental health professions. Psychotherapists, like any professionals, are confronted with ethical problems in the course of their work. We discuss the importance of the adoption of professional codes and standards for guiding one's professional practice. It is important to recognize, however, that ethical codes do not address many complex and multifaceted issues. Many existing "gray areas" are often subject to debate by different professionals at different times in history regarding the interpretation of various guidelines within ethical codes. Furthermore, "most ethical codes are discipline or organization specific, and as such, do not apply to everyone outside the discipline or organization but still within the profession" (Tymchuk, 1981, p. 23; see Dalglish, 1976). However, the *Ethical Principles of Psychologists* (APA, 1989) has a footnote stating: "These revised *Ethical Principles* . . . are also intended for the guidance of *nonmembers* of the Association who are engaged in psychological research or practice of the Association who are engaged in psychological research or practice." (emphasis added).

In this chapter, we will concentrate on different official codes of ethical conduct adopted by some of the major professional mental health organizations. We have chosen to examine the following six professional organizations' codes of ethics as representative of a variety of mental health disciplines: (a) the American Psychological Association (APA; 1989), (b) the American Psychiatric Association (AmPsyA; American Medical Association, *Principles of Medical Ethics*, 1989), (c) the American Association for Counseling and Development (AACD; 1988), (d) the American Association for Marriage and Family Therapy (AAMFT; 1988a), (e) the National Association of Social Workers (NASW; 1984), and (f) the Association for Specialists in Group Work (ASGW; 1989). The codes of ethics of these six organizations are included in Appendix D. Four of these organizations (APA, AACD, AAMFT, and NASW) are considered "parent" organizations, while the American Psychiatric Association (referred to as "AmPsyA" here to avoid confusion with "APA") is a division of the American Medical Association (AMA), and ASGW is one of the 15 divisions of AACD. We felt that it was worthwhile to include ASGW's code because group work is a specialty within various mental health disciplines. There is a professional "parent" organization called the American Group Psychotherapy Association (AGPA), however, at the time of this writing, AGPA had not adopted an official code of ethics. Although APA has several codes that can be termed *ethical codes*, including *Ethical Principles in the Conduct of Research with Human Participants* (1982) and *General Guidelines for Providers of Psychological Services* (1987b), we will focus only on the *Ethical Principles of Psychologists* (1989).

In this chapter, we also discuss the inherent limitations of ethical codes, the development of ethical codes, and different categories of unethical complaints filed against psychotherapists as well as identifying some specific types of unethical behavior. The topics of ethical decision making, and ethics committee rules and procedures for disciplinary action of professional organization members who violate ethical codes, are also addressed in this chapter. Finally, there is a major focus on the similarities and differences between the six codes of ethics chosen for examination.

Definitions: Ethics, Values, Morality, Professionalism, and Law

The terms *ethics, values, morality, professionalism,* and *law* are closely related yet different in meaning. Several academic curricula geared to train professional counselors and psychotherapists have courses titled with any of these terms, singly or in various combinations. Before engaging in a discussion on ethical decision making, and to avoid any confusion on the part of the reader, we thought it would be beneficial to define each of these five terms.

The terms *ethics* and *value* are often used interchangeably, although the two are not identical (Loewenberg & Dolgoff, 1988). Differences exist between the terms in that *ethics* focuses on what is considered "right" and "correct," while the term *values* concerns what is "good" and "desirable." Furthermore, "ethics are deduced from values and must be in consonance with them" (Loewenberg & Dolgoff, 1988, p. 17). We concur with Corey, Corey, and Callanan's (1988, p. 67) position that "it's crucial for counselors [and psychotherapists] to be clear about their own values" and understand how values permeate the psychotherapeutic process. As noted by Van Hoose and Kottler (1985, p. 3), "Ethics, values, and morality are an intrinsic part of therapy practice." Based on the premise that "your values will significantly affect your work with clients, it is incumbent on you to clarify your values and the ways they enter the therapeutic process" (Corey, Corey, & Callanan, 1988, p. 68). Tymchuk (1981) discusses how values derive from three major areas including religion, economics, and philosophies of thought. It is our intent not to discuss in detail how these various disciplines influence one's values but to communicate how values may affect one's ethical decision making.

Stadler (1986, p. 6) discusses how "ethical behavior and professional codes of ethics are grounded in the study of moral philosophy." The terms *ethics* and *morality* overlap and are often used synonymously. However, there are some subtle differences in meaning. Although both terms refer to what may be considered "good and bad behavior or the study of human conduct and values" (Van Hoose & Kottler, 1985, p. 2), variations of meaning have been identified. Mowrer (1967, cited in Van Hoose & Kottler, 1985) explains that *morality* may imply force or coercion, while *ethics* signifies reason and objectivity.

"Ethics is generally defined as a philosophical discipline concerned with human conduct and moral decision making" (Van Hoose & Kottler, 1985, p. 3, emphasis added). The term connotes *normative standards of conduct or actions* and "generally involves behavior of individuals that positively or negatively affects other human beings and, in some instances, animals" (Carroll, Schneider, & Wesley, 1985, p. 5). *Ethics* focuses on questions that have no absolute answers. The cultural context must also be considered whenever determining what constitutes ethical behavior (Williams, 1989). For example, ethical behavior in one culture is not necessarily considered to be ethical behavior in another culture. Furthermore, professional organizations provide "guidelines," "standards," or "principles" for ethical behavior.

Morality, on the other hand, involves an *evaluation* or *judgment* of action, including both the ends themselves as well as the means to achieve the ends. Issues of morality arise when one person's welfare may be affected by another person based upon a choice or decision that is made. "Morality . . . seems to be a social institution with a code of learnable rules" (Beauchamp, 1982, p. 6). "Morality is usually contrasted with prudence or self-interest, *because* morality does require taking into account the interests of others" (Beauchamp, 1982, p. 7). Therefore, the same type of conduct may be called either "moral" or "immoral" on the basis of the community standard. Conduct regarded in one community as being socially important defines "moral" while the same type of conduct in another community is not called either "moral" or "immoral," because neither its behavior nor its neglect is regarded as socially important.

Professionalism relates to a code of etiquette and may be differentiated from a code of ethics (Carroll, Schneider, & Wesley, 1985). "If a professional does not abide by the code of professional etiquette in his or her field, we say that person is acting unprofessionally" (Carroll, Schneider, & Wesley, 1985, p. 1). Although a psychotherapist who acts unethically is also considered to have acted unprofessionally, one who acts unprofessionally is not necessarily considered to have acted unethically. There are some subtle differences between what constitutes ethical behavior and professionalism. First, of all, "while all professions have normative codes or standards, not all professional standards are ethical standards" (Carroll, Schneider, & Wesley, 1985, p. 2). Second, not all professional mental health organizations have adopted a professional code of ethics, and one must have been violated before a professional may be considered to have acted unethically; otherwise, we could only consider an individual's conduct to have been unprofessional. At the time of this writing, only 6 of the 16 divisions of AACD had adopted their own ethical codes or standards. These 6 divisions include the American College Personnel Association (ACPA), the American Mental Health Counselors Association (AMHCA), the American School Counselor Association (ASCA), the American Rehabilitation Counseling Association (ARCA), the Association for Specialists in Group Work (ASGW), and the National Career Development Association (NCDA).

A person may only be considered to have behaved unethically, if the behavior is defined as such in his or her respective professional organization's code of ethics. For example, among the six codes examined herein, only APA (1981) specifies the importance of responding to inquiries: "Members also respond promptly and completely to inquiries from duly constituted state association ethics committees and professional standards review committees" (Preamble). Therefore, psychologists who do not respond promptly in these situations would be considered both unprofessional and unethical. However, in the same type of situation, a counselor for individuals (AACD, 1988a) or groups (ASGW, 1989), a social worker (NASW, 1984), a marriage and family therapist (AAMFT, 1988), or a psychiatrist (AmPsyA, 1989) would be considered only unprofessional, but *not* unethical, because their respective professional organizations codes do not specify such expected behavior. Some confusion exists regarding the complexity of differentiating unprofessional and unethical behavior. For example, AACD has a document titled *Policies and Procedures for Processing Complaints of Ethical Violations* (1988b, hereinafter referred to as *AACD Policies and Procedures*) that clearly outlines specific steps and the time frame to be followed by the chairperson of the AACD Ethics Committee while processing ethical complaints. One of the steps includes the chairperson directing "a letter to the accused member informing the member of the accusations lodged against him/her, asking for a response and requesting that relevant information be submitted to the Chairperson within thirty (30) days" ("Processing Complaints," 2. [d]). Because this statement is not included in AACD's code of ethics and is only contained in the *AACD Policies and Procedures* (1988b), a document that was adopted "to facilitate the work of the AACD Ethics Committee" and not to serve to educate the AACD membership (as is a purpose of AACD's ethics code), an AACD member who did not respond promptly (as in the situation described above) or within 30 days would only be considered to have behaved unprofessionally but *not* unethically. Recently, Barbara Herlihy (past chair of the AACD Ethics Committee) and Larry Golden published the *AACD Ethical Standards Casebook* (1989), which includes several vignettes applicable to the *AACD Ethical Standards* (1988a) as well as a variety of essays dealing with select ethical topics.

Another example to help clarify how a psychotherapist may be considered to be unprofessional, without being unethical, would be someone who wears dirty clothes and appears unkempt while conducting a counseling session. Other examples include a psychotherapist who frequently cancels and reschedules client appointments or one who is frequently late for scheduled counseling sessions. Mental health professionalism, as a form of etiquette, involves psychotherapists adhering to certain socially accepted norms and behaviors that clients expect of them. Such client and societal expectations are not necessarily included in professional organizations' codes of ethics.

There is a close relationship between *ethics and law*, yet distinct differences exist. "In general, the *law* provides specific statements about appropriate or inappropriate actions and is designed to apply to the population as a whole" (Bray, Shepherd, & Hays, 1985, p. 51, emphasis added). The law specifies *minimum* standards of acceptable behavior, while ethical standards are also designed to regulate conduct; however, they represent the ideal rather than the minimum and are relevant only within a profession (Bray, Shepherd, & Hays, 1985; Van Hoose & Kottler, 1985). One may conceptualize professional ethics by differentiating the terms *mandatory ethics* and *aspirational ethics*. *Mandatory ethics* describes a minimum level of ethical functioning, characterized by following the ethical codes of one's profession and by compliance with the law. In contrast is *aspirational ethics*, which entails a higher level of ethical functioning, whereby practitioners do more than comply with the codes and the law. These individuals function at a higher level of moral reasoning by continuously assessing the effects of their interventions on the welfare of their clients. Mappes, Robb, and Engels (1985) discuss how the ethical standards of the mental health professions seem to conflict with the law in such areas as advertising, confidentiality, and clients' rights of access to their own files.

"As with codes of ethics, how the law is applied is open to interpretation" (Tymchuk, 1981, p. 510). "In the absence of any clear statutory authority or case law precedent to guide a court of law in judging a case involving the conduct of a counselor [or psychotherapist], courts

generally apply the standard of care given similarly suited professionals, in this case other counselors [or psychotherapists]" (Hopkins &
Anderson, 1985, p. 3). Courts may refer to a psychotherapist's professional organization's code of ethics to determine liability.

Reasons for Adopting a Professional Code of Ethics

We have heard puzzled colleagues comment: "Why do we need a
professional code of ethics? Anyone entering the mental health profession already has a genuine interest in helping others and has common
sense regarding appropriate ethical behavior." Also, "Why waste time
developing a professional code of ethics. Not many members will even
spend the time to read the code, yet alone understand it."

We firmly believe there are several reasons that make it necessary
for professional mental health organizations to adopt a code of ethics.
First, if we are to call our counseling and psychotherapy a "profession,"
we need to conform to the characteristics of a profession, one of which
is the adoption of a code of ethical standards by the members of the
profession. The existence of a professional code of ethics communicates that a profession is no longer "emerging" but has achieved "maturity." In other words, professional codes of ethics serve to increase
the prestige of the profession (Mappes, Robb, & Engels, 1985). Second,
they provide standards of practice to aid psychotherapists in deciding
what to do when conflicts arise. Simply stated, ethical codes provide
some guidelines for "right" or "wrong" behavior of members of the organization. In addition, they help in controlling internal disagreements
and bickering among professionals within the organization and accel-
erate the process of consensual behavior (Mappes, Robb, & Engels,
1985). Third, they clarify the psychotherapist's responsibility to clients,
to the profession, and to society. They provide clients and prospective clients some protection from incompetence and charlatanism in
the knowledge that a psychotherapist belongs to a professional organization that has a code of ethics (Swanson, 1983). Also, they provide the
mental health professions some measure of assurance that the behavior
of individual psychotherapists will not be detrimental to the profession.
In addition, codes of ethics help to protect psychotherapists from the
public, especially in regard to malpractice suits (Talbutt, 1981). Fourth,
a psychotherapist's professional freedom and integrity are safeguarded

with ethical standards. They enable the profession to regulate itself
and function autonomously, without being solely controlled by the
government or by governmental regulations (Van Hoose & Kottler,
1985). Fifth, they "provide supervisors, consultants, and other professionals with a basis for appraising and evaluating practitioner activities" (Loewenberg & Dolgoff, 1988, p. 23). Sixth, ethical guidelines
may assist counselor educators in designing and implementing counselor training courses (Williams, 1990).

Limitations of Ethical Codes

Although codes of ethics are helpful—indeed essential—they are not
free from ambiguity. In other words, as noted by Mabe and Rollin
(1986), "a professional code is necessary but not sufficient for the
exercise of professional responsibility. An awareness of a code's limitations is a key element in developing an adequate account of professional responsibility" (p. 294). Although some of the issues that arise
in the mental health professions are concrete, others are philosophical.
Consequently, no universally "right" answer exists for many of them.
Several writers have recognized the limitations of professional codes
(Corey, Corey, and Callanan, 1988; Mabe & Rollin, 1986; Mappes,
Robb, & Engels, 1985; Talbutt, 1981; Tymchuk, 1981).

- Some issues cannot be resolved by sole reliance on ethical codes.
- Difficulties exist in enforcing ethical codes.
- Ethical codes are temporarily and culturally determined by their environ-
  mental context and frequently require revision.
- Ethical guidelines tend to be reactive rather than proactive (i.e., they are
  usually established after difficult dilemmas have occurred rather than
  helping practitioners decide what to do before the previously inconceiv-
  able situation).
- Sometimes conflicts exist within ethical codes as well as between different
  organizations' codes of ethics.
- Sometimes codes of ethics conflict with the law.
- Ethical codes may conflict with institutional policies.
- An ethical code may conflict with the values of the members of the
  professional organization to which the code applies.
- Because codes of ethics are usually formally established by an ethics
  committee representing a professional organization, not all members of the
  organization will necessarily agree with all of the guidelines of their
  organization's code of ethics.

Thus there are several inherent limitations of professional codes of ethics, and answers will not always be provided for the practitioner seeking a quick solution in a complex situation. Initially, ethical codes were developed to protect the profession from outside regulation. It is important to realize that they are developed to serve merely as guidelines, rather than as blueprints, to assist practitioners when difficult dilemmas arise. As Tennyson and Strom (1986) note, ethical standards cannot tell therapists what to do or why they should behave in a certain way. Furthermore, because of the sometimes existing conflicts between different organizations' codes of ethics, practitioners who belong to several professional organizations may become confused. Despite knowing that professional organizations' codes of ethics do not often offer specific direction about what to do with a given ethical dilemma, and have several other shortcomings, it is important for psychotherapists to first consult with the codes for some helpful guidelines in resolving their difficult dilemmas.

Ethical Decision Making

You may pose the question: "Why be ethical?" Or, "why should I be so concerned about ethics?" "After all, the worst that can happen to me if I'm found to have acted unethically is that I'll get expelled from the association and could possibly lose my certification and licensure." Thus there appears to be a very small deterrent for behaving unethically and, for some, very little punishment at all. As noted by Stadler (1986b, p. 1). "Professional organizations can only take action against *members*. Withdrawal of membership and notification of certifying or licensing boards is the harshest sanction an association can impose upon a member. An association has no other kind of leverage."

We agree with Corey and Corey (1989), who profess that psychotherapists need to be honest with themselves while examining their motives for choosing a career in the helping professions. In addition, we believe that one cannot separate being an "ethical professional" from being an "ethical person." A person's professional conduct is a reflection of his or her individual standards of morality and dignity. Those therapists who focus upon the potential punishment for not behaving ethically, rather than examining how they may aspire to a higher level of ethical functioning (i.e., aspirational ethics), are functioning at a lower level of moral development. Furthermore, we believe that such individuals contribute to making psychotherapy potentially more harmful. Unethical behavior creates potential adverse effects not only on clients but on other professional practitioners, on counselor trainees, on the mental health profession, on society, and on the unethical professionals themselves. We believe that ethical codes are developed to serve as a minimum standard of expected professional behavior.

Kitchener's (1984) critical-evaluative model provides counselors a framework for logical thinking when they are not pressed to respond immediately and suggests there are different levels of moral reasoning, hierarchically arranged, that affect our ethical decisions. Four fundamental moral principles, borrowed from the discipline of philosophy, have been identified for use by counselors to find direction in ethical decision making. These include (a) *autonomy*, (b) *beneficence*, (c) *nonmaleficence*, and (d) *justice* and *fairness*.

Autonomy means to promote self-determination. Specifically related to counseling, it means that the client has the freedom to choose his or her own course of action. This principle entails the counselor reporting the client's right to informed consent and privacy.

Beneficence means to promote good for others and to prevent harm. In the context of counseling, this principle has significance for the flourishing of the profession. The belief that counseling contributes to the growth and general welfare of clients encourages people to seek such services. Society supports the continuation of the profession based upon the notion that counseling "does good" for humanity. Dishonest and incompetent counselors who cause harm to their clients undermine the profession and may cause the public to become disillusioned and lose its faith in the profession.

Nonmaleficence means not doing harm. This principle includes the counselor's both avoiding inflicting harm on clients and refraining from actions that risk harming them. Examples of actions that may be harmful to clients include reliance on traditional diagnostic labels, misuse of assessment, and the use of aversive techniques (Kitchener, 1984).

Justice and *fairness* mean that all people are to be treated equally. Applying these concepts to counseling suggests that all people, regardless of age, sex, disability, race, socioeconomic status, religion, and so on, should have equal access to professional mental health services. In addition, professional helpers are to promote the worth and dignity of each individual by having a concern that equal treatment be provided for all individuals.

Carroll, Schneider, and Wesley (1985) discuss three ethical theories that commonly enter into discussions of mental health professionals encountering moral problems. These theories include (a) *ethical relativism* in which the determination of right and wrong actions is based upon what is approved of by the client or by society; (b) *utilitarianism*, the view that counselors ought to do that act that promotes the greatest happiness for the largest number of people; and (c) a theory developed with *Kant's moral philosophy* as a foundation, the perspective that psychotherapists' moral decisions should be universalizable, that psychotherapists always value the worth of the client by treating the client with respect and dignity, and that they honor the preservation and protection of fundamental human rights (e.g., the autonomy of individuals). As noted by the authors, all three of these theories are reflected in the *Ethical Principles* (APA, 1982, 1989) as well as other mental health professional organizations' codes of ethics.

Several writers have developed different models for ethical decision making. We recommend that you refer to these different models to determine which one best fits you (Kitchener, 1984; Paradise & Siegelwaks, 1982; Stadler, 1986a; Tymchuk, 1981). As research has indicated, although certain theoretical approaches to counseling and psychotherapy have been found to be most effective in treating specific types of problems (e.g., cognitive-behavioral approaches in treating depression, systematic desensitization in treating phobias), no single theory has been found to be most effective in treating all types of client problems (Garfield & Bergin, 1978). Therefore, similarly, we believe that you as mental health practitioners need to select a model of ethical decision making that seems to work best for you. Included here is just one of many possible models specifying "a process of ethical decision making" for your consideration. We have modified and expanded a model developed by Paradise and Siegelwaks (1982) by including some of our own additional guidelines and questions for you to consider while following the steps in the decision-making process.

(1) *Identify the problem or dilemma.*

- What is the source of conflict for the client?
- Is the conflict with another person, client, group of people or family member?
- Is the conflict between the client and the therapist?
- Does the conflict involve legal, moral, ethical, religious, cultural, gender, or value issues?

(2) *Consider all (ethical code) guidelines or principles that exist relevant to the resolution of the dilemma.*

- Refer to *Williams' Index of Ethical Code Terminology* (Williams, in process). This includes a referencing categorization system for indexing 79 descriptor words that pertain to the content of six professional organizations' codes of ethics (AACD, 1988a; AAMFT, 1988; American Psychiatric Association, 1989; APA, 1989; ASGW, 1989; NASW, 1984).
- Do guidelines, principles, or laws exist that are relevant to the dilemmas and may provide a possible solution?
- Are the therapist's values, ethics, or morals in conflict with the relevant principles or guidelines?
- Is the therapist aware of the effect of values and does he or she have a rationale for the behavior?
- Consult with professional colleagues, if available.

(3) *Generate possible and probable courses of action.*

- What are the possible and probable alternatives? (Brainstorming without evaluating is helpful at this stage.)

(4) *Consider the probable consequences of each course of action.*

- What are the implications for the client?
- What are the implications for others?
- What are the implications for you, the therapist?

(5) *Select the best source of action.*

- What course of action is in the best interest of appropriate professional conduct?
- Holly A. Stadler, past chairperson of the AACD Ethics Committee, offers some very helpful thoughts to consider before taking a course of action. Put it to the tests of "universality," "publicity," and "justice." As stated by Stadler (1986b), "The test of universality hinges on whether the chosen course of action could be recommended to others in similar circumstances" (p. 9). "Would I condone my behavior in anyone else?" (Stadler, 1986a, p. 4). Passing the test of publicity means, "Would I tell other counselors [therapists] what I intend to do? Would I be willing to have my actions and rationale for them described on the front page of the local newspaper" (Stadler, 1986b, p. 9) or "reported on the evening news?" (Stadler, 1986a, p. 4). Stadler (1986a, p. 4) states, "If your answers are

'no,' there is a good chance the behavior you are contemplating may be unethical." "Finally, the test of justice judges the fairness of actions. Would I treat another client or family in the same situation differently?" (Stadler, 1986b, p. 9). For example, if this were a well-known political leader of the community, would I treat the person differently? Answers of "no" to these questions pass the test of justice.

Development of Ethical Codes

While researching the existence of professional state association ethics committees, one of the authors was startled by a comment heard from one of the state "leaders." It was stated that "there is no need to have an ethics committee in our state since our membership is small enough for us to discuss any ethical problems that occur." We strongly disagree with this individual's comment. We see a tremendous value in state, as well as national, association ethics committees to develop ethical codes that are representative of the professional membership. In this section, we discuss early history in the development of some national codes of ethics for mental health professionals.

Golann (1970) discusses the development of ethical standards among American psychologists since the 1930s. In 1939, a special APA committee on ethical matters recommended the establishment of a standing committee, which was established the following year. During the 1940s, there was much interest in and discussion on developing an ethical code. In 1948, the membership of APA were solicited by survey to share descriptions of ethical problems they had encountered in practice and to share an explanation of what other members perceived to be the ethical implications of the examples. The collection of over 1,000 cases was then classified into five different areas of professional work: (a) public responsibility, (b) client relationships, (c) teaching, (d) research, and (e) professional relationships. APA adopted its first code of ethics in 1953. The code was first revised in 1959 and an entirely new code (shifting from a medical to a psychological focus) was adopted in 1981, following the controversy over Stanley Milgram's studies (1963) on obedience to authority figures, in which research subjects were instructed and led to believe that they were inflicting increasing voltages of electric shock and pain to other people. The 1981 code changed the former title of *Ethical Standards of Psychologists* (1959) to *Ethical Principles of Psychologists* and included an entirely new section, titled

"Principle 10: Care and Use of Animals." In addition, as specified in a footnote of the code, "the revised *Ethical Principles* contain both substantive and grammatical changes in each of the nine ethical principles constituting the *Ethical Standards of Psychologists* [revision] previously adopted by the Council of Representatives in 1979" (APA, 1981, footnote). The current 1989 revision of the code retained the same title as the 1981 version. For examples of different vignettes on how to apply APA's code of ethics, you may refer to a book titled *Casebook on Ethical Principles of Psychologists* (APA, 1987a).

AACD (formerly named, and at the time, the American Personnel and Guidance Association) established its first standards based upon the original APA code of ethics (Allen, 1986). The first AACD Code of Ethics was adopted in 1961 and three subsequent revisions were made in 1974, in 1981, and in the current 1988 *Ethical Standards*. To date, as mentioned earlier in this chapter, 6 of the 16 divisions of AACD have adopted their own codes of ethics. Several of the other divisions are in the process of developing their initial codes. Similar to APA, which publishes a casebook relating to its ethical code, AACD published a book citing a variety of ethical dilemma vignettes applicable to the AACD *Ethical Standards* (1988a) that is titled *Ethical Standards Casebook* (1989).

AAMFT (founded in 1942 and formerly known as AAMC—the American Association of Marriage Counselors) adopted its first code of ethics in 1962, titled *American Association of Marriage and Family Counselors: Code of Ethics*. A first revision of the code was adopted in 1975 and titled *Code of Professional Ethics*. In 1967, AAMC became the American Association of Marriage and Family Counselors (AAMFC) and, in the late 1970s, the current name, American Association for Marriage and Family Therapy (AAMFT), was adopted. A second revision of the code was made in January 1979 and titled *AAMFT: Code of Professional Ethics and Standards for Public Information and Advertising*. In July 1982, a third revision was made and titled *AAMFT: Code of Ethical Principles for Family Therapists*. Five months later, in December 1982, a fourth revision was made and titled *AAMFT: Ethical Principles for Family Therapists*. In September 1985, a fifth revision was made and titled *AAMFT: Code of Ethical Principles for Marriage and Family Therapists*. The sixth and most recent revision of the ethics code was adopted in August 1988, retaining the same title as the 1985 version (Barbara W. Stone, AAMFT professional standards coordinator, personal communication, August 10, 1989). The organization has been revising its code about every three years, with the next revision expected in August 1992. For those of you who are interested in the history of AAMFT, you may refer to a book titled *Handbook of Marriage Counseling* (1976), edited by Ben N. Ard. Especially worth reading is Chapter 40, titled "The AAMFT and the AAMC: Nearly 40 Years of Form and Function."

NASW published its first *Code of Ethics* in October 1960. A first revision was adopted in April 1967 and the current, second revision of the NASW *Code of Ethics* was approved in July 1980.

In 1973, the American Psychiatric Association (AmPsyA), a division of the American Medical Association (AMA), added to the already existing *The Principles of Medical Ethics* and titled the document, *The Principles of Medical Ethics, with Annotations Especially Applicable to Psychiatry*. These "annotations especially applicable to psychiatry" do not in any way change the already existing seven sections of the AMA code but include additions to each of the seven sections. Revisions are made almost annually and the code is under constant review and revision (Robert Moore, consultant to the American Psychiatric Association Ethics Committee, personal communication, July 31, 1989).

The Association for Specialists in Group Work (ASGW) was established as the 11th division of the currently named American Association for Counseling and Development (AACD; formerly called the American Personnel and Guidance Association—APGA) in December 1973. Within a few years, ASGW adopted its initial code of professional ethics. A first revision of the original *Ethical Guidelines for Group Leaders* was made in 1980, and Corey, Corey, and Callanan (1982) wrote an instructor's resource manual, titled *A Casebook of Ethical Guidelines for Group Leaders*, while referring to the 1980 *Ethical Guidelines for Group Leaders*. A second revision was made in 1989, changing the ethics code title to the current *Ethical Guidelines for Group Counselors* (1989) and including major substantive content, format, and grammatical changes from the earlier version. ASGW dedicated the September 1982 and May 1990 issues of the *Journal for Specialists in Group Work* to ethical issues in group work.

Similarities and Differences Among the Codes

Ethical standards in helping professions usually govern conduct in three areas: (a) interactions with the recipients of our services (e.g., clients, students, employees, supervisees), (b) interactions with peers and other professionals, and (c) interactions with the public. At the core of any code appears to be the practitioner-client interaction. An extensive review of the professional literature reveals a lack of any in-depth discussion comparing various codes of ethics in terms of similarities and differences. We've discovered that only Corey, Corey, and Callanan (1988) have published different categories for comparing ethical codes. They have compared some of the earlier versions of the ethical codes of AAMFT (1985), APA (1982), American Psychiatric Association (1986), NASW (1979), AACD (1981), and the American Psychoanalytic Association (1981) on the four dimensions of (a) competence, (b) the rights of clients and informed consent, (c) confidentiality, and (d) sexual relations in therapy.

In this section we'll remain focused on the six codes mentioned earlier (i.e., APA, AmPsyA, AACD, AAMFT, NASW, and ASGW). We'll use two broad categories to examine these codes: (a) the structural format and (b) the content.

Several differences exist regarding the structural formats of the six respective ethical codes. The choice of words in the titles vary in that three of the codes (APA, AmPsyA, AAMFT) use *principles*, one uses *standards* (AACD), another uses *guidelines* (ASGW), and still another does not use *principles*, *standards*, or *guidelines* but states succinctly *Code of Ethics, National Association of Social Workers*. Also, the choice of words used for subheadings varies among the codes. *Section* is used as the sole word, excluding the respective number, by the AmPsyA and is the stem word for the subheadings of the AACD code. The word *principle* is used by APA, a few different key word descriptors are used by AAMFT and ASGW, and phrases of words are used by NASW. AACD is the only code that uses letters (i.e., A-H) for chronologically ordering the subsections, whereas the other five codes chronologically order the subsections by number (e.g. 1-7). AAMFT is the only code without a "preamble." However, AAMFT is also the only code in which the reader does not need to refer to the preceding subheading to understand the exact referencing of each ethical principle. Each of the principles is numbered chronologically, consistent with the respective subheading number (i.e., 1-7). For example, the document contains printed numbers that correspond to the respective ethical principle, such as 1.1, 1.2, 1.3, . . . 2.1, 2.2.

The length of the codes vary with AmPsyA being the shortest and APA and AACD being the longest codes. The number of subsections within the codes differ with NASW having six, AmPsyA and AAMFT having seven, AACD having eight, APA having ten, and ASGW having sixteen.

Williams' Index of Ethical Code Terminology (Williams, in process) includes a referencing categorization system that pertains to the six professional organization's codes of ethics discussed in this chapter. Of the 79 descriptor words in the index, 23 are referred to in all six codes. The 23 common themes discussed in each of the codes are as follows:

- client records
- colleague relationships
- community standards/standards of the profession
- confidentiality/privacy
- conflict of interest
- continuing education
- danger
- discrimination
- exploitation for personal gain/undue influence
- fees
- fraud/deception
- governmental laws/regulations and advising, consulting
- measurement and evaluation/research/testing/assessment
- personal problems/conduct
- professional competence (development)/accountability/integrity
- protection of clients/participants
- referrals
- refusal of treatment
- reporting colleagues who are incompetent, unethical
- research/scholarship
- sexual intimacies
- teaching/training
- use of techniques/skills

We refer you to *Williams' Index of Ethical Code Terminology* (Williams, in process) for a comprehensive guide to the six professional organization's codes of ethics (AACD, 1988; AAMFT, 1988; ASGW, 1989; American Psychiatric Association, 1989; APA, 1989; NASW, 1984).

The content of all six codes stresses the confidential nature of the professional relationship. Each code certifies the professional *member's* responsibility to inform the appropriate, responsible authorities when there is evidence of *serious* danger. In addition, APA (1989) specifies that the "revised *Ethical Principles* apply [not only] to psychologists, [but] to students of psychology, and to others who do work of a psychological nature under the supervision of a psychologist. They are also intended for the guidance of *nonmembers* of the Association who are engaged in psychological research or practice" (footnote, emphasis added). Using different terminology, each of the codes takes a firm position regarding the duty to breach confidentiality when there is either "danger" (NASW, 1979, 1 E3), "clear danger" (APA, 1989, Principle 5), "imminent danger" (AmPsyA, 1989, 4[8]), "clear and imminent danger" (AACD, 1988a, 84; ASGW, 1989, 3[a]), and "clear and immediate danger" (AAMFT, 1988, 2.1 [2]). However, "it is not entirely clear whether the code provision on revealing confidences in matters of *potential* danger is mandatory or discretionary on the psychologist's [or therapist's] part" (Curran, McGarry, & Shah, 1986, p. 51, emphasis added). However, according to the literature, violence cannot be predicted. The reader is encouraged to consider the following:

(1) Alden (1976): "psychiatrists do not have specific training to diagnose or predict dangerous behavior"
(2) Cooke (1980, p. 190): "empirical data indicate that clinicians are most inclined to overpredict violence and classify an excessive number of people as dangerous"
(3) Halleck (1971, p. 348): "our criteria for predicting who will commit a dangerous act are totally inadequate"
(4) Spielberger (1970, p. 98): "there are few, if any structures or projective tests which adequately predict or even postdict, violent behavior"
(5) Wenk, Ribison, and Smith (1972, p. 393): "criminal offender studies show between 86-99% false positive predictions"

Unfortunately, many courts perpetuate the myth that the licensed mental health professional possesses the power to predict violence. The significance of such foolishness can be derived from Monahan (1981), who concluded that, at best, psychiatrists and psychologists were accurate one third of the time in predicting violent behavior. If 250 million people in the United States were to be evaluated, and we assumed that 1 in 1,000 were potential killers, we would identify 250,000 people who would kill if we were 100% accurate. However, we would have two-thirds false positives, or 500,000 people who would not kill but would be identified as potential killers. It is obvious that among these false positives would be judges, lawyers, psychiatrists, and their spouses.

Other subtle differences exist with the wording of the different organizational code guidelines. For instance, AACD (1988a) standard B4 states, "When the client's condition indicates that there is clear and imminent danger to the client or others, the member must take reasonable personal action or inform responsible authorities," while ASGW (1989) guideline 3(a) specifies, "When a group member's condition indicates that there is clear and imminent danger to the client or others, the member must take reasonable personal action or inform responsible authorities," while ASGW (1989) guideline 3(a) specifies, "When a group member's condition indicates that there is clear and imminent danger to the member, others, *or physical property*, the group counselor takes reasonable personal action and/or informs responsible authorities" (emphasis added). AAMFT's (1988) code states, in Principle 2.1, "Marriage and family therapists cannot disclose client confidences to anyone except: (1) as mandated by law; (2) to prevent a clear and immediate danger to a person or persons." The importance of varying state laws appears to be acknowledged in AAMFT's (1988) code. For example, in the state of Maryland, "both statute and court action indicate that confidentiality may not be breached even when the lives of others are at risk. It may be possible for psychotherapists in Maryland to be found guilty of a breach of confidentiality if they attempt to warn probable victims of a life-threatening danger from their clients" (Mappes, Robb, & Engels, 1985, p. 249). On September 17, 1985, California Governor George Deukmejiian signed a law that limits the duties and liabilities of psychotherapists to potential victims of violence. Monetary liability was eliminated except when the patient communicated to the therapist a threat of violence against a reasonably identifiable victim or victims. If the therapist can prove that a reasonable effort was made to communicate the threat to law enforcement and to potential victim(s), liability is then eliminated.

Disciplinary Action for Violating the Ethics Code

Five of the six professional organizations focused upon in this chapter (AAMFT, NASW, AACD, AmPsyA, and APA) have policies specifying various disciplinary actions for accused members found guilty of violating their professional organization's ethical standards. ASGW (the sixth professional organization discussed) has a section titled "Safe-guarding Ethical Practices and Procedures for Reporting Unethical Behavior" at the end of its ethical code, directing persons to file ethical complaints against group counselors to the Ethics Committee of AACD (i.e., ASGW's parent organization). Although AACD is covered for liability and ASGW, as well as the other 14 divisions of AACD, are not, all complaints of ethical violation are filed with the AACD Ethics Committee rather than the ASGW Ethics Committee. In addition to the safeguard of liability, this reporting procedure avoids the problem of having the same case heard by two different ethics committees (AACD, ASGW) that could potentially reach different decisions regarding an alleged violator. In other words, it would be a difficult dilemma to have either the AACD or the ASGW Ethics Committee find a member guilty and the other committee find the same person innocent (Barbara Herlihy, AACD Ethics Committee chair, personal communication, April 1989).

Both APA and AACD have detailed documents for handling complaint reports for ethical violations filed against their respective organization members. APA has a document titled *Rules and Procedures* and AACD has a document titled *Policies and Procedures for Processing Complaints of Ethical Violations* (AACD, 1988b, hereinafter referred to as *AACD Policies and Procedures*). "The purpose of this document is to facilitate the work of the AACD Ethics Committee by specifying procedures for processing cases of alleged violations of the AACD Code of Ethics, codifying options for sanctioning members, and stating appeal procedures" (p. 1).

In 1984, AmPsyA implemented "Procedures for Handling Complaints of Unethical Conduct." These procedures are specified in a six-page section added to the organization's existing nine-page ethics code. All 15 pages, both the ethics code and the procedures section, are contained in a small booklet.

Each of the five professional organizations' ethics committees (AAMFT, NASW, AACD, AmPsyA, and APA) that process complaints may discipline the accused violator of the ethical standards by any of several actions. As specified in the *AACD Policies and Procedures* (1988b), the AACD Ethics Committee may take any of the following actions:

(a) issue a reprimand with recommendations for corrective action, subject to review by the Committee, or

(b) withdraw eligibility for membership in AACD for a specified period of time, or

(c) place the member on probation for a specified period of time, subject to review by the Committee, or

(d) expel the member from AACD permanently. (App. C, "Appropriate Discipline")

"Of the six (6) voting members of the [AACD Ethics] Committee, a vote of four (4) is necessary to conduct business, and a unanimous vote is necessary to expel a member from the association" (AACD, 1988b, App. C).

Professional members who have been found guilty of violating their ethical standards, following a formal hearing and deliberation with their respective professional organization's ethics committee, have a right to appeal. After any right to appeal has been exhausted, the respective ethics committee will usually inform the appropriate state licensing board(s) of the disciplined member's status with the professional organization. For instance, as stated in the *AACD Policies and Procedures* (1988b), one of the consequences of discipline by the AACD Ethics Committee is as follows:

> After any right to appeal has been exhausted, the Committee will notify the appropriate State Licensing Board(s) of the disciplined member's status with AACD. Notice will also be given to the National Board for Certified Counselors, the AACD divisions of which the disciplined party is a member, the members of AACD, and the complainant. Such notice shall only state the discipline imposed and the sections of the AACD Ethical Standards that were violated. Further elaboration shall not be disclosed. ("Recommended Hearing Procedures," 4.C. [3] D.)

To date (i.e., May 1, 1990), only once has the name of a disciplined AACD member been published. The notification appeared in the AACD *Guidepost*, the newspaper of the American Association for Counseling and Development published at three-week intervals (with the exception of special issues). Below is a quotation of the published announcement as it appeared in the *Guidepost* on August 20, 1987 (Vol. 30, No. 2, p. 12).

> To the editor:
> As prescribed by the AACD Policies and Procedures and under the direction of AACD President, you are to give notice to the members of

AACD that an AACD MEMBER . . . has been found to be in violation of the AACD Ethical Standards Section A #8 and Section B #1 and #11.

The discipline imposed as a result of this violation is suspension from membership for one year followed by one year of probationary membership status.

Virginia B. Allen, Chair
AACD Ethics Committee

ASGW does not currently have a provision for publishing the names of those who are disciplined for violating the standards of their respective professional codes. In contrast, APA, AmPsyA, AAMFT, and NASW all provide a list to members of those who have been disciplined along with a notation of the specific area of the code that has been violated. APA publishes the names of those members who violated the ethics code in an annual mailing that is sent to all APA members in the fall each year.

AAMFT has two ways to list the names of persons whose memberships were terminated as a result of violating the ethical code, and the respective ethical violations are cited: (a) *Family Therapy News*, which is published bimonthly (i.e., every other month) and (b) listings of names sent to all organization members accompanying the annual dues notices. In addition, AAMFT contacts state regulatory organizations, other professional organizations, and any other institutions that have jurisdiction over the individual (e.g., the employing universities for those persons working as professors or the church in which he or she may be serving as a minister; Steven L. Preister, AAMFT deputy director, personal communication, July 28, 1989).

NASW publishes a list of those members who have been "sanctioned for violating the code" (i.e., NASW's Code of Ethics). The lists have been published since the early 1980s in *NASW News*, the monthly newsletter sent to all members (Myles Davis, NASW certification associate, personal communication, July 28, 1989).

"If a complaint of unethical conduct against a member [of the AmPsyA] is sustained, the member shall receive a sanction ranging from admonishment to expulsion. Any decision to expel a member must be approved by a two-thirds affirmative vote of all members of the Board present and voting" (1989, p. 10). The names of those psychiatrists *expelled* from AmPsyA for violating the code of ethics are listed in two different publications: (a) *Psychiatric News*, which is published every two weeks and sent to all AmPsyA members, and (b) the district branch newsletters, which are generally published bimonthly. In addition to listing the names of the psychiatrists expelled, the publications cite the section or sections of the seven-section code that were violated. The specifics of the violation are not spelled out, only the section or section numbers are included. For those psychiatrists who are *suspended* from AmPsyA for violating the code of ethics, the decision on whether or not to publish the names is based upon the prevailing circumstances. Therefore, it is not obligatory to publish the names as is the case for those expelled. If a psychiatrist *resigns* from AmPsyA while under examination for violating the ethics code, his or her name is included in the same publications as those listing the expelled members.

Summary

The topic of "ethics" initiates many different thoughts among mental health professionals. The terms *ethics, values, morality, professionalism,* and *law* are closely related, yet differences exist. Psychotherapists need to be cognizant of their professional organization's code of ethics and behave accordingly. Although, to date, we are aware of only one court case in which the judge referred to a professional mental health association's code of ethics, we believe that such a practice will increase in the immediate future. However, it is important to realize that there may be instances in which the law conflicts with the profession's code of ethics. And we encourage psychotherapists to function at a higher level of moral reasoning (i.e., aspirational ethics) than simply complying with the law and the profession's codes of ethics.

We refer you to the six professional codes of ethics included in Appendix D. The Association for Specialists Group Work's *Ethical Guidelines for Group Counselors* (1989), as well as Appendix C of this book, which includes the names and addresses of several professional mental health associations.

Vignettes

You are treating a 15-year-old boy who informs you that he was involved in a robbery on a military base. He stole one case of land mines and buried them because he didn't know what else to do with the material. What might you do in this situation according to the ethical and legal issues in your state?

Questions to Consider

(1) Why do we need professional ethics codes?

(2) Would it be better only to have laws that govern behavior?

(3) What are some drawbacks to the ethics codes?

(4) What are some similarities between different ethics codes? What are some differences? Are there more similarities or more differences?

(5) How ethical are you being if you predict "dangerousness" when the literature shows violence cannot be predicted?

PART IV

18

Epilogue

From the outcome of malpractice cases reviewed in Chapters 2-16, we conclude that a psychotherapist has many responsibilities in the delivery of mental health services, as follows:

- A psychotherapist must obtain informed consent for treatment.
- Adequate records must be maintained.
- Confidentiality must be maintained except where contraindicated.
- There is a responsibility not to invade the privacy of a client.
- A psychotherapist has a responsibility to protect human life (clients'/others').
- Sexual contact with a client must be avoided.
- Psychotherapists must practice competently and not injure clients.
- A diagnosis should not be arrived at in a negligent manner.
- When authorized, psychotherapists have a responsibility to transfer/obtain information pertaining to clients.
- Psychotherapists have a responsibility not to release a client who is still considered to be dangerous.
- Undue influence must be avoided with clients.
- Clients must not be abandoned, and there is a responsibility to provide a termination experience for a client.

- Psychotherapists have a responsibility to refrain from defamatory comments.
- When a psychotherapist undertakes the responsibility of supervising another, this supervision must not be done in a negligent manner.

PRACTICE IN A RESPONSIBLE MANNER

In summary, it is our opinion that you will greatly reduce your chances of a malpractice suit, as well as improve the quality of service to your clients, if you adhere to the following suggestions:

(1) Do not work outside the areas of your competence.

(2) Use effective communication.

(3) Watch your statements regarding your effectiveness.

(4) Have knowledge about alternative modes of therapy.

(5) Discuss with clients the risks of therapy as well as their other alternatives.

(6) Obtain informed consent for all therapy.

(7) Only treat minors with parental consent, unless there is a legal exception.

(8) Make sure the patient has understood and voluntarily agreed to therapy.

(9) If you are in an institutional setting, make sure you employ the "least restrictive environment."

(10) Carefully evaluate high-risk clients and treat them accordingly (that is, outpatient therapy as "least restrictive versus risk of suicide/assault").

(11) Maintain careful records on all clients. This includes history, homicide/suicide attempts/threats, written treatment plans, and any failure to follow suggestions.

(12) Don't forget to utilize consultations with colleagues and record these in the case files.

(13) Take reasonable precautions regarding keeping records confidential.

(14) Remember that the client holds the privilege, not you, but that you must claim the privilege for the client unless the court orders you to testify. If ordered to testify, you might consider requesting to the court judge that the case be heard "in camera."

(15) If you supervise, do so closely. Make sure you discuss *all* cases.

(16) Don't forget to report all cases of suspected child abuse, as mandated by law in all states.

(17) Report cases of suspected adult/elder abuse if required by state law.

(18) Keep up to date with legal and ethical changes by active involvement in professional associations (e.g., reading the literature, attending conferences).

(19) Maintain and understand your professional liability insurance coverage.

(20) Keep up with the literature in your field so that you know the most modern methods of treatment, evaluation, and so on.

IF SUED

(1) Don't panic: Recognize the crisis and seek appropriate professional assistance.

(2) Notify your insurance broker immediately. Consult your personal attorney. Do not discuss the case without safeguards on privileged communication.

(3) Be patient; the process of litigation usually takes years. Do not attempt to settle the matter yourself without legal guidance. Refrain from sending angry letters to the client(s) involved.

(4) Review your records in a systematic manner. Organize your data but do not show your information to anyone without the approval of your attorney. Watch out for the "friendly" attorney for the plaintiff who "just wants to settle this unfortunate matter."

(5) If you consult with a fellow psychotherapist, do so in hypothetical terms to maintain the anonymity of your client.

IF AN ETHICAL COMPLAINT IS FILED

(1) Be cooperative with the ethics committee. Don't refuse to respond to their inquiries; however, do not be impulsive when responding.

(2) Review the "ethics rules and procedures" and the "ethical principles/ standards/guidelines" of the professional organizations in which you hold membership.

(3) Make sure your response is within the time frame given (or request an extension of time to prepare your reply).

(4) Systematically review the chronology and documentation of the case.

(5) Consider asking to meet face to face with the ethics committee to present your documents.

(6) Consider obtaining the guidance of your attorney.

(7) Consider consultation with a colleague.

(8) Remember that you have the right to appeal procedural errors or if significant additional evidence is available.

Questions to Consider

The following are ideas for discussion and questions that could not be answered based on the case reviews in the preceding chapters of the text. We include them here to further stimulate your thinking regarding malpractice in psychotherapy.

(1) Discuss the concepts of treatment in the "least restrictive environment" versus "potential danger to self/others/physical property."

(2) Discuss the risks involved in psychotherapy.

(3) If your focus is on family therapy, are you open to being sued by a dissatisfied family member for neglect of his or her individual rights?

(4) What responsibilities does a psychotherapist have to his or her clients?

(5) What is more important--breaking confidentiality or risking a suicide? How does a therapist determine whether or not he or she is breaking confidentiality unnecessarily?

(6) How much responsibility should the therapist have to change a client?

(7) Who is responsible for a client's recovery?

(8) As a therapist, how might you determine who potential victims of your client might be if your client refuses to divulge such information?

(9) What can family members do to make sure their loved ones are receiving proper care while hospitalized? After referring a client for hospitalization, what might you do to make certain your client is receiving proper treatment?

(10) If your client had AIDS, a deadly disease, and was unwilling to tell his or her spouse, would you breach confidentiality to warn the client's spouse about the danger?

(11) How long are you held liable following the termination of the psychotherapeutic relationship with a client?

(12) Does a psychotherapist have a duty to report a client's prior crimes? What if your client is currently involved in a crime?

(13) What would you do if a fire destroyed all of your client records?

(14) If a "confidential communication between client and therapist" includes information transmitted in the course of therapy, would it be a breach of confidentiality to reveal any of the following: (a) client's name, (b) date(s) seen, (c) length of session(s), (d) diagnosis, or (e) prognosis?

(15) After a client dies, is it okay to release information about him or her? (States that permit a legal representative of a deceased patient from posthumous disclosures are Alaska, Arizona, California, Florida, Hawaii, Illinois, Indiana, Maine, Nevada, New Jersey, Mexico, North Dakota, Ohio, Oklahoma, Rhode Island, South Dakota, Texas, and Wisconsin; Stromberg et al., 1988, p. 430).

(16) Can tape-recorded counseling sessions be subpoenaed by the court?

(17) If you do not have hospital privileges and you refer a client for hospitalization, how would you evaluate his or her care and treatment?

(18) How does a therapist determine whether or not he or she is breaching confidentiality unnecessarily?

(19) What is your state law regarding clients' access to their records? What might be the value of permitting your client to review your written case notes when there is high probability that the client will attempt suicide? What might be the disadvantages of such a practice?

(20) If the therapist feels that a certain intervention should not be revealed on paper (in case notes), should that intervention not be used?

(21) Do you believe that psychotherapists should *ever* be permitted to have a sexual relationship with a former client given the law and professional organization codes of ethics? If so, what period of time do you believe needs to elapse following the termination of the psychotherapeutic relationship?

(22) Do you believe that psychotherapists should be permitted to have a social relationship with a former client? If so, what period of time do you believe needs to elapse following the psychotherapeutic relationship?

(23) A 45-year-old client last saw a psychotherapist at the age of 40. Should the new psychotherapist request a release of information from the former therapist? What if the same client last saw a psychotherapist at age 25? What if the last time were at age 15? What period of time from a client's former experience in therapy might you determine to mean there is no need to receive such information? How might the client's presenting problem to you as a therapist or the client's reporting of past issues dealt with in therapy determine whether or not you would question your client to sign a release for you to obtain such past information?

(24) To whom is it appropriate to disclose information about a client when trying to save a client's life? What and how much information should you disclose about this client? How might your response differ based upon such factors as client age, inpatient versus outpatient client status, and so on?

(25) What would you do if you were unable to contact your suicidal client about needing to cancel his or her next scheduled appointment because of an unexpected emergency that requires you to be unavailable for several days?

(26) You have been seeing a patient or an inpatient in a mental health hospital facility. Before hospital discharge and returning to his or her home in another state, the patient requests to continue psychotherapy with you as an outpatient by telephone therapy sessions. What might you do?

Appendix A:
Legal Citations

	In re Subpoena served upon Pierce (1983)
Minnesota:	*State of Minnesota v. Gullekson* (1986)
New Jersey:	*State of New Jersey v. McBride* (1986)
Oregon:	*State of Oregon v. Miller* (1985)
South Dakota:	*Schaffer v. Spicer* (1974)
Texas:	*Tumlinson v. The State of Texas* (1983)

CHAPTER 4: PRIVACY

Massachusetts:	*Bratt v. International Business Machines Corp.* (1986)
New York:	*Doe v. Roe* (1977)
West Virginia:	*Davis v. Monsanto Company* (1986)

CHAPTER 5: DEFAMATION OF CHARACTER

Utah:	*Berry v. Moench* (1958)

CHAPTER 6: FAILURE TO WARN AND PROTECT

California:	*Tarasoff v. the Regents of the University of California* (1975)
	Jablonski v. U.S.A. (1983)
	Hedlund v. the Superior Court of Orange County (1983)
	Doyle and Doyle v. U.S.A. (1982)
	Thompson v. County of Alameda (1980)
Colorado:	*Brady, McCarthy, and Delahanty v. Hopper* (1983)
District of	
Columbia:	*White v. U.S.A.* (1986)
Iowa:	*Heltsely v. Votteler* (1982)
Louisiana:	*Phillips v. Gibson's Inc., Sentry Insurance and State of Louisiana* (1986)
Maryland:	*Shaw v. Glickman* (1980)
	Hansenei v. U.S.A. (1982)
Michigan:	*Davis v. Lhim* (1983)
	Chrite v. U.S.A. (1983)
Minnesota:	*Cairl et al. v. State of Minnesota et al.* (1982)
Nebraska:	*Lipari & the Bank of Elkorn v. Sears Roebuck & Co. & U.S.A.* (1980)
New Jersey:	*McIntosh v. Milano* (1979)
Pennsylvania:	*Leedy and Leedy v. Hartnett & Lebanon Veterans Administration Hospital* (1981)

CHAPTER 7: FAILURE TO TAKE PRECAUTIONS AGAINST SUICIDE

California:	*Bellah v. Greenson* (1977)
	Johnson v. County of Los Angeles (1983)
Illinois:	*Pietrucha v. Grant Hospital* (1971)
Missouri:	*Gregory v. Robinson* (1960)
New York:	*Eady v. Alter* (1976)
	Cohen v. State of New York (1976)

CHAPTER 8: SEXUAL CONTACT WITH A CLIENT

Florida:	*Solloway v. Department of Professional Regulation* (1982)
Missouri:	*Zipkin v. Freeman* (1968)
New York:	*Roy v. Hartogs* (1976)
North Carolina:	*Mazza v. Huffaker* (1983)
Wisconsin:	*L. L. v. Medical Protective Co.* (1984)

CHAPTER 9: INJURY FROM NONTRADITIONAL THERAPY

California:	*Solano County Dept. of Social Services v. Ron B.* (1987)
New York:	*Hammer v. Rosen* (1960)

CHAPTER 10: DIAGNOSIS

Alabama:	*North American Company for Life and Health Insurance v. Berger* (1981)
Iowa:	*Baker v. United States* (1964)

CHAPTER 11: INADEQUATE TERMINATION OR ABANDONMENT

Illinois:	*Mary and Crystal v. Ramsden* (1980)

CHAPTER 12: RELEASING OR OBTAINING INFORMATION AND INFORMED CONSENT TO TREAT

Alabama:	*Underwood v. U.S.A.* (1966)
California:	*Jablonski v. United States* (1983)
Michigan:	*Stowers v. Wolodzko* (1971)
North Dakota:	*Merchants National Bank v. U.S.A.* (1967)

Vermont:	*Peck v. The Counseling Service of Addison County* (1985)
Illinois:	*Dymek v. Nyquist* (1984)

CHAPTER 13: ILLEGAL DETAINMENT

District of Columbia:	*Rouse v. Cameron* (1966)
	Lake v. Cameron (1966)
Florida:	*O'Connor v. Donaldson* (1975)
New York:	*Whitree v. State of New York* (1968)

CHAPTER 14: WRONGFUL RELEASE

Kansas:	*Durflinger v. Artiles* (1981)
Washington, D.C.:	*Semler v. Psychiatric Institute of Washington* (1976)

CHAPTER 15: UNDUE INFLUENCE

Michigan:	*Flemming v. Hall (1965)*
New York:	*Geis v. Landau* (1983)
Wisconsin:	*Patterson v. Jensen et al.* (1945)

CHAPTER 16: NEGLIGENT SUPERVISION

New York:	*Cohen v. State of New York* (1976)

Appendix B:
Sample Forms

PERMISSION TO USE AUDIO AND/OR VIDEOTAPE

Agreement entered into this _____ day of _____ between
Dr. _____

Whereas, Dr. _____ is desirous of using videotape and/or audiotape for the purpose of professional education, treatment and research, and is desirous of endorsing and supporting the use of such videotape, for the purpose of professional education treatment and research.

It is agreed by both parties hereto as follows:

1. The client consents to the use of videotape, and/or audiotape hereinafter to be taken in the office of Dr. _____ during the course of individual treatment.

2. The said videotape and/or audiotape will be used solely in the interest of the advancement of mental health programs and only for the purpose of professional education, treatment or research activities connected with such programs, and will not be used for any other purpose.

3. Dr. _____ agrees not to use or permit the use of the name of _____ in connection with any direct or indirect use or exhibition of such videotape and/or audiotape.

4. I agree that Dr. _____ is to be the sole owner of all rights in and to the said videotape and/or audiotape for all purposes herein set forth.

5. There shall be no financial compensation for the use of such videotape and/or audiotape.

_____
Psychotherapist

_____
Patient

_____
Witness

INFORMED CONSENT

I, _____ , assert that I have discussed the goals, objectives, methods and time frame of my Treatment Plan with my psychotherapist. I understand that the above may be modified as therapy progresses. I understand that I have the right to refuse treatment or to terminate psychotherapy should I choose. I understand fully the risks, alternatives and the nature of the treatment to be employed. I am aware that my psychotherapist will discuss these or any other issues should I request. At this time, I consent to work toward the achievement of the objectives stated in my Treatment Plan. I further specifically limit my therapist's use of any information which can in any way identify me to others unless I have offered my specific written permission. It is without any pressure or coercion that I sign this consent. I agree to compensate my therapist at the rate of $ _____ per _____ session.

Date _____

Signature _____

Witness _____

AGREEMENT

I, _____ agree to call _____ at
(__) _____ when needed for depression or when I have suicidal thoughts.
Should Dr. _____ not be available I will call Dr. _____
at (__) _____ . In the event Dr. _____ is not
available I will call Dr. _____ at (__) _____ .
If I am unable to reach one of the above I will contact the Suicide Crisis Hotline
at (__) _____ . If I cannot reach the Crisis Hotline I will contact [nearest
relative(s)]. If I fail to reach any of the above I will call [friend(s)]. If I fail to
reach any of the above I will call [employee(s)]. Ultimately, I can hospitalize
myself at _____ , _____ , _____ .
　　　　　　　　　(Hospital name)　　　　(address)　　　　(telephone)

SIGNED: _____

DATE: _____

WITNESS: _____

PROGRESS NOTES

Name _____   Date _____

Apt. Length: 15 _____   30 _____   45 _____   60 _____

Individual _____   Canceled _____   Emergency ____

Couple _____   Late Canc. _____   No Show _____

Family _____   On Time _____   Late _____

Group _____

Observations/Appearance/Affect: _____

_____

_____

Significant/Recent Events: _____

_____

_____

Content/Topics: _____

_____

_____

Assignments/Homework: _____

_____

_____

Diagnosis (Same/Different): _____

_____

_____

Treatment Plan: Same or Replace _____

_____

_____

Suicide: Y N   Violence: Y N   Ref: Medical _____

                                            Psychiatric _____

                                            Neurological _____

Next Session: _____   Signature: _____

NAME: _____

THERAPY PLAN

PROBLEM AREA:

    1.

    2.

    3.

    4.

BEHAVIORAL OBJECTIVE:

    1.

    2.

    3.

    4.

TIME FRAME:

    1.

    2.

    3.

    4.

CONCEPTS/SKILLS TO DEVELOP:

    1.

    2.

    3.

    4.

MATERIALS/ACTIVITIES:

    1.

    2.

    3.

    4.

Appendix C:
Names and Addresses of
Professional Organizations

American Association for Counseling and Development (AACD)
5999 Stevenson Avenue
Alexandria, Virginia 22304
(703) 823-9800
AACD Ethical Standards (1988)

American Association for Marriage and Family Therapy (AAMFT)
1717 K Street, N.W.
Suite 407
Washington, DC 20006
(202) 429-1825
AAMFT Code of Ethical Principles for Marriage and Family Therapists (1988)

American College Personnel Association (ACPA)
c/o American Association for Counseling and Development
5999 Stevenson Avenue
Alexandria, Virginia 22304

(703) 823-9800
Statement of Ethical Principles and Standards (1989)

American Mental Health Counselors Association (AMHCA)
c/o American Association for Counseling and Development
5999 Stevenson Avenue
Alexandria, Virginia 22304
(703) 823-9800
Code of Ethics for Mental Health Counselors (1987)

American Psychiatric Association
1400 K Street, N.W.
Washington, DC 20005
(202) 682-6000
*Principles of Medical Ethics, with
Annotations Especially Applicable to Psychiatry* (1989)

American Psychological Association (APA)
1200 Seventeenth Street, N.W.
Washington, DC 20036
(202) 955-7600
(703) 247-7705 (Order Department in Virginia)
Ethical Principles of Psychologists, APA (1989)

American Rehabilitation Counselors Association (ARCA)
c/o American Association for Counseling and Development
5999 Stevenson Avenue
Alexandria, Virginia 22304
(703) 823-9800
Rehabilitation Counselor Code of Ethics

American School Counselor Association (ASCA)
c/o American Association for Counseling and Development
5999 Stevenson Avenue
Alexandria, Virginia 22304
(703) 823-9800
*American School Counselor Association Ethical Standards for
School Counselors* (1972)

Association for Specialists in Group Work (ASGW)
c/o American Association for Counseling and Development
5999 Stevenson Ave.
Alexandria, Virginia 22304

(703) 823-9800
Ethical Guidelines for Group Counselors (1989)

National Association of Social Workers (NASW)
7981 Eastern Ave.
Silver Spring, Maryland 20910
(301) 565-0333
Code of Ethics, NASW (1984)

National Board for Certified Counselors, Inc. (NBCC)
5999 Stevenson Avenue
Alexandria, Virginia 22304
(703) 823-9800
NBCC Code of Ethics

National Career Development Association (NCDA)
c/o American Association for Counseling and Development
5999 Stevenson Avenue
Alexandria, Virginia 22304
(703) 823-9800
National Career Development Association Ethical Standards (1987)

Appendix D:
Ethics Codes

AAMFT Code of Ethical Principles for Marriage and Family Therapists

The Board of Directors of the American Association for Marriage and Family Therapy (AAMFT) hereby promulgates, pursuant to Article II, Section (1)(C) of the Association's Bylaws, the Revised AAMFT Code of Ethical Principles for Marriage and Family Therapists, effective August 1, 1988.

The AAMFT Code of Ethical Principles for Marriage and Family Therapists is binding on all Members of AAMFT (Clinical, Student, and Associate) and on all AAMFT Approved Supervisors.

If an AAMFT Member or an AAMFT Approved Supervisor resigns in anticipation of or during the course of an ethics investigation, the Ethics Committee will complete its investigation. Any publication of action taken by the Association will include the fact that the Member attempted to resign during the investigation.

Marriage and family therapists are encouraged to report alleged unethical behavior of colleagues to appropriate professional associations and state regulatory bodies.

1. Responsibility to Clients

Marriage and family therapists are dedicated to advancing the welfare of families and individuals, including respecting the rights of those persons seeking their assistance, and making reasonable efforts to ensure that their services are used appropriately.

SOUCE: *AAMFT Code of Ethical Principles for Marriage and Family Therapists* reprinted by permission. This revised code of ethics was approved August 1, 1988. AAMFT can make further revisions to the code at any time, as the Association deems necessary.

1.1 Marriage and family therapists do not discriminate against or refuse professional service to anyone on the basis of race, sex, religion, or national origin.

1.2 Marriage and family therapists are cognizant of their potentially influential position with respect to clients, and they avoid exploiting the trust and dependency of such persons. Marriage and family therapists therefore make every effort to avoid dual relationships with clients that could impair their professional judgment or increase the risk of exploitation. Examples of such dual relationships include, but are not limited to, business or close relationships with clients. Sexual intimacy with clients is prohibited. Sexual intimacy with former clients for two years following the termination of therapy is prohibited.

1.3 Marriage and family therapists do not use their professional relationship with clients to further their own interests.

1.4 Marriage and family therapists respect the right of clients to make decisions and help them to understand the consequences of these decisions. Marriage and family therapists clearly advise a client that a decision on marital status is the responsibility of the client.

1.5 Marriage and family therapists continue therapeutic relationships only so long as it is reasonably clear that clients are benefiting from the relationship.

1.6 Marriage and family therapists assist persons in obtaining other therapeutic services if a marriage and family therapist is unable or unwilling, for appropriate reasons, to see a person who has requested professional help.

1.7 Marriage and family therapists do not abandon or neglect clients in treatment without making reasonable arrangements for the continuation of such treatment.

1.8 Marriage and family therapists obtain informed consent of clients before taping, recording, or permitting third party observation of their activities.

2. Confidentiality

Marriage and family therapists have unique confidentiality problems because the "client" in a therapeutic relationship may be more than one person. The overriding principle is that marriage and family therapists respect the confidences of their client(s).

2.1 Marriage and family therapists cannot disclose client confidences to anyone, except: (1) as mandated by law; (2) to prevent a clear and immediate danger to a person or persons; (3) where the marriage and family therapist is a defendant in a civil, criminal or disciplinary action arising from the therapy (in which case client confidences may only be disclosed in the course of that action); or (4) if there is a waiver previously obtained in writing, and then such information may only be revealed in accordance with the terms of the waiver. In circumstances where more than one person in a family is receiving therapy, each

such family member who is legally competent to execute a waiver must agree
to the waiver required by sub-paragraph (4). Absent such a waiver from each
family member legally competent to execute a waiver, a marriage and family
therapist cannot disclose information received from any family member.

2.2 Marriage and family therapists use client and/or clinical materials in
teaching, writing, and public presentations only if a written waiver has been
received in accordance with sub-principle 2.1(4), or when appropriate steps have
been taken to protect client identity.

2.3 Marriage and family therapists store or dispose of client records in ways
that maintain confidentiality.

3. Professional Competence and Integrity

Marriage and family therapists are dedicated to maintaining high standards of
professional competence and integrity.

3.1 Marriage and family therapists who (a) are convicted of felonies, (b) are
convicted of misdemeanors (related to their qualifications or functions), (c)
engage in conduct which could lead to conviction of felonies, or misdemeanors
related to their qualifications or functions, (d) are expelled from other professional organizations, (e) have their licenses or certificates suspended or revoked,
(f) are no longer competent to practice marriage and family therapy because they
are impaired due to physical or mental causes or the abuse of alcohol or other
substances, or (g) fail to cooperate with the Association at any stage of an
investigation of an ethical complaint of his/her conduct by the AAMFT Ethics
Committee or Judicial Council, are subject to termination of membership or
other appropriate action.

3.2 Marriage and family therapists seek appropriate professional assistance
for their own personal problems or conflicts that are likely to impair their work
performance and their clinical judgment.

3.3 Marriage and family therapists, as teachers, are dedicated to maintaining
high standards of scholarship and presenting information that is accurate.

3.4 Marriage and family therapists seek to remain abreast of new developments in family therapy knowledge and practice through both educational
activities and clinical experiences.

3.5 Marriage and family therapists do not engage in sexual or other harassment or exploitation of clients, students, trainees, employees, colleagues, research subjects, or actual or potential witnesses or complainants in ethical
proceedings.

3.6 Marriage and family therapists do not attempt to diagnose, treat, or advise
on problems outside the recognized boundaries of their competence.

3.7 Marriage and family therapists attempt to prevent the distortion or misuse
of their clinical and research findings.

3.8 Marriage and family therapists are aware that, because of their ability to influence and alter the lives of others, they must exercise special care when making public their professional recommendations and opinions through testimony or other public statements.

4. Responsibility to Students, Employees, and Supervisees

Marriage and family therapists do not exploit the trust and dependency of students, employees, and supervisees.

4.1 Marriage and family therapists are cognizant of their potentially influential position with respect to students, employees, and supervisees, and they avoid exploiting the trust and dependency of such persons. Marriage and family therapists, therefore, make every effort to avoid dual relationships that could impair their professional judgment or increase the risk of exploitation. Examples of such dual relationships include, but are not limited to, provision of therapy to students, employees, or supervisees, and business or close personal relationships with students, employees, or supervisees. Sexual intimacy with students or supervisees is prohibited.

4.2 Marriage and family therapists do not permit students, employees, or supervisees to perform or to hold themselves out as competent to perform professional services beyond their training, level of experience, and competence.

5. Responsibility to the Profession

Marriage and family therapists respect the rights and responsibilities of professional colleagues; carry out research in an ethical manner; and participate in activities which advance the goals of the profession.

5.1 Marriage and family therapists remain accountable to the standards of the profession when acting as members or employees of organizations.

5.2 Marriage and family therapists assign publication credit to those who have contributed to a publication in proportion to their contributions and in accordance with customary professional publication practices.

5.3 Marriage and family therapists who are the authors of books or other materials that are published or distributed should cite appropriately persons to whom credit for original ideas is due.

5.4 Marriage and family therapists who are the authors of books or other materials published or distributed by an organization take reasonable precautions to ensure that the organization promotes and advertises the materials accurately and factually.

5.5 Marriage and family therapists, as researchers, must be adequately informed of and abide by relevant laws and regulations regarding the conduct of research with human participants.

5.6 Marriage and family therapists recognize a responsibility to participate in activities that contribute to a better community and society, including devoting a portion of their professional activity to services for which there is little or no financial return.

5.7 Marriage and family therapists are concerned with developing laws and regulations pertaining to marriage and family therapy that serve the public interest, and with altering such laws and regulations that are not in the public interest.

5.8 Marriage and family therapists encourage public participation in the designing and delivery of services and in the regulation of practitioners.

6. Financial Arrangements

Marriage and family therapists make financial arrangements with clients and third party payors that conform to accepted professional practices and that are reasonably understandable.

6.1 Marriage and family therapists do not offer or accept payment for referrals.

6.2 Marriage and family therapists do not charge excessive fees for services.

6.3 Marriage and family therapists disclose their fee structure to clients at the onset of treatment.

6.4 Marriage and family therapists are careful to represent facts to clients and third party payors regarding services rendered.

7. Advertising

Marriage and family therapists engage in appropriate informational activities, including those that enable laypersons to choose marriage and family services on an informed basis.

7.1 Marriage and family therapists accurately represent their competence, education, training, and experience relevant to their practice of marriage and family therapy.

7.2 Marriage and family therapists claim as evidence of educational qualifications in conjunction with their AAMFT membership only those degrees (a) from regionally-accredited institutions or (b) from institutions recognized by states which license or certify marriage and family therapists, but only if such regulation is accepted by AAMFT.

7.3 Marriage and family therapists assure that advertisements and publications, whether in directories, announcement cards, newspapers, or on radio or television, are formulated to convey information that is necessary for the public to make an appropriate selection. Information could include: (1) office information, such as name, address, telephone number, credit card acceptability, fee structure, languages spoken, and office hours; (2) appropriate degrees, state licensure and/or certification, and AAMFT Clinical Member status; and (3) description of practice.

7.4 Marriage and family therapists do not use a name which could mislead the public concerning the identity, responsibility, source, and status of those practicing under that name and do not hold themselves out as being partners or associates of a firm if they are not.

7.5 Marriage and family therapists do not use any professional identification (such as a professional card, office sign, letterhead, or telephone or association directory listing) if it includes a statement or claim that is false, fraudulent, misleading, or deceptive. A statement is false, fraudulent, misleading, or deceptive if it (a) contains a material misrepresentation of fact; (b) fails to state any material fact necessary to make the statement, in light of all circumstances, not misleading; or (c) is intended to or is likely to create an unjustified expectation.

7.6 Marriage and family therapists correct, wherever possible, false, misleading, or inaccurate information and representations made by others concerning the marriage and family therapist's qualifications, services, or products.

7.7 Marriage and family therapists make certain that the qualifications of persons in their employ are represented in a manner that is not false, misleading, or deceptive.

7.8 Marriage and family therapists may represent themselves as specializing within a limited area of marriage and family therapy, but may not hold themselves out as specialists without being able to provide evidence of training, education, and supervised experience in settings which meet recognized professional standards.

7.9 Only marriage and family therapist Clinical Members, Approved Supervisors, and Fellows—*not* Associate Members, Student Members, or organizations—may identify these AAMFT designations in public information or advertising materials.

7.10 Marriage and family therapists may not use the initials AAMFT following their name in the manner of an academic degree.

7.11 Marriage and family therapists may not use the AAMFT name, logo, and the abbreviated initials AAMFT. The Association (which is the sole owner of its name, logo, and the abbreviated initials AAMFT) and its committees and regional divisions, operating as such, may use the name, logo, and the abbreviated initials AAMFT. A regional division of AAMFT may use the AAMFT insignia to list its individual Clinical Members as a group (e.g., in the Yellow Pages); when all Clinical Members practicing within a directory district have been invited to list themselves in the directory, any one or more members may do so.

7.12 Marriage and family therapists use their membership in AAMFT only in connection with their clinical and professional activities.

Violations of this Code should be brought in writing to the attention of the AAMFT Committee on Ethics and Professional Practices at the central office of AAMFT, 1717 K Street, N.W., Suite 407, Washington DC 20003. *Effective August 1, 1988*

The American Association for
Marriage and Family Therapy
1717 K Street, NW, Suite 407
Washington DC 20006
202/429-1825

Ethical Standards of the American Association for Counseling and Development (3rd Revision, AACD Governing Council, March 1988)

Preamble

The Association is an educational, scientific, and professional organization whose members are dedicated to the enhancement of the worth, dignity, potential, and uniqueness of each individual and thus to the service of society.

The Association recognizes that the role definitions and work settings of its members include a wide variety of academic disciplines, levels of academic preparation, and agency services. This diversity reflects the breadth of the Association's interest and influence. It also poses challenging complexities in efforts to set standards for the performance of members, desired requisite preparation or practice, and supporting social, legal, and ethical controls.

The specification of ethical standards enables the Association to clarify to present and future members and to those served by members the nature of ethical responsibilities held in common by its members.

The existence of such standards serves to stimulate greater concern by members for their own professional functioning and for the conduct of fellow professionals such as counselors, guidance and student personnel workers, and others in the helping professions. As the ethical code of the Association, this document establishes principles that define the ethical behavior of Association members. Additional ethical guidelines developed by the Association's Divisions for their specialty areas may further define a member's ethical behavior.

Section A: General

1. The member influences the development of the profession by continuous efforts to improve professional practices, teaching, services, and research. Professional growth is continuous throughout the member's career and is exemplified by the development of a philosophy that explains why and how a member functions in the helping relationship. Members must gather data on their effectiveness and be guided by the findings. Members recognize the need for continuing education to ensure competent service.

2. The member has a responsibility both to the individual who is served and to the institution within which the service is performed to maintain high standards of professional conduct. The member strives to maintain the highest levels of professional services offered to the individuals to be served. The member also strives to assist the agency, organization, or institution in providing the highest caliber of professional services. The acceptance of employment in an institution implies that the member is in agreement with the general policies and principles of the institution. Therefore the professional activities of the member are also in accord with the objectives of the institution. If, despite concerted efforts, the member cannot reach agreement with the employer as to acceptable standards of conduct that allow for changes in institutional policy conducive to the positive growth and development of clients, then terminating the affiliation should be seriously considered.

3. Ethical behavior among professional associates, both members and nonmembers, must be expected all times. When information is possessed that raises doubt as to the ethical behavior of professional colleagues, whether Association members or not, the member must take action to attempt to rectify such a condition. Such action shall use the institution's channels first and then use procedures established by the Association.

4. The member neither claims nor implies professional qualifications exceeding those possessed and is responsible for correcting any misrepresentations of these qualifications by others.

5. In establishing fees for professional counseling services, members must consider the financial status of clients and locality. In the event that the established fee structure is inappropriate for a client, assistance must be provided in finding comparable services of acceptable cost.

6. When members provide information to the public or to subordinates, peers, or supervisors, they have a responsibility to ensure that the content is general, unidentified client information that is accurate, unbiased, and consists of objective, factual data.

7. Members recognize their boundaries of competence and provide only those services and use only those techniques for which they are qualified by training or experience. Members should only accept those positions for which they are professionally qualified.

8. In the counseling relationship, the counselor is aware of the intimacy of the relationship and maintains respect for the client and avoids engaging in activities that seek to meet the counselor's personal needs at the expense of that client.

9. Members do not condone or engage in sexual harassment which is defined as deliberate or repeated comments, gestures, or physical contacts of a sexual nature.

10. The member avoids bringing personal issues into the counseling relationship, especially if the potential for harm is present. Through awareness of the negative impact of both racial and sexual stereotyping and discrimination, the counselor guards the individual rights and personal dignity of the client in the counseling relationship.

11. Products or services provided by the member by means of classroom instruction, public lectures, demonstrations, written articles, radio or television programs, or other types of media must meet the criteria cited in these standards.

Section B: Counseling Relationship

This section refers to practices and procedures of individual and/or group counseling relationships.

The member must recognize the need for client freedom of choice. Under those circumstances where this is not possible, the member must apprise clients of restrictions that may limit their freedom of choice.

1. The member's primary obligation is to respect the integrity and promote the welfare of the client(s), whether the client(s) is (are) assisted individually or in a group relationship. In a group setting, the member is also responsible for taking reasonable precautions to protect individuals from physical and/or psychological trauma resulting from interaction within the group.

2. Members make provisions for maintaining confidentiality in the storage and disposal of records and follow an established record retention and disposition policy. The counseling relationship and information resulting therefrom must be kept confidential, consistent with the obligations of the member as a professional person. In a group counseling setting, the counselor must set a norm of confidentiality regarding all group participants' disclosures.

3. If an individual is already in a counseling relationship with another professional person, the member does not enter into a counseling relationship without first contacting and receiving the approval of that other professional. If the member discovers that the client is in another counseling relationship after the counseling relationship begins, the member must gain the consent of the

other professional or terminate the relationship, unless the client elects to terminate the other relationship.

4. When the client's condition indicates that there is clear and imminent danger to the client or others, the member must take reasonable personal action or inform responsible authorities. Consultation with other professionals must be used where possible. The assumption of responsibility for the client's(s') behavior must be taken only after careful deliberation. The client must be involved in the resumption of responsibility as quickly as possible.

5. Records of the counseling relationship, including interview notes, test data, correspondence, tape recordings, electronic data storage, and other documents are to be considered professional information for use in counseling, and they should not be considered a part of the records of the institution or agency in which the counselor is employed unless specified by state statute or regulation. Revelation to others of counseling material must occur only upon the expressed consent of the client.

6. In view of the extensive data storage and processing capacities of the computer, the member must ensure that data maintained on a computer is: (a) limited to information that is appropriate and necessary for the services being provided; (b) destroyed after it is determined that the information is no longer of any value in providing services; and (c) restricted in terms of access to appropriate staff members involved in the provision of services by using the best computer security methods available.

7. Use of data derived from a counseling relationship for purposes of counselor training or research shall be confined to content that can be disguised to ensure full protection of the identity of the subject client.

8. The member must inform the client of the purposes, goals, techniques, rules of procedure, and limitations that may affect the relationship at or before the time that the counseling relationship is entered. When working with minors or persons who are unable to give consent, the member protects these clients' best interests.

9. In view of common misconceptions related to the perceived inherent validity of computer generated data and narrative reports, the member must ensure that the client is provided with information as part of the counseling relationship that adequately explains the limitations of computer technology.

10. The member must screen prospective group participants, especially when the emphasis is on self-understanding and growth through self-disclosure. The member must maintain an awareness of the group participants' compatibility throughout the life of the group.

11. The member may choose to consult with any other professionally competent person about a client. In choosing a consultant, the member must avoid placing the consultant in a conflict of interest situation that would preclude the consultant's being a proper party to the member's efforts to help the client.

12. If the member determines an inability to be of professional assistance to the client, the member must either avoid initiating the counseling relationship

or immediately terminate that relationship. In either event, the member must suggest appropriate alternatives. (The member must be knowledgeable about referral resources so that a satisfactory referral can be initiated.) In the event the client declines the suggested referral, the member is not obligated to continue the relationship.

13. When the member has other relationships, particularly of an administrative, supervisory, and/or evaluative nature with an individual seeking counseling services, the member must not serve as the counselor but should refer the individual to another professional. Only in instances where such an alternative is unavailable and where the individual's situation warrants counseling intervention should the member enter into and/or maintain a counseling relationship. Dual relationships with clients that might impair the member's objectivity and professional judgment (e.g., as with close friends or relatives) must be avoided and/or the counseling relationship terminated through referral to other competent professional.

14. The member will avoid any type of sexual intimacies with clients. Sexual relationships with clients are unethical.

15. All experimental methods of treatment must be clearly indicated to prospective recipients, and safety precautions are to be adhered to by the member.

16. When computer applications are used as a component of counseling services, the member must ensure that: (a) the client is intellectually, emotionally, and physically capable of using the computer application; (b) the computer application is appropriate for the needs of the client; (c) the client understands the purpose and operation of the computer application; and (d) a follow-up of client use of a computer application is provided to both correct possible problems (misconceptions or inappropriate use) and assess subsequent needs.

17. When the member is engaged in short-term group treatment/training programs (e.g., marathons and other encounter-type or growth groups), the member ensures that there is professional assistance available during and following the group experience.

18. Should the member be engaged in a work setting that calls for any variation from the above statements, the member is obligated to consult with other professionals whenever possible to consider justifiable alternatives.

19. The member must ensure that members of various ethnic, racial, religious, disability, and socioeconomic groups have equal access to computer applications used to support counseling services and that the content of available computer applications does not discriminate against the groups described above.

20. When computer applications are developed by the member for use by the general public as self-help/stand-alone computer software, the member must ensure that: (a) self-help computer applications are designed from the beginning to function in a stand-alone manner, as opposed to modifying software that was originally designed to require support from a counselor; (b) self-help computer applications will include within the program statements regarding intended user

outcomes, suggestions for using the software, a description of the conditions under which self-help computer applications might not be appropriate, and a description of when and how counseling services might be beneficial; and (c) the manual for such applications will include the qualifications of the developer, the development process, validation data, and operating procedures.

Section C: Measurement and Evaluation

The primary purpose of educational and psychological testing is to provide descriptive measures that are objective and interpretable in either comparative or absolute terms. The member must recognize the need to interpret the statements that follow as applying to the whole range of appraisal techniques including test and nontest data. Test results constitute only one of a variety of pertinent sources of information for personnel, guidance, and counseling decisions.

1. The member must provide specific orientation or information to the examinee(s) prior to and following the test administration so that the results of testing may be placed in proper perspective with other relevant factors. In so doing, the member must recognize the effects of socioeconomic, ethnic, and cultural factors on test scores. It is the member's professional responsibility to use additional unvalidated information carefully in modifying interpretation of the test results.

2. In selecting tests for use in a given situation or with a particular client, the member must consider carefully the specific validity, reliability, and appropriateness of the test(s). General validity, reliability, and related issues may be questioned legally as well as ethically when tests are used for vocational and educational selection, placement, or counseling.

3. When making any statements to the public about tests and testing, the member must give accurate information and avoid false claims or misconceptions. Special efforts are often required to avoid unwarranted connotations of such terms as IQ and grade equivalent scores.

4. Different tests demand different levels of competence for administration, scoring, and interpretation. Members must recognize the limits of their competence and perform only those functions for which they are prepared. In particular, members using computer-based test interpretations must be trained in the construct being measured and the specific instrument being used prior to using this type of computer application.

5. In situations where a computer is used for test administration and scoring, the member is responsible for ensuring that administration and scoring programs function properly to provide clients with accurate test results.

6. Tests must be administered under the same conditions that were established in their standardization. When tests are not administered under standard conditions or when unusual behavior or irregularities occur during the testing session, those conditions must be noted and the results designated as invalid or of questionable validity. Unsupervised or inadequately supervised test-taking,

such as the use of tests through the mails, is considered unethical. On the other hand, the use of instruments that are so designed or standardized to be self-administered and self-scored, such as interest inventories, is to be encouraged.

7. The meaningfulness of test results used in personnel, guidance, and counseling functions generally depends on the examinees unfamiliarity with the specific items on the test. Any prior coaching or dissemination of the test materials can invalidate test results. Therefore, test security is one of the professional obligations of the member. Conditions that produce most favorable test results must be made known to the examinee.

8. The purpose of testing and the explicit use of the results must be made known to the examinee prior to testing. The counselor must ensure that instrument limitations are not exceeded and that periodic review and/or retesting are made to prevent client stereotyping.

9. The examinee's welfare and explicit prior understanding must be the criteria for determining the recipients of the test results. The member must see that specific interpretation accompanies any release of individual or group test data. The interpretation of test data must be related to the examinee's particular concerns.

10. Members responsible for making decisions based on test results have an understanding of educational and psychological measurement, validation criteria, and test research.

11. The member must be cautious when interpreting the results of research instruments possessing insufficient technical data. The specific purposes for the use of such instruments must be stated explicitly to examinees.

12. The member must proceed with caution when attempting to evaluate and interpret the performance of minority group members or other persons who are not represented in the norm group on which the instrument was standardized.

13. When computer-based test interpretations are developed by the member to support the assessment process, the member must ensure that the validity of such interpretations is established prior to the commercial distribution of such a computer application.

14. The member recognizes that test results may become obsolete. The member will avoid and prevent the misuse of obsolete test results.

15. The member must guard against the appropriation, reproduction, or modification of published tests or parts thereof without acknowledgment and permission from the previous publisher.

16. Regarding the preparation, publication, and distribution of tests, reference should be made to:

   a. "Standards for Educational and Psychological Testing," revised edition, 1985, published by the American Psychological Association on behalf of itself, the American Educational Research Association, and the National Council on Measurement in Education.
   b. "The Responsible Use of Tests: A Position Paper of AMEG, APGA, and NCME," *Measurement and Evaluation in Guidance*, 1972, 5, 385-388.

    c. "Responsibilities of Users of Standardized Tests," APGA, *Guidepost*, October 5, 1978, pp. 5-8.

Section D: Research and Publication

1. Guidelines on research with human subjects shall be adhered to, such as:

    a. *Ethical Principles in the Conduct of Research with Human Participants*, Washington, D.C.: American Psychological Association, Inc., 1982.

    b. Code of Federal Regulation, Title 45, Subtitle A, Part 46, as currently issued.

    c. *Ethical Principles of Psychologists*, American Psychological Association, Principle #9: Research with Human Participants.

    d. Family Educational Rights and Privacy Act (the Buckley Amendment).

    e. Current federal regulations and various state rights privacy acts.

2. In planning any research activity dealing with human subjects, the member must be aware of and responsive to all pertinent ethical principles and ensure that the research problem, design, and execution are in full compliance with them.

3. Responsibility for ethical research practice lies with the principal researcher, while others involved in the research activities share ethical obligation and full responsibility for their own actions.

4. In research with human subjects, researchers are responsible for the subjects' welfare throughout the experiment, and they must take all reasonable precautions to avoid causing injurious psychological, physical, or social effects on their subjects.

5. All research subjects must be informed of the purpose of the study except when withholding information or providing misinformation to them is essential to the investigation. In such research the member must be responsible for corrective action as soon as possible following completion of the research.

6. Participation in research must be voluntary. Involuntary participation is appropriate only when it can be demonstrated that participation will have no harmful effects on subjects and is essential to the investigation.

7. When reporting research results, explicit mention must be made of all variables and conditions known to the investigator that might affect the outcome of the investigation or the interpretation of the data.

8. The member must be responsible for conducting and reporting investigations in a manner that minimizes the possibility that results will be misleading.

9. The member has an obligation to make available sufficient original research data to qualified others who may wish to replicate the study.

10. When supplying data, aiding in the research of another person, reporting research results, or making original data available, due care must be taken to disguise the identity of the subjects in the absence of specific authorization from such subjects to do otherwise.

11. When conducting and reporting research, the member must be familiar with and give recognition to previous work on the topic, as well as to observe all copyright laws and follow the principles of giving full credit to all to whom credit is due.

12. The member must give due credit through joint authorship, acknowledgment, footnote statements, or other appropriate means to those who have contributed significantly to the research and/or publication, in accordance with such contributions.

13. The member must communicate to other members the results of any research judged to be of professional or scientific value. Results reflecting unfavorably on institutions, programs, services, or vested interests must not be withheld for such reasons.

14. If members agree to cooperate with another individual in research and/or publication, they incur an obligation to cooperate as promised in terms of punctuality of performance and with full regard to the completeness and accuracy of the information required.

15. Ethical practice requires that authors not submit the same manuscript or one essentially similar in content for simultaneous publication consideration by two or more journals. In addition, manuscripts published in whole or in substantial part in another journal or published work should not be submitted for publication without acknowledgment and permission from the previous publication.

Section E: Consulting

Consultation refers to a voluntary relationship between a professional helper and help-needing individual, group, or social unit in which the consultant is providing help to the client(s) in defining and solving a work-related problem with a client or client system.

1. The member acting as consultant must have a high degree of self-awareness of his/her own values, knowledge, skills, limitations, and needs in entering a helping relationship that involves human and/or organizational change and that the focus of the relationship be on the issues to be resolved and not on the person(s) presenting the problem.

2. There must be understanding and agreement between member and client for the problem definition, change of goals, and prediction of consequences of interventions selected.

3. The member must be reasonably certain that she/he or the organization represented has the necessary competencies and resources for giving the kind of help that is needed now or may be needed later and that appropriate referral resources are available to the consultant.

4. The consulting relationship must be one in which client adaptability and growth toward self-direction are encouraged and cultivated. The member must

maintain this role consistently and not become a decision maker for the client or create a future dependency on the consultant.

5. When announcing consultant availability for services, the member conscientiously adheres to the Association's Ethical Standards.

6. The member must refuse a private fee or other remuneration for consultation with persons who are entitled to these services through the member's employing institution or agency. The policies of a particular agency may make explicit provisions for private practice with agency clients by members of its staff. In such instances, the client must be apprised of other options open to them should they seek private counseling services.

Section F: Private Practice

1. The member should assist the profession by facilitating the availability of counseling services in private as well as public settings.

2. In advertising services as a private practitioner, the member must advertise the services in a manner that accurately informs the public of professional services, expertise, and techniques of counseling available. A member who assumes an executive leadership role in the organization shall not permit his/her name to be used in professional notices during periods when he/she is not actively engaged in the private practice of counseling.

3. The member may list the following: highest relevant degree, type and level of certification and/or license, address, telephone number, office hours, type and/or description of services, and other relevant information. Such information must not contain false, inaccurate, misleading, partial, out-of-context, or deceptive material or statements.

4. Members do not present their affiliation with any organization in such a way that would imply inaccurate sponsorship or certification by that organization.

5. Members may join in partnership/corporation with other members and/or other professionals provided that each member of the partnership or corporation makes clear the separate specialties by name in compliance with the regulations of the locality.

6. A member has an obligation to withdraw from a counseling relationship if it is believed that employment will result in violation of the Ethical Standards. If the mental or physical condition of the member renders it difficult to carry out an effective professional relationship or if the member is discharged by the client because the counseling relationship is no longer productive for the client, then the member is obligated to terminate the counseling relationship.

7. A member must adhere to the regulations for private practice of the locality where the services are offered.

8. It is unethical to use one's institutional affiliation to recruit clients for one's private practice.

Section G: Personnel Administration

It is recognized that most members are employed in public or quasi-public institutions. The functioning of a member within an institution must contribute to the goals of the institution and vice versa if either is to accomplish their respective goals or objectives. It is therefore essential that the member and the institution function in ways to: (a) make the institution's goals explicit and public; (b) make the member's contribution to institutional goals specific; and (c) foster mutual accountability for goal achievement.

To accomplish these objectives, it is recognized that the member and the employer must share responsibilities in the formulation and implementation of personnel policies.

1. Members must define and describe the parameters and levels of their professional competency.

2. Members must establish interpersonal relations and working agreements with supervisors and subordinates regarding counseling or clinical relationships, confidentiality, distinction between public and private material, maintenance and dissemination of recorded information, work load, and accountability. Working agreements in each instance must be specified and made known to those concerned.

3. Members must alert their employers to conditions that may be potentially disruptive or damaging.

4. Members must inform employers of conditions that may limit their effectiveness.

5. Members must submit regularly to professional review and evaluation.

6. Members must be responsible for inservice development of self and/or staff.

7. Members must inform their staff of goals and programs.

8. Members must provide personnel practices that guarantee and enhance the rights and welfare of each recipient of their service.

9. Members must select competent persons and assign responsibilities compatible with their skills and experiences.

10. The member, at the onset of a counseling relationship, will inform the client of the member's intended use of supervisors regarding the disclosure of information concerning this case. The member will clearly inform the client of the limits of confidentiality in the relationship.

11. Members, as either employers or employees, do not engage in or condone practices that are inhumane, illegal, or unjustifiable (such as considerations based on sex, handicap, age, race) in hiring, promotion, or training.

Section H: Preparation Standards

Members who are responsible for training others must be guided by the preparation standards of the Association and relevant Division(s). The member who functions in the capacity of trainer assumes unique ethical responsibilities that frequently go beyond that of the member who does not function in a training capacity. These ethical responsibilities are outlined as follows:

1. Members must orient students to program expectations, basic skills development, and employment prospects prior to admission to the program.

2. Members in charge of learning experiences must establish programs that integrate academic study and supervised practice.

3. Members must establish a program directed toward developing students' skills, knowledge, and self-understanding, stated whenever possible in competency or performance terms.

4. Members must identify the levels of competencies of their students in compliance with relevant Division standards. These competencies must accommodate the paraprofessional as well as the professional.

5. Members, through continual student evaluation and appraisal, must be aware of the personal limitations of the learner that might impede future performance. The instructor must not only assist the learner in securing remedial assistance but also screen from the program those individuals who are unable to provide competent services.

6. Members must provide a program that includes training in research commensurate with levels of role functioning. Paraprofessional and technician-level personnel must be trained as consumers of research. In addition, personnel must learn how to evaluate their own and their program's effectiveness. Graduate training, especially at the doctoral level, would include preparation for original research by the member.

7. Members must make students aware of the ethical responsibilities and standards of the profession.

8. Preparatory programs must encourage students to value the ideals of service to individuals and to society. In this regard, direct financial remuneration or lack thereof must not influence the quality of service rendered. Monetary considerations must not be allowed to overshadow professional and humanitarian needs.

9. Members responsible for educational programs must be skilled as teachers and practitioners.

10. Members must present thoroughly varied, theoretical positions so that students may make comparisons and have the opportunity to select a position.

11. Members must develop clear policies within their educational institutions regarding field placement and the roles of the student and the instructor in such placement.

12. Members must ensure that forms of learning focusing on self-understanding or growth are voluntary, or if required as part of the educational program, are made known to prospective students prior to entering the program. When the educational program offers a growth experience with an emphasis on self-disclosure or other relatively intimate or personal involvement, the member must

have no administrative, supervisory, or evaluating authority regarding the participant.

13. The member will at all times provide students with clear and equally acceptable alternatives for self-understanding or growth experiences. The member will assure students that they have a right to accept these alternatives without prejudice or penalty.

14. Members must conduct an educational program in keeping with the current relevant guidelines of the Association.

... Principles of Medical Ethics, with Annotations Especially Applicable to Psychiatry, *American Psychiatric Association*

Following are the AMA Principles of Medical Ethics printed separately, along with annotations especially applicable to psychiatry. (Statements in italics are taken directly from the American Medical Association's Principles of Medical Ethics.)

Preamble

The medical profession has long subscribed to a body of ethical statements developed primarily for the benefit of the patient. As a member of this profession, a physician must recognize responsibility not only to patients, but also to society, to other health professionals, and to self. The following Principles, adopted by the American Medical Association, are not laws, but standards of conduct which define the essentials of honorable behavior for the physician.

Section 1

A physician shall be dedicated to providing competent medical service with compassion and respect for human dignity.

SOURCE: *The Principles of Medical Ethics, with Annotations Especially Applicable to Psychiatry*, by the American Psychiatric Association. Copyright 1986 by the American Psychiatric Association. Reprinted by permission.

1. The patient may place his/her trust in his/her psychiatrist knowing that the psychiatrist's ethics and professional responsibilities preclude him/her gratifying his/her own needs by exploiting the patient. This becomes particularly important because of the essentially private, highly personal, and sometimes intensely emotional nature of the relationship established with the psychiatrist.

2. A psychiatrist should not be a party to any type of policy that excludes, segregates, or demeans the dignity of any patient because of ethic origin, race, sex, creed, age, socioeconomic status, or sexual orientation.

3. In accord with the requirements of law and accepted medical practice, it is ethical for a physician to submit his/her work to peer review and to the ultimate authority of the medical staff executive body and the hospital administration and its governing body. In case of dispute, the ethical psychiatrist has the following steps available:

a. Seek appeal from the medical staff decision to a joint conference committee, including members of the medical staff executive committee and the executive committee of the governing board. At this appeal, the ethical psychiatrist could request that outside opinions be considered.

b. Appeal to the governing body itself.

c. Appeal to state agencies regulating licensure of hospitals if, in the particular state, they concern themselves with matters of professional competency and quality of care.

d. Attempt to educate colleagues through development of research projects and data and presentations at professional meetings and in professional journals.

e. Seek redress in local courts, perhaps through an enjoining injunction against the governing body.

f. Public education as carried out by an ethical psychiatrist would not utilize appeals based solely upon emotion, but would be presented in a professional way and without any potential exploitation of patients through testimonials.

4. A psychiatrist should not be a participant in a legally authorized execution.

Section 2

A physician shall deal honestly with patients and colleagues, and strive to expose those physicians deficient in character or competence, or who engage in fraud or deception.

1. The requirement that the physician conduct himself with propriety in his/her profession and in all the actions of his/her life is especially important in the case of the psychiatrist because the patient tends to model his/her behavior after that of his/her therapist by identification. Further, the necessary intensity of the therapeutic relationship may tend to activate sexual and other needs and fantasies on the part of both patient and therapist, while weakening the objectivity necessary for control. Sexual activity with a patient is unethical.

2. The psychiatrist should diligently guard against exploiting information furnished by the patient and should not use the unique position of power afforded him/her by the psychotherapeutic situation to influence the patient in any way not directly relevant to the treatment goals.

3. A psychiatrist who regularly practices outside his/her area of professional competence should be considered unethical. Determination of professional competence should be made by peer review boards or other appropriate bodies.

4. Special consideration should be given to those psychiatrists who, because of mental illness, jeopardize the welfare of their patients and their own reputations and practices. It is ethical, even encouraged, for another psychiatrist to intercede in such situations.

5. Psychiatric services, like all medical services, are dispensed in the context of a contractual arrangement between the patient and the treating physician. The provisions of the contractual arrangement, which are binding on the physician as well as on the patient, should be explicitly established.

6. It is ethical for the psychiatrist to make a charge for a missed appointment when this falls within the terms of the specific contractual agreement with the patient. Charging for a missed appointment or for one not canceled 24 hours in advance need not, in itself, be considered unethical if a patient is fully advised that the physician will make such a charge. The practice, however, should be resorted to infrequently and always with the utmost consideration of the patient and his/her circumstances.

7. An arrangement in which a psychiatrist provides supervision or administration to other physicians or nonmedical persons for a percentage of their fees or gross income is not acceptable; this would constitute fee-splitting. In a team of practitioners, or a multidisciplinary team, it is ethical for the psychiatrist to receive income for administration, research, education, or consultation. This should be based upon a mutually agreed upon and set fee or salary, open to renegotiation when a change in the time demand occurs. (See also Section 5, Annotations 2, 3, and 4.)

8. When a member has been found to have behaved unethically by the American Psychiatric Association or one of its constituent district branches, there should not be automatic reporting to the local authorities responsible for medical licensure, but the decision to report should be decided upon the merits of the case.

Section 3

A physician shall respect the law and also recognize a responsibility to seek changes in those requirements which are contrary to the best interests of the patient.

1. It would seem self-evident that a psychiatrist who is a lawbreaker might be ethically unsuited to practice his/her profession. When such illegal activities

bear directly upon his/her practice, this would obviously be the case. However, in other instances, illegal activities such as those concerning the right to protest social injustices might not bear on either the image of the psychiatrist or the ability of the specific psychiatrist to treat his/her patient ethically and well. While no committee or board could offer prior assurance that any illegal activity would not be considered unethical, it is conceivable that an individual could violate a law without being guilty of professionally unethical behavior. Physicians lose no right of citizenship on entry into the profession of medicine.

2. Where not specifically prohibited by local laws governing medical practice, the practice of acupuncture by a psychiatrist is not unethical per se. The psychiatrist should have professional competence in the use of acupuncture. Or, if he/she is supervising the use of acupuncture by nonmedical individuals, he/she should provide proper medical supervision. (See also Section 5, Annotations 3 and 4.)

Section 4

A physician shall respect the rights of patients, of colleagues, and of other health professionals, and shall safeguard patient confidences within the constraints of the law.

1. Psychiatric records, including even the identification of a person as a patient, must be protected with extreme care. Confidentiality is essential to psychiatric treatment. This is based in part on the special nature of psychiatric therapy as well as on the traditional ethical relationship between physician and patient. Growing concern regarding the civil rights of patients and the possible adverse effects of computerization, duplication equipment, and data banks makes the dissemination of confidential information an increasing hazard. Because of the sensitive and private nature of the information with which the psychiatrist deals, he/she must be circumspect in the information that he/she chooses to disclose to others about a patient. The welfare of the patient must be a continuing consideration.

2. A psychiatrist may release confidential information only with the authorization of the patient or under proper legal compulsion. The continuing duty of the psychiatrist to protect the patient includes fully apprising him/her of the connotations of waiving the privilege of privacy. This may become an issue when the patient is being investigated by a government agency, is applying for a position, or is involved in legal action. The same principles apply to the release of information concerning treatment to medical departments of government agencies, business organizations, labor unions, and insurance companies. Information gained in confidence about patients seen in student health services should not be released without the student's explicit permission.

3. Clinical and other materials used in teaching and writing must be adequately disguised in order to preserve the anonymity of the individuals involved.

4. The ethical responsibility of maintaining confidentiality holds equally for the consultations in which the patient may not have been present and in which the consultee was not a physician. In such instances, the physician consultant should alert the consultee to his/her duty of confidentiality.

5. Ethically the psychiatrist may disclose only that information which is relevant to a given situation. He/she should avoid offering speculation as fact. Sensitive information such as an individual's sexual orientation or fantasy material is usually considered unnecessary.

6. Psychiatrists are often asked to examine individuals for security purposes, to determine suitability for various jobs, and to determine legal competence. The psychiatrist must fully describe the nature and purpose and lack of confidentiality of the examination to the examinee at the beginning of the examination.

7. Careful judgment must be exercised by the psychiatrist in order to include, when appropriate, the parents or guardian in the treatment of a minor. At the same time the psychiatrist must assure the minor proper confidentiality.

8. Psychiatrists at times may find it necessary, in order to protect the patient or the community from imminent danger, to reveal confidential information disclosed by the patient.

9. When the psychiatrist is ordered by the court to reveal the confidences entrusted to him/her by patients, he/she may comply or he/she may ethically hold the right to dissent within the framework of the law. When the psychiatrist is in doubt, the right of the patient to confidentiality and, by extension, to unimpaired treatment should be given priority. The psychiatrist should reserve the right to raise the question of adequate need for disclosure. In the event that the necessity for legal disclosure is demonstrated by the court, the psychiatrist may request the right to disclosure of only that information which is relevant to the legal question at hand.

10. With regard for the person's dignity and privacy and with truly informed consent, it is ethical to present a patient to a scientific gathering, if the confidentiality of the presentation is understood and accepted by the audience.

11. It is ethical to present a patient or former patient to a public gathering or to the news media only if that patient is fully informed of enduring loss of confidentiality, is competent, and consents in writing without coercion.

12. When involved in funded research, the ethical psychiatrist will advise human subjects of the funding source, retain his/her freedom to reveal data and results, and follow all appropriate and current guidelines relative to human subject protection.

13. Ethical considerations in medical practice preclude the psychiatric evaluation of any adult charged with criminal acts prior to access to, or availability of, legal counsel. The only exception is the rendering of care to the person for the sole purpose of medical treatment.

Section 5

A physician shall continue to study, apply, and advance scientific knowledge, make relevant information available to patients, colleagues, and the public, obtain consultation, and use the talents of other health professionals when indicated.

1. Psychiatrists are responsible for their own continuing education and should be mindful of the fact that theirs must be a lifetime of learning.

2. In the practice of his/her specialty, the psychiatrist consults associates, collaborates, or integrates his/her work with that of many professionals, including psychologists, psychometricians, social workers, alcoholism counselors, marriage counselors, public health nurses, etc. Furthermore, the nature of modern psychiatric practice extends his/her contacts to such people as teachers, juvenile and adult probation officers, attorneys, welfare workers, agency volunteers, and neighborhood aids. In referring patients for treatment, counseling, or rehabilitation to any of these practitioners, the psychiatrist should ensure that the allied professional or paraprofessional with whom he/she is dealing is a recognized member of his/her own discipline and is competent to carry out the therapeutic task required. The psychiatrist should have the same attitude toward members of the medical profession to whom he/she refers patients. Whenever he/she has reason to doubt the training, skill, or ethical qualifications of the allied professional, the psychiatrist should not refer cases to him/her.

3. When the psychiatrist assumes a collaborative or supervisory role with another mental health worker, he/she must extend sufficient time to assure that proper care is given. It is contrary to the interests of the patient and to patient care if he/she allows himself/herself to be used as a [sic] figurehead.

4. In relationships between psychiatrists and practicing licensed psychologists, the physician should not delegate to the psychologist or, in fact, to any nonmedical person any matter requiring the exercise of professional medical judgment.

5. The psychiatrist should agree to the request of a patient for consultation or to such a request from the family of an incompetent or minor patient. The psychiatrist may suggest possible consultants, but the patient or family should be given free choice of the consultant. If the psychiatrist disapproves of the professional qualifications of the consultant or if there is a difference of opinion that the primary therapist cannot resolve, he/she may, after suitable notice, withdraw from the case. If this disagreement occurs within an institution or agency framework, the difference should be resolved by the mediation or arbitration of higher professional authority within the institution or agency.

Section 6

A physician shall, in the provision of appropriate patient care, except in emergencies, be free to choose whom to serve, with whom to associate, and the environment in which to provide medical services.

1. Physicians generally agree that the doctor-patient relationship is such a vital factor in effective treatment of the patient that preservation of optimal conditions for development of a sound working relationship between a doctor and his/her patient should take precedence over all other considerations. Professional courtesy may lead to poor psychiatric care for physicians and their families because of embarrassment over the lack of a complete give-and-take contract.

2. An ethical psychiatrist may refuse to provide psychiatric treatment to a person who, in the psychiatrist's opinion, cannot be diagnosed as having a mental illness amenable to psychiatric treatment.

Section 7

A physician shall recognize a responsibility to participate in activities contributing to an improved community.

1. Psychiatrists should foster the cooperation of those legitimately concerned with the medical, psychological, social, and legal aspects of mental health and illness. Psychiatrists are encouraged to serve society by advising and consulting with the executive, legislative, and judiciary branches of the government. A psychiatrist should clarify whether he/she speaks as an individual or as a representative of an organization. Furthermore, psychiatrists should avoid cloaking their public statements with the authority of the profession (e.g., "Psychiatrists know that . . .").

2. Psychiatrists may interpret and share with the public their expertise in the various psychosocial issues that may affect mental health and illness. Psychiatrists should always be mindful of their separate roles as dedicated citizens and as experts in psychological medicine.

3. On occasion psychiatrists are asked for an opinion about an individual who is in the light of public attention, or who has disclosed information about himself/herself through public media. It is unethical for a psychiatrist to offer a professional opinion unless he/she has conducted an examination and has been granted proper authorization for such a statement.

4. The psychiatrist may permit his/her certification to be used for the involuntary treatment of any person only following his/her personal examination of that person. To do so, he/she must find that the person, because of mental illness, cannot form a judgment as to what is in his/her own best interests and that, without such treatment, substantial impairment is likely to occur to the person or others.

Ethical Principles of Psychologists
(Ammended June 2, 1989)

Preamble

Psychologists respect the dignity and worth of the individual and strive for the preservation and protection of fundamental human rights. They are committed to increasing knowledge of human behavior and of people's understanding of themselves and others and to the utilization of such knowledge for the promotion of human welfare. While pursuing these objectives, they make every effort to protect the welfare of those who seek their services and of the research participants that may be the objects of study. They use their skills only for purposes consistent with these values and do not knowingly permit their misuse by others. While demanding for themselves freedom of inquiry and communication, psychologists accept the responsibility this freedom requires: competence, objectivity in the application of skills, and concern for the best interests of clients, colleagues, students, research participants, and society. In the pursuit of these ideals, psychologists subscribe to principles in the following areas: 1. Responsibility, 2. Competence, 3. Moral and Legal Standards, 4. Public Statements, 5. Confidentiality, 6. Welfare of the Consumer, 7. Professional Relationships, 8. Assessment Techniques, 9. Research with Human Participants, and 10. Care and Use of Animals.

Acceptance of membership in the American Psychological Association commits the member to adherence to these principles.

SOURCE: American Psychological Association. (1990). Ethical Principles of Psychologists (amended June 2, 1989). *American Psychologist, 45,* 390-395. Reprinted by permission of the publisher.

This version of the *Ethical Principles of Psychologists* was adopted by the American Psychological Association's Board of Directors on June 2, 1989. On that date, the Board of Directors resinded several sections of the Ethical Principles that had been adopted by the APA Council of Representatives on

Psychologists cooperate with duly constituted committees of the American Psychological Association, in particular, the Committee on Scientific and Professional Ethics and Conduct, by responding to inquiries promptly and completely. Members also respond promptly and completely to inquiries from duly constituted state association ethics committees and professional standards review committees.

Principle 1: Responsibility

In providing services, psychologists maintain the highest standards of their profession. They accept responsibility for the consequences of their acts and make every effort to ensure that their services are used appropriately.

a. As scientists, psychologists accept responsibility for the selection of their research topics and the methods used in investigation, analysis, and reporting. They plan their research in ways to minimize the possibility that their findings will be misleading. They provide thorough discussion of the limitations of their data, especially where their work touches on social policy or might be construed to the detriment of persons in specific age, sex, ethnic, socioeconomic, or other social groups. In publishing reports of their work, they never suppress disconfirming data, and they acknowledge the existence of alternative hypotheses and explanations of their findings. Psychologists take credit only for work they have actually done.

b. Psychologists clarify in advance with all appropriate persons and agencies the expectations for sharing and utilizing research data. They avoid relationships

---

January 24, 1981. Inquires concerning the substance or interpretation of the *Ethical Principles of Psychologists* should be addressed to the Administrative Director, Office of Ethics, American Psychological Association, 1200 Seventeenth Street, NW., Washington, DC 20036.

These *Ethical Principles* apply to psychologists, to students of psychology, and to others who do work of a psychological nature under the supervision of a psychologist. They are also intended for the guidance of nonmembers of the Association who are engaged in psychological research or practice.

The Ethical Principles have previously been published as follows:

American Psychological Association. (1953). *Ethical Standards of Psychologists,* Washington, DC.
American Psychological Association. (1958). Standards of ethical behavior for psychologists. *American Psychologist, 13,* 268-271.
American Psychological Association. (1959). Ethical standards of psychologists. *American Psychologist, 14,* 279-282.
American Psychological Association. (1963). Ethical standards of psychologists. *American Psychologist, 18,* 56-60.
American Psychological Association. (1968). Ethical standards of psychologists. *American Psychologist, 23,* 357-361.
American Psychological Association. (1977, March). Ethical standards of psychologists. *The APA Monitor,* pp. 22-23.
American Psychological Association. (1979). *Ethical Standards of Psychologists.* Washington, DC: Author.
American Psychological Association. (1981). Ethical principles of psychologists. *American Psychologists, 36,* 633-638.

Request copies of the *Ethical Principles of Psychologists* from the APA Order Department, P.O. Box 2710, Hyattsville, MD 20784; or phone (703) 247-7705.

that may limit their objectivity or create a conflict of interest. Interference with the milieu in which data are collected is kept to a minimum.

c. Psychologists have the responsibility to attempt to prevent distortion, misuse, or suppression of psychological findings by the institution or agency of which they are employees.

d. As members of governmental or other organizational bodies, psychologists remain accountable as individuals to the highest standards of their profession.

e. As teachers, psychologists recognize their primary obligation to help others acquire knowledge and skill. They maintain high standards of scholarship by presenting psychological information objectively, fully, and accurately.

f. As practitioners, psychologists know that they bear a heavy social responsibility because their recommendations and professional actions may alter the lives of others. They are alert to personal, social, organizational, financial, or political situations and pressures that might lead to misuse of their influence.

Principle 2: Competence

The maintenance of high standards of competence is a responsibility shared by all psychologists in the interest of the public and the profession as a whole. Psychologists recognize the boundaries of their competence and the limitations of their techniques. They only provide services and only use techniques for which they are qualified by training and experience. In those areas in which recognized standards do not yet exist, psychologists take whatever precautions are necessary to protect the welfare of their clients. They maintain knowledge of current scientific and professional information related to the services they render.

a. Psychologists accurately represent their competence, education, training, and experience. They claim as evidence of educational qualifications only those degrees obtained from institutions acceptable under the Bylaws and Rules of Council of the American Psychological Association.

b. As teachers, psychologists perform their duties on the basis of careful preparation so that their instruction is accurate, current, and scholarly.

c. Psychologists recognize the need for continuing education and are open to new procedures and changes in expectations and values over time.

d. Psychologists recognize differences among people, such as those that may be associated with age, sex, socioeconomic, and ethnic backgrounds. When necessary, they obtain training, experience, or counsel to assure competent service or research relating to such persons.

e. Psychologists responsible for decisions involving individuals or policies based on test results have an understanding of psychological or educational measurement, validation problems, and test research.

f. Psychologists recognize that personal problems and conflicts may interfere with professional effectiveness. Accordingly, they refrain from undertaking any activity in which their personal problems are likely to lead to inadequate performance or harm to a client, colleague, student, or research participant. If engaged in such activity when they become aware of their personal problems, they seek competent professional assistance to determine whether they should suspend, terminate, or limit the scope of their professional and/or scientific activities.

Principle 3: Moral and Legal Standards

Psychologists' moral and ethical standards of behavior are a personal matter to the same degree as they are for any other citizen, except as these may compromise the fulfillment of their professional responsibilities or reduce the public trust in psychology and psychologists. Regarding their own behavior, psychologists are sensitive to prevailing community standards and to the possible impact that conformity to or deviation from these standards may have upon the quality of their performance as psychologists. Psychologists are also aware of the possible impact of their public behavior upon the ability of colleagues to perform their professional duties.

a. As teachers, psychologists are aware of the fact that their personal values may affect the selection and presentation of instructional materials. When dealing with topics that may give offense, they recognize and respect the diverse attitudes that students may have toward such materials.

b. As employees or employers, psychologists do not engage in or condone practices that are inhumane or that result in illegal or unjustifiable actions. Such practices include, but are not limited to, those based on considerations of race, handicap, age, gender, sexual preference, religion, or national origin in hiring, promotion, or training.

c. In their professional roles, psychologists avoid any action that will violate or diminish the legal and civil rights of clients or of others who may be affected by their actions.

d. As practitioners and researchers, psychologists act in accord with Association standards and guidelines related to practice and to the conduct of research with human beings and animals. In the ordinary course of events, psychologists adhere to relevant governmental law and institutional regulations. When federal, state, provincial, organizational, or institutional laws, regulations, or practices are in conflict with Association standards and guidelines, psychologists make known their commitment to Association standards and guidelines and, wherever possible, work toward a resolution of the conflict. Both practitioners and researchers are concerned with the development of such legal and quasi-legal regulations as best serve the public interest, and they work toward changing existing regulations that are not beneficial to the public interest.

Principle 4: Public Statements

Public statements, announcements of services, advertising, and promotional activities of psychologists serve the purpose of helping the public make informed judgments and choices. Psychologists represent accurately and objectively their professional qualifications, affiliations, and functions, as well as those of the institutions or organizations with which they or the statements may be associated. In public statements providing psychological information or professional opinions or providing information about the availability of psychological products, publications, and services, psychologists base their statements on scientifically acceptable psychological findings and techniques with full recognition of the limits and uncertainties of such evidence.

a. When announcing or advertising professional services, psychologists may list the following information to describe the provider and services provided: name, highest relevant academic degree earned from a regionally accredited institution, date, type, and level of certification or licensure, diplomate status, APA membership status, address, telephone number, office hours, a brief listing of the type of psychological services offered, an appropriate presentation of fee information, foreign languages spoken, and policy with regard to third-party payments. Additional relevant or important consumer information may be included if not prohibited by other sections of these Ethical Principles.

b. In announcing or advertising the availability of psychological products, publications, or services, psychologists do not present their affiliation with any organization in a manner that falsely implies sponsorship or certification by that organization. In particular and for example, psychologists do not state APA membership or fellow status in a way to suggest that such status implies specialized professional competence or qualifications. Public statements include, but are not limited to, communication by means of periodical, book, list, directory, television, radio, or motion picture. They do not contain (i) a false, fraudulent, misleading, deceptive, or unfair statement; (ii) a misinterpretation of fact or a statement likely to mislead or deceive because in context it makes only a partial disclosure of relevant facts; (iii) a statement intended or likely to create false or unjustified expectations of favorable results.

c. Psychologists do not compensate or give anything of value to a representative of the press, radio, television, or other communication medium in anticipation of or in return for professional publicity in a news item. A paid advertisement must be identified as such, unless it is apparent from the context that it is a paid advertisement. If communicated to the public by use of radio or television, an advertisement is prerecorded and approved for broadcast by the psychologist, and a recording of the actual transmission is retained by the psychologist.

d. Announcements or advertisements of "personal growth groups," clinics, or agencies give a clear statement of purpose and a clear description of the experiences to be provided. The education, training, and experience of the staff members are appropriately specified.

e. Psychologists associated with the development or promotion of psychological devices, books, or other products offered for commercial sale make reasonable efforts to ensure that announcements and advertisements are presented in a professional, scientifically acceptable, and factually informative manner.

f. Psychologists do not participate for personal gain in commercial announcements or advertisements recommending to the public the purchase or use of proprietary or single-source products or services when that participation is based solely upon their identification as psychologists.

G. Psychologists present the science of psychology and offer their services, products, and publications fairly and accurately, avoiding misrepresentation through sensationalism, exaggeration, or superficiality. Psychologists are guided by the primary obligation to aid the public in developing informed judgments, opinions, and choices.

h. As teachers, psychologists ensure that statements in catalogs and course outlines are accurate and not misleading, particularly in terms of subject matter to be covered, bases for evaluating progress, and the nature of course experiences. Announcements, brochures, or advertisements describing workshops, seminars, or other educational programs accurately describe the audience for which the program is intended as well as eligibility requirements, educational objectives, and nature of the materials to be covered. These announcements also accurately represent the education, training, and experience of the psychologists presenting the programs and any fees involved.

i. Public announcements or advertisements soliciting research participants in which clinical services or other professional services are offered as an inducement make clear the nature of the services as well as the costs and other obligations to be accepted by participants in the research.

j. A psychologist accepts the obligation to correct others who represent the psychologist's professional qualifications, or associations with products or services, in a manner incompatible with these guidelines.

k. Individual diagnostic and therapeutic services are provided only in the context of a professional psychological relationship. When personal advice is given by means of public lectures or demonstrations, newspaper or magazine articles, radio or television programs, mail or similar media, the psychologist utilizes the most current relevant data and exercises the highest level of professional judgment.

l. Products that are described or presented by means of public lectures or demonstrations, newspaper or magazine articles, radio or television programs, or similar media meet the same recognized standards as exist for products used in the context of a professional relationship.

Principle 5: Confidentiality

Psychologists have a primary obligation to respect the confidentiality of information obtained from persons in the course of their work as psychologists. They reveal such information to others only with the consent of the person or the person's legal representative, except in those unusual circumstances in which not to do so would result in clear danger to the person or to others. Where appropriate, psychologists inform their clients of the legal limits of confidentiality.

a. Information obtained in clinical or consulting relationships, or evaluative data concerning children, students, employees, and others, is discussed only for professional purposes and only with persons clearly concerned with the case. Written and oral reports present only data germane to the purposes of the evaluation, and every effort is made to avoid undue invasion of privacy.

b. Psychologists who present personal information obtained during the course of professional work in writings, lectures, or other public forums either obtain adequate prior consent to do so or adequately disguise all identifying information.

c. Psychologists make provisions for maintaining confidentiality in the storage and disposal of records.

d. When working with minors or other persons who are unable to give voluntary, informed consent, psychologists take special care to protect these persons' best interests.

Principle 6: Welfare of the Consumer

Psychologists respect the integrity and protect the welfare of the people and groups with whom they work. When conflicts of interest arise between clients and psychologists' employing institutions, psychologists clarify the nature and direction of their loyalties and responsibilities and keep all parties informed of their commitments. Psychologists fully inform consumers as to the purpose and nature of an evaluative, treatment, educational, or training procedure, and they freely acknowledge that clients, students, or participants in research have freedom of choice with regard to participation.

a. Psychologists are continually cognizant of their own needs and of their potentially influential position vis-à-vis persons such as clients, students, and subordinates. They avoid exploiting the trust and dependency of such persons. Psychologists make every effort to avoid dual relationships that could impair their professional judgment or increase the risk of exploitation. Examples of such dual relationships include, but are not limited to, research with and treatment of employees, students, supervisees, close friends, or relatives. Sexual intimacies with clients are unethical.

b. When a psychologist agrees to provide services to a client at the request of a third party, the psychologist assumes the responsibility of clarifying the nature of the relationships to all parties concerned.

c. Where the demands of an organization require psychologists to violate these Ethical Principles, psychologists clarify the nature of the conflict between the demands and these principles. They inform all parties of psychologists' ethical responsibilities and take appropriate action.

d. Psychologists make advance financial arrangements that safeguard the best interests of and are clearly understood by their clients. They neither give nor receive any remuneration for referring clients for professional services. They contribute a portion of their services to work for which they receive little or no financial return.

e. Psychologists terminate a clinical or consulting relationship when it is reasonably clear that the consumer is not benefiting from it. They offer to help the consumer locate alternative sources of assistance.

Principle 7: Professional Relationships

Psychologists act with due regard for the needs, special competencies, and obligations of their colleagues in psychology and other professions. They respect the prerogatives and obligations of the institutions or organizations with which these other colleagues are associated.

a. Psychologists understand the areas of competence of related professions. They make full use of all the professional, technical, and administrative resources that serve the best interests of consumers. The absence of formal relationships with other professional workers does not relieve psychologists of the responsibility of securing for their clients the best possible professional service, nor does it relieve them of the obligation to exercise foresight, diligence, and tact in obtaining the complementary or alternative assistance needed by clients.

b. Psychologists know and take into account the traditions and practices of other professional groups with whom they work and cooperate fully with such groups. If a psychologist is contacted by a person who is already receiving similar services from another professional, the psychologist carefully considers that professional relationship and proceeds with caution and sensitivity to the therapeutic issues as well as the client's welfare. The psychologist discusses these issues with the client so as to minimize the risk of confusion and conflict.

c. Psychologists who employ or supervise other professionals or professionals in training accept the obligation to facilitate the further professional development of these individuals. They provide appropriate working conditions, timely evaluations, constructive consultation, and experience opportunities.

d. Psychologists do not exploit their professional relationships with clients, supervisees, students, employees, or research participants sexually or otherwise.

Psychologists do not condone or engage in sexual harassment. Sexual harassment is defined as deliberate or repeated comments, gestures, or physical contacts of a sexual nature that are unwanted by the recipient.

e. In conducting research in institutions or organizations, psychologists secure appropriate authorization to conduct such research. They are aware of their obligations to future research workers and ensure that host institutions receive adequate information about the research and proper acknowledgment of their contributions.

f. Publication credit is assigned to those who have contributed to a publication in proportion to their professional contributions. Major contributions of a professional character made by several persons to a common project are recognized by joint authorship, with the individual who made the principal contribution listed first. Minor contributions of a professional character and extensive clerical or similar nonprofessional assistance may be acknowledged in footnotes or in an introductory statement. Acknowledgment through specific citations is made for unpublished as well as published material that has directly influenced the research or writing. Psychologists who compile and edit material of others for publication publish the material in the name of the originating group, if appropriate, with their own name appearing as chairperson or editor. All contributors are to be acknowledged and named.

g. When psychologists know of an ethical violation by another psychologist, and it seems appropriate, they informally attempt to resolve the issue by bringing the behavior to the attention of the psychologist. If the misconduct is of a minor nature and/or appears to be due to lack of sensitivity, knowledge, or experience, such an informal solution is usually appropriate. Such informal corrective efforts are made with sensitivity to any rights to confidentiality involved. If the violation does not seem amenable to an informal solution, or is of a more serious nature, psychologists bring it to the attention of the appropriate local, state, and/or national committee on professional ethics and conduct.

Principle 8: Assessment Techniques

In the development, publication, and utilization of psychological assessment techniques, psychologists make every effort to promote the welfare and best interests of the client. They guard against the misuse of assessment results. They respect the client's right to know the results, the interpretations made, and the bases for their conclusions and recommendations. Psychologists make every effort to maintain the security of tests and other assessment techniques within limits of legal mandates. They strive to ensure the appropriate use of assessment techniques by others.

a. In using assessment techniques, psychologists respect the right of clients to have full explanations of the nature and purpose of the techniques in language the client can understand, unless an explicit exception to this right has been agreed upon in advance. When the explanations are to be provided by others, psychologists establish procedures for ensuring the adequacy of these explanations.

b. Psychologists responsible for the development and standardization of psychological tests and other assessment techniques utilize established scientific procedures and observe the relevant APA standards.

c. In reporting assessment results, psychologists indicate any reservations that exist regarding validity or reliability because of the circumstances of the assessment or the inappropriateness of the norms for the person tested. Psychologists strive to ensure that the results of assessments and their interpretations are not misused by others.

d. Psychologists recognize that assessment results may become obsolete. They make every effort to avoid and prevent the misuse of obsolete measures.

e. Psychologists offering scoring and interpretation services are able to produce appropriate evidence for the validity of the programs and procedures used in arriving at interpretations. The public offering of an automated interpretation service is considered a professional-to-professional consultation. Psychologists make every effort to avoid misuse of assessment reports.

f. Psychologists do not encourage or promote the use of psychological assessment techniques by inappropriately trained or otherwise unqualified persons through teaching, sponsorship, or supervision.

Principle 9: Research with Human Participants

The decision to undertake research rests upon a considered judgment by the individual psychologist about how best to contribute to psychological science and human welfare. Having made the decision to conduct research, the psychologist considers alternative directions in which research energies and resources might be invested. On the basis of this consideration, the psychologist carries out the investigation with respect and concern for the dignity and welfare of the people who participate and with cognizance of federal and state regulations and professional standards governing the conduct of research with human participants.

a. In planning a study, the investigator has the responsibility to make a careful evaluation of its ethical acceptability. To the extent that the weighing of scientific and human values suggests a compromise of any principle, the investigator incurs a correspondingly serious obligation to seek ethical advice and to observe stringent safeguards to protect the rights of human participants.

b. Considering whether a participant in a planned study will be a "subject at risk" or a "subject at minimal risk," according to recognized standards, is of primary ethical concern to the investigator.

c. The investigator always retains the responsibility for ensuring ethical practice in research. The investigator is also responsible for the ethical treatment of research participants by collaborators, assistants, students, and employees, all of whom, however, incur obligations.

d. Except in minimal-risk research, the investigator establishes a clear and fair agreement with research participants, prior to their participation, that clarifies the obligations and responsibilities of each. The investigator has the obligation to honor all promises and commitments included in that agreement. The investigator informs the participants of all aspects of the research that might reasonably be expected to influence willingness to participate and explains all other aspects of the research about which the participants inquire. Failure to make full disclosure prior to obtaining informed consent requires additional safeguards to protect the welfare and dignity of the research participants. Research with children or with participants who have impairments that would limit understanding and/or communication requires special safeguarding procedures.

e. Methodological requirements of a study may make the use of concealment or deception necessary. Before conducting such a study, the investigator has a special responsibility to (i) determine whether the use of such techniques is justified by the study's prospective scientific, educational, or applied value; (ii) determine whether alternative procedures are available that do not use concealments or deception; and (iii) ensure that the participants are provided with sufficient explanation as soon as possible.

f. The investigator respects the individual's freedom to decline to participate in or to withdraw from the research at any time. The obligation to protect this freedom requires careful thought and consideration when the investigator is in a position of authority or influence over the participant. Such positions of authority include, but are not limited to, situations in which research participation is required as part of employment or in which the participant is a student, client, or employee of the investigator.

g. The investigator protects the participant from physical and mental discomfort, harm, and danger that may arise from research procedures. If risks of such consequences exist, the investigator informs the participant of that fact. Research procedures likely to cause serious or lasting harm to a participant are not used unless the failure to use these procedures might expose the participant to risk of greater harm, or unless the research has great potential benefit and fully informed and voluntary consent is obtained from each participant. The participant should be informed of procedures for contacting the investigator within a reasonable time period following participation should stress, potential harm, or related questions or concerns arise.

h. After the data are collected, the investigator provides the participant with information about the nature of the study and attempts to remove any misconceptions that may have arisen. Where scientific or humane values justify delaying or withholding this information, the investigator incurs a special responsibility to monitor the research and to ensure that there are no damaging consequences for the participant.

i. Where research procedures result in undesirable consequences for the individual participant, the investigator has the responsibility to detect and remove or correct these consequences, including long-term effects.

j. Information obtained about a research participant during the course of an investigation is confidential unless otherwise agreed upon in advance. When the possibility exists that others may obtain access to such information, this possibility, together with the plans for protecting confidentiality, is explained to the participant as part of the procedure for obtaining informed consent.

Principle 10: Care and Use of Animals

An investigator of animal behavior strives to advance understanding of basic behavioral principles and/or to contribute to the improvement of human health and welfare. In seeking these ends, the investigator ensures the welfare of animals and treats them humanely. Laws and regulations notwithstanding, an animal's immediate protection depends upon the scientist's own conscience.

a. The acquisition, care, use, and disposal of all animals are in compliance with current federal, state or provincial, and local laws and regulations.

b. A psychologist trained in research methods and experienced in the care of laboratory animals closely supervises all procedures involving animals and is responsible for ensuring appropriate consideration of their comfort, health, and humane treatment.

c. Psychologists ensure that all individuals using animals under their supervision have received explicit instruction in experimental methods and in the care, maintenance, and handling of the species being used. Responsibilities and activities of individuals participating in a research project are consistent with their respective competencies.

d. Psychologists make every effort to minimize discomfort, illness, and pain of animals. A procedure subjecting animals to pain, stress, or privation is used only when an alternative procedure is unavailable and the goal is justified by its prospective scientific, educational, or applied value. Surgical procedures are performed under appropriate anesthesia; techniques to avoid infection and minimize pain are followed during and after surgery.

e. When it is appropriate that the animal's life be terminated, it is done rapidly and painlessly.

Ethical Guidelines for Group Counselors

Preamble

One characteristic of any professional group is the possession of a body of knowledge, skills, and voluntarily, self-professed standards for ethical practice. A Code of Ethics consists of those standards that have been formally and publicly acknowledged by the members of a profession to serve as the guidelines for professional conduct, discharge of duties, and the resolution of moral dilemmas. By this document, the Association for Specialists in Group Work (ASGW) has identified the standards of conduct appropriate for ethical behavior among its members.

The Association for Specialists in Group Work recognizes the basic commitment of its members to the Ethical Standards of its parent organization, the American Association for Counseling and Development (AACD) and nothing in this document shall be construed to supplant that code. These standards are intended to complement the AACD standards in the area of group work by clarifying the nature of ethical responsibility of the counselor in the group setting and by stimulating a greater concern for competent group leadership.

The group counselor is expected to be a professional agent and to take the processes of ethical responsibility seriously. ASGW views "ethical process" as being integral to group work and views group counselors as "ethical agents." Group counselors, by their very nature in being responsible and responsive to their group members, necessarily embrace a certain potential for ethical vulnerability. It is incumbent upon group counselors to give considerable attention to

SOURCE: These guidelines, drafted June 1, 1989, by the Association for Specialists in Group Work (ASGW), have been reprinted by permission of the American Association for Counseling and Development (AACD), 5999 Stevenson Avenue, Alexandria, VA 22304.

the intent and context of their actions because the attempts of counselors to influence human behavior through group work always have ethical implications.

The following ethical guidelines have been developed to encourage ethical behavior of group counselors. These guidelines are written for students and practitioners, and are meant to stimulate reflection, self-examination, and discussion of issues and practices. They address the group counselor's responsibility for providing information about group work to clients and the group counselor's responsibility for providing group counseling services to clients. A final section discusses the group counselor's responsibility for safeguarding ethical practice and procedures for reporting unethical behavior. Group counselors are expected to make known these standards to group members.

Ethical Guidelines

1. Orientation and providing information: Group counselors adequately prepare prospective or new group members by providing as much information about the existing or proposed group as necessary.

- Minimally, information related to each of the following areas should be provided.

(a) Entrance procedures, time parameters of the group experience, group participation expectations, methods of payment (where appropriate), and termination procedures are explained by the group counselor as appropriate to the level of maturity of group members and the nature and purpose(s) of the group.

(b) Group counselors have available for distribution, a professional disclosure statement that includes information on the group counselor's qualifications and group services that can be provided, particularly as related to the nature and purpose(s) of the specific group.

(c) Group counselors communicate the role expectations, rights, and responsibilities of group members and group counselor(s).

(d) The group goals are stated as concisely as possible by the group counselor including "whose" goal it is (the group counselor's, the institution's, the parent's, the law's, society's, etc.) and the role of group members in influencing or determining the group's goal(s).

(e) Group counselors explore with group members the risks of potential life changes that may occur because of the group experience and help members explore their readiness to face these possibilities.

(f) Group members are informed by the group counselor of unusual or experimental procedures that might be expected in their group experience.

(g) Group counselors explain, as realistically as possible, what services can and cannot be provided within the particular group structure offered.

(h) Group counselors emphasize the need to promote full psychological functioning and presence among group members. They inquire from prospective group members whether they are using any kind of drug or medication that may affect functioning in the group. They do not permit any use of alcohol and/or illegal drugs during group sessions and they discourage the use of alcohol and/or drugs (legal or illegal) prior to group meetings which may affect the physical or emotional presence of the member or other group members.

(i) Group counselors inquire from prospective group members whether they have ever been a client in counseling or psychotherapy. If a prospective group member is already in a counseling relationship with another professional person, the group counselor advises the prospective group member to notify the other professional of their participation in the group.

(j) Group counselors clearly inform group members about the policies pertaining to the group counselor's willingness to consult with them between group sessions.

(k) In establishing fees for group counseling services, group counselors consider the financial status and the locality of prospective group members. Group members are not charged fees for group sessions where the group counselor is not present and the policy of charging for sessions missed by a group member is clearly communicated. Fees for participating as a group member are contracted between group counselor and group member for a specified period of time. Group counselors do not increase fees for group counseling services until the existing contracted fee structure has expired. In the event that the established fee structure is inappropriate for a prospective member, group counselors assist in finding comparable services of acceptable cost.

2. Screening of members: The group counselor screens prospective group members (when appropriate to their theoretical orientation). Insofar as possible, the counselor selects group members whose needs and goals are compatible with the goals of the group, who will not impede the group process, and whose well-being will not be jeopardized by the group experience. An orientation to the group (i.e., ASGW Ethical Guideline #1), is included during the screening process.

- Screening may be accomplished in one or more ways, such as the following:

    (a) Individual interview,
    (b) Group interview of prospective group members,
    (c) Interview as part of a team staffing, and
    (d) Completion of a written questionnaire by prospective group members.

3. Confidentiality: Group counselors protect members by defining clearly what confidentiality means, why it is important, and the difficulties involved in enforcement.

(a) Group counselors take steps to protect members by defining confidentiality and the limits of confidentiality (i.e., when a group member's condition indicates that there is clear and imminent danger to the member, others, or physical property, the group counselor takes reasonable personal action and/or informs responsible authorities).

(b) Group counselors stress the importance of confidentiality and set a norm of confidentiality regarding all group participants' disclosures. The importance of maintaining confidentiality is emphasized before the group begins and at various times in the group. The fact that confidentiality cannot be guaranteed is clearly stated.

(c) Members are made aware of the difficulties involved in enforcing and ensuring confidentiality in a group setting. The counselor provides examples of how confidentiality can non-maliciously be broken to increase members' awareness, and help to lessen the likelihood that this breach of confidence will occur. Group counselors inform group members about the potential consequences of intentionally breaching confidentiality.

(d) Group counselors can only ensure confidentiality on their part and not on the part of the members.

(e) Group counselors video or audio tape a group session only with the prior consent, and the members' knowledge of how the tape will be used.

(f) When working with minors, the group counselor specifies the limits of confidentiality.

(g) Participants in a mandatory group are made aware of any reporting procedures required of the group counselor.

(h) Group counselors store or dispose of group member records (written audio, video, etc.) in ways that maintain confidentiality.

(i) Instructors of group counseling courses maintain the anonymity of group members whenever discussing group counseling cases.

4. Voluntary/involuntary participation: Group counselors inform members whether participation is voluntary or involuntary.

(a) Group counselors take steps to ensure informed consent procedures in both voluntary and involuntary groups.

(b) When working with minors in a group, counselors are expected to follow the procedures specified by the institution in which they are practicing.

(c) With involuntary groups, every attempt is made to enlist the cooperation of the members and their continuance in the group on a voluntary basis.

(d) Group counselors do not certify that group treatment has been received by members who merely attend sessions, but did not meet the defined group expectations. Group members are informed about the consequences for failing to participate in a group.

5. Leaving a group: Provisions are made to assist a group member to terminate in an effective way.

(a) Procedures to be followed for a group member who chooses to exit a group prematurely are discussed by the counselor with all group members either before the group begins, during a pre-screening interview, or during the initial group session.

(b) In the case of legally mandated group counseling, group counselors inform members of the possible consequences for premature self termination.

(c) Ideally, both the group counselor and the member can work cooperatively to determine the degree to which a group experience is productive or counter-productive for that individual.

(d) Members ultimately have a right to discontinue membership in the group, at a designated time, if the predetermined trial period proves to be unsatisfactory.

(e) Members have the right to exit a group, but it is important that they be made aware of the importance of informing the counselor and the group members prior to deciding to leave. The counselor discusses the possible risks of leaving the group prematurely with a member who is considering this option.

(f) Before leaving a group, the group counselor encourages members (if appropriate) to discuss their reasons for wanting to discontinue membership in the group. Counselors intervene if other members use undue pressure to force a member to remain in the group.

6. Coercion and pressure: Group counselors protect member rights against physical threats, intimidation, coercion, and undue peer pressure insofar as is reasonably possible.

(a) It is essential to differentiate between "therapeutic pressure" that is part of any group and "undue pressure," which is not therapeutic.

(b) The purpose of a group is to help participants find their own answer, not to pressure them into doing what the group thinks is appropriate.

(c) Counselors exert care not to coerce participants to change in directions which they clearly state they do not choose.

(d) Counselors have a responsibility to intervene when others use undue pressure or attempt to persuade members against their will.

(e) Counselors intervene when any member attempts to act out aggression in a physical way that might harm another member or themselves.

(f) Counselors intervene when a member is verbally abusive or inappropriately confrontive to another member.

7. Imposing counselor values: Group counselors develop an awareness of their own values and needs and the potential impact they have on the interventions likely to be made.

(a) Although group counselors take care to avoid imposing their values on members, it is appropriate that they expose their own beliefs, decisions, needs, and values, when concealing them would create problems for the members.

(b) There are values implicit in any group, and these are made clear to potential members before they join the group. (Examples of certain values include: expressing feelings, being direct and honest, sharing personal material with others, learning how to trust, improving interpersonal communication, and deciding for oneself.)

(c) Personal and professional needs of group counselors are not met at the members' expense.

(d) Group counselors avoid using the group for their own therapy.

(e) Group counselors are aware of their own values and assumptions and how these apply in a multicultural context.

(f) Group counselors take steps to increase their awareness of ways that their personal reactions to members might inhibit the group process and they monitor their countertransference. Through an awareness of the impact of stereotyping and discrimination (i.e., biases based on age, disability, ethnicity, gender, race, religion, or sexual preference), group counselors guard the individual rights and personal dignity of all group members.

8. Equitable treatment: Group counselors make every reasonable effort to treat each member individually and equally.

(a) Group counselors recognize and respect differences (e.g., cultural, racial, religious, lifestyle, age, disability, gender) among group members.

(b) Group counselors maintain an awareness of their behavior toward individual group members and are alert to the potential detrimental effects of favoritism or partiality toward any particular group member to the exclusion or detriment of any other member(s). It is likely that group counselors will favor some members over others, yet all group members deserve to be treated equally.

(c) Group counselors ensure equitable use of group time for each member by inviting silent members to become involved, acknowledging nonverbal attempts to communicate, and discouraging rambling and monopolizing of time by members.

(d) If a large group is planned, counselors consider enlisting another qualified professional to serve as a co-leader for the group sessions.

9. Dual relationships: Group counselors avoid dual relationships with group members that might impair their objectivity and professional judgment, as well as those which are likely to compromise a group member's ability to participate fully in the group.

(a) Group counselors do not misuse their professional role and power as group leader to advance personal or social contacts with members throughout the duration of the group.

(b) Group counselors do not use their professional relationship with group members to further their own interest either during the group or after the termination of the group.

(c) Sexual intimacies between group counselors and members are unethical.

(d) Group counselors do not barter (exchange) professional services with group members for services.

(e) Group counselors do not admit their own family members, relatives, employees, or personal friends as members to their groups.

(f) Group counselors discuss with group members the potential detrimental effects of group members engaging in intimate inter-member relationships outside of the group.

(g) Students who participate in a group as a partial course requirement for a group course are not evaluated for an academic grade based upon their degree of participation as a member in a group. Instructors of group counseling courses take steps to minimize the possible negative impact on students when they participate in a group course by separating course grades from participation in the group and by allowing students to decide what issues to explore and when to stop.

(h) It is inappropriate to solicit members from a class (or institutional affiliation) for one's private counseling or therapeutic groups.

10. Use of techniques: Group counselors do not attempt any technique unless trained in its use or under supervision by a counselor familiar with the intervention.

(a) Group counselors are able to articulate a theoretical orientation that guides their practice, and they are able to provide a rationale for their interventions.

(b) Depending upon the type of an intervention, group counselors have training commensurate with the potential impact of a technique.

(c) Group counselors are aware of the necessity to modify their techniques to fit the unique needs of various cultural and ethnic groups.

(d) Group counselors assist members in translating in-group learnings to daily life.

11. Goal development: Group counselors make every effort to assist members in developing their personal goals.

(a) Group counselors use their skills to assist members in making their goals specific so that others present in the group will understand the nature of the goals.

(b) Throughout the course of a group, group counselors assist members in assessing the degree to which personal goals are being met, and assist in revising any goals when it is appropriate.

(c) Group counselors help members clarify the degree to which the goals can be met within the context of a particular group.

12. Consultation: Group counselors develop and explain policies about between-session consultation to group members.

(a) Group counselors take care to make certain that members do not use between-session consultations to avoid dealing with issues pertaining to the group that would be dealt with best in the group.

(b) Group counselors urge members to bring the issues discussed during between-session consultations into the group if they pertain to the group.

(c) Group counselors seek out consultation and/or supervision regarding ethical concerns or when encountering difficulties which interfere with their effective functioning as group leaders.

(d) Group counselors seek appropriate professional assistance for their own personal problems or conflicts that are likely to impair their professional judgment and work performance.

(e) Group counselors discuss their group cases only for professional consultation and educational purposes.

(f) Group counselors inform members about policies regarding whether consultations will be held confidential.

13. Termination from the group: Depending upon the purpose of participation in the group, counselors promote termination of members from the group in the most efficient period of time.

(a) Group counselors maintain a constant awareness of the progress made by each group member and periodically invite the group members to explore and reevaluate their experiences in the group. It is the responsibility of group counselors to help promote the independence of members from the group in a timely manner.

14. Evaluation and follow-up: Group counselors make every attempt to engage in ongoing assessment and to design follow-up procedures for their groups.

(a) Group counselors recognize the importance of ongoing assessment of a group, and they assist members in evaluating their own progress.

(b) Group counselors conduct evaluation of the total group experience at the final meeting (or before termination), as well as ongoing evaluation.

(c) Group counselors monitor their own behavior and become aware of what they are modeling in the group.

(d) Follow-up procedures might take the form of personal contact, telephone contact, or written contact.

(e) Follow-up meetings might be with individuals, or groups, or both to determine the degree to which: (i) members have reached their goals, (ii) the group had a positive or negative effect on the participants, (iii) members could profit from some type of referral, and (iv) as information for possible modification of future groups. If there is no follow-up meeting, provisions are made available for individual follow-up meetings to any member who needs or requests such a contact.

15. Referrals: If the needs of a particular member cannot be met within the type of group being offered, the group counselor suggests other appropriate professional referrals.

(a) Group counselors are knowledgeable of local community resources for assisting group members regarding professional referrals.

(b) Group counselors help members seek further professional assistance, if needed.

16. Professional development: Group counselors recognize that professional growth is a continuous, ongoing, developmental process throughout their career.

(a) Group counselors maintain and upgrade their knowledge and skill competencies through educational activities, clinical experiences, and participation in professional development activities.

(b) Group counselors keep abreast of research findings and new developments as applied to groups.

Safeguarding Ethical Practice and Procedures for Reporting Unethical Behavior

The preceding remarks have been advanced as guidelines which are generally representative of ethical and professional group practice. They have not been proposed as rigidly defined prescriptions. However, practitioners who are thought to be grossly unresponsive to the ethical concerns addressed in this document may be subject to a review of their practices by the AACD Ethics Committee and ASGW peers.

- For consultation and/or questions regarding these ASGW Ethical Guidelines or group ethical dilemmas, you may contact the Chairperson of the ASGW Ethics Committee. The name, address, and telephone number of the current ASGW Ethics Committee Chairperson may be acquired by telephoning the AACD office in Alexandria, Virginia[,] at (703) 823-9800.
- If a group counselor's behavior is suspected as being unethical, the following procedures are to be followed:

(a) Collect more information and investigate further to confirm the unethical practice as determined by the ASGW Ethical Guidelines.

(b) Confront the individual with the apparent violation of ethical guidelines for the purposes of protecting the safety of any clients and to help the group counselor correct any inappropriate behaviors. If satisfactory resolution is not reached through this contact then:

(c) A complaint should be made in writing, including the specific facts and dates of the alleged violation and all relevant supporting data. The complaint should be included in an envelope marked "CONFIDENTIAL" to ensure confidentiality for both the accuser(s) and the alleged violator(s) and forwarded to all of the following sources:

1. The name and address of the Chairperson of the state Counselor Licensure Board for the respective state, if in existence.

2. The Ethics Committee
c/o The President
American Association for Counseling and Development
5999 Stevenson Avenue
Alexandria, Virginia 22304

3. The name and address of all private credentialing agencies [in which] the alleged violator maintains credentials or holds professional membership. Some of these include the following:

National Board for Certified Counselors, Inc.
5999 Stevenson Avenue
Alexandria, Virginia 22304

National Council for Credentialing of Career Counselors
c/o NBCC
5999 Stevenson Avenue
Alexandria, Virginia 22304

National Academy for Certified Clinical Mental Health Counselors
5999 Stevenson Avenue
Alexandria, Virginia 22304

Commission on Rehabilitation Counselor Certification
162 North State Street, Suite 317
Chicago, Illinois 60601

American Association for Marriage and Family Therapy
1717 K Street, N.W., Suite 407
Washington, D.C. 20006

American Psychological Association
1200 Seventeenth Street, N.W.
Washington, D.C. 20036

American Group Psychotherapy Association, Inc.
25 East 21st Street, 6th Floor
New York, New York 10010

. . . Code of Ethics,
National Association of Social Workers

Preamble

This code is intended to serve as a guide to the everyday conduct of members of the social work profession and as a basis for the adjudication of issues in ethics when the conduct of social workers is alleged to deviate from the standards expressed or implied in this code. It represents standards of ethical behavior for social workers in professional relationships with those served, with colleagues, with employers, with other individuals and professions, and with the community and society as a whole. It also embodies standards of ethical behavior governing individual conduct to the extent that such conduct is associated with an individual's status and identity as a social worker.

This code is based on the fundamental values of the social work profession that include the worth, dignity, and uniqueness of all persons as well as their rights and opportunities. It is also based on the nature of social work, which fosters conditions that promote these values.

In subscribing to and abiding by this code, the social worker is expected to view ethical responsibility in as inclusive a context as each situation demands and within which ethical judgment is required. The social worker is expected to take into consideration all the principles in this code that have a bearing upon any situation in which ethical judgment is to be exercised and professional intervention or conduct is planned. The course of action that the social worker chooses is expected to be consistent with the spirit as well as the letter of this code.

In itself, this code does not represent a set of rules that will prescribe all the behaviors of social workers in all the complexities of professional life. Rather, it offers general principles to guide conduct, and the judicious appraisal of conduct, in situations that have ethical implications. It provides the basis for making judgments about ethical actions before and after they occur. Frequently, the particular situation determines the ethical principles that apply and the manner of their application. In such cases, not only the particular ethical principles are taken into immediate consideration, but also the entire code and its spirit. Specific applications of ethical principles must be judged within the

SOURCE: This Code of Ethics as adopted by the 1979 NASW Delgate Assembly, effective July 1, 1980, and reapproved by the 1984 NASW Delegate Assembly is reprinted with the permission of the National Association of Social Workers.

context in which they are being considered. Ethical behavior in a given situation must satisfy not only the judgment of the individual social worker, but also the judgment of an unbiased jury of professional peers.

This code should not be used as an instrument to deprive any social worker of the opportunity or freedom to practice with complete professional integrity; nor should any disciplinary action be taken on the basis of this code without maximum provision for safeguarding the rights of the social worker affected.

The ethical behavior of social workers results not from edict, but from a personal commitment of the individual. This code is offered to affirm the will and zeal of all social workers to be ethical and to act ethically in all that they do as social workers.

The following codified ethical principles should guide social workers in the various roles and relationships and at the various levels of responsibility in which they function professionally. These principles also serve as a basis for the adjudication by the National Association of Social Workers of issues in ethics.

In subscribing to this code, social workers are required to cooperate in its implementation and abide by any disciplinary rulings based on it. They should also take adequate measures to discourage, prevent, expose, and correct the unethical conduct of colleagues. Finally, social workers should be equally ready to defend and assist colleagues unjustly charged with unethical conduct.

I. The Social Worker's Conduct and Comportment as a Social Worker

A. Propriety. The social worker should maintain high standards of personal conduct in the capacity or identity as social worker.

1. The private conduct of the social worker is a personal matter to the same degree as is any other person's, except when such conduct compromises the fulfillment of professional responsibilities.

2. The social worker should not participate in, condone, or be associated with dishonesty, fraud, deceit, or misrepresentation.

3. The social worker should distinguish clearly between statements and actions made as a private individual and as a representative of the social work profession or an organization or group.

B. Competence and professional development. The social worker should strive to become and remain proficient in professional practice and the performance of professional functions.

1. The social worker should accept responsibility or employment only on the basis of existing competence or the intention to acquire the necessary competence.

2. The social worker should not misrepresent professional qualifications, education, experience, or affiliations.

C. Service. The social worker should regard as primary the service obligation of the social work profession.

1. The social worker should retain ultimate responsibility for the quality and extent of the service that individual assumes, assigns, or performs.

2. The social worker should act to prevent practices that are inhumane or discriminatory against any person or group of persons.

D. Integrity. The social worker should act in accordance with the highest standards of professional integrity and impartiality.

1. The social worker should be alert to and resist the influences and pressures that interfere with the exercise of professional discretion and impartial judgment required for the performance of professional functions.

2. The social worker should not exploit professional relationships for personal gain.

E. Scholarship and research. The social worker engaged in study and research should be guided by the conventions of scholarly inquiry.

1. The social worker engaged in research should consider carefully its possible consequences for human beings.

2. The social worker engaged in research should ascertain that the consent of participants in the research is voluntary and informed, without any implied deprivation or penalty for refusal to participate, and with due regard for participants' privacy and dignity.

3. The social worker engaged in research should protect participants from unwarranted physical or mental discomfort, distress, harm, danger, or deprivation.

4. The social worker who engages in the evaluation of services or cases should discuss them only for the professional purposes and only with persons directly and professionally concerned with them.

5. Information obtained about participants in research should be treated as confidential.

6. The social worker should take credit only for work actually done in connection with scholarly and research endeavors and credit contributions made by others.

II. The Social Worker's Ethical Responsibility to Clients

F. Primacy of clients' interests. The social worker's primary responsibility is to clients.

1. The social worker should serve clients with devotion, loyalty, determination, and the maximum application of professional skill and competence.

2. The social worker should not exploit relationships with clients for personal advantage, or solicit the clients of one's agency for private practice.

3. The social worker should not practice, condone, facilitate, or collaborate with any form of discrimination on the basis of race, sex, sexual orientation, age, religion, national origin, marital status, political belief, mental or physical handicap, or any other preference or personal characteristic, condition, or status.

4. The social worker should avoid relationships or commitments that conflict with the interests of clients.

5. The social worker should under no circumstances engage in sexual activities with clients.

6. The social worker should provide clients with accurate and complete information regarding the extent and nature of the services available to them.

7. The social worker should apprise clients of their risks, rights, opportunities, and obligations associated with social service to them.

8. The social worker should seek advice and counsel of colleagues and supervisors whenever such consultation is in the best interest of clients.

9. The social worker should terminate service to clients, and professional relationships with them, when such service and relationships are no longer required or no longer serve the clients' needs or interests.

10. The social worker should withdraw services precipitously only under unusual circumstances, giving careful consideration to all factors in the situation and taking care to minimize possible adverse effects.

11. The social worker who anticipates the termination or interruption of service to clients should notify clients promptly and seek the transfer, referral, or continuation of services in relation to the clients' needs and preferences.

G. Rights and prerogatives of clients. The social worker should make every effort to foster maximum self-determination on the part of clients.

1. When the social worker must act on behalf of a client who has been adjudged legally incompetent, the social worker should safeguard the interests and rights of that client.

2. When another individual has been legally authorized to act in behalf of a client, the social worker should deal with that person always with the client's best interest in mind.

3. The social worker should not engage in any action that violates or diminishes the civil or legal rights of clients.

H. Confidentiality and privacy. The social worker should respect the privacy of clients and hold in confidence all information obtained in the course of professional service.

1. The social worker should share with others confidences revealed by clients, without their consent, only for compelling professional reasons.

2. The social worker should inform clients fully about the limits of confidentiality in a given situation, the purposes for which information is obtained, and how it may be used.

3. The social worker should afford clients reasonable access to any official social work records concerning them.

4. When providing clients with access to records, the social worker should take due care to protect the confidences of others contained in those records.

5. The social worker should obtain informed consent of clients before taping, recording, or permitting third party observation of their activities.

I. Fees. When setting fees, the social worker should ensure that they are fair, reasonable, considerate, and commensurate with the service performed and with due regard for the clients' ability to pay.

1. The social worker should not divide a fee or accept or give anything of value for receiving or making a referral.

III. The Social Worker's Ethical Responsibility to Colleagues

J. Respect, fairness, and courtesy. The social worker should treat colleagues with respect, courtesy, fairness, and good faith.

1. The social worker should cooperate with colleagues to promote professional interests and concerns.

2. The social worker should respect confidences shared by colleagues in the course of their professional relationships and transactions.

3. The social worker should create and maintain conditions of practice that facilitate ethical and competent professional performance by colleagues.

4. The social worker should treat with respect, and represent accurately and fairly, the qualifications, views, and findings of colleagues and use appropriate channels to express judgments on these matters.

5. The social worker who replaces or is replaced by a colleague in professional practice should act with consideration for the interest, character, and reputation of that colleague.

6. The social worker should not exploit a dispute between a colleague and employers to obtain a position or otherwise advance the social worker's interest.

7. The social worker should seek arbitration or mediation resolution for compelling professional reasons.

8. The social worker should extend to colleagues of other professions the same respect and cooperation that is extended to social work colleagues.

9. The social worker who serves as an employer, supervisor, or mentor to colleagues should make orderly and explicit arrangements regarding the conditions of their continuing professional relationship.

10. The social worker who has the responsibility for employing and evaluating the performance of other staff members should fulfill such responsibility in a fair, considerate, and equitable manner, on the basis of clearly enunciated criteria.

11. The social worker who has the responsibility for evaluating the performance of employees, supervisees, or students should share evaluations with them.

K. Dealing with colleagues' clients. The social worker has the responsibility to relate to the clients of colleagues with full professional consideration.

1. The social worker should not solicit the clients of colleagues.

2. The social worker should not assume professional responsibility for the clients of another agency for a colleague without appropriate communication with that agency or colleague.

3. The social worker who serves the clients of colleagues, during a temporary absence or emergency, should serve those clients with the same consideration as that afforded any clients.

IV. The Social Worker's Ethical Responsibility to Employers and Employing Organizations

L. Commitments to employing organization. The social worker should adhere to commitments made to the employing organization.

1. The social worker should work to improve the employing agency's policies and procedures, and the efficiency and effectiveness of its services.

2. The social worker should not accept employment or arrange student field placements in an organization which is currently under public sanction by NASW for violating personnel standards, or imposing limitations on or penalties for professional actions on behalf of clients.

3. The social worker should act to prevent and eliminate discrimination in the employing organization's work assignments and in its employment policies and practices.

4. The social worker should use with scrupulous regard, and only for the purpose for which they are intended, the resources of the employing organization.

V. The Social Worker's Ethical Responsibility to the Social Work Profession

M. Maintaining the integrity of the profession. The social worker should uphold and advance the values, ethics, knowledge, and mission of the profession.

1. The social worker should protect and enhance the dignity and integrity of the profession and should be responsible and vigorous in discussion and criticism of the profession.

2. The social worker should take action through appropriate channels against unethical conduct by any other member of the profession.

3. The social worker should act to prevent the unauthorized and unqualified practice of social work.

4. The social worker should make no misrepresentation in advertising as to qualifications, competence, service, or results to be achieved.

N. Community service. The social worker should assist the profession in making social services available to the general public.

1. The social worker should contribute time and professional expertise to activities that promote respect for the utility, the integrity, and the competence of the social work profession.

2. The social worker should support the formulation, development, enactment, and implementation of social policies of concern to the profession.

O. Development of knowledge. The social worker should take responsibility for identifying, developing, and fully utilizing knowledge for professional practice.

1. The social worker should base practice upon recognized knowledge relevant to social work.

2. The social worker should critically examine and keep current with emerging knowledge relevant to social work.

3. The social worker should contribute to the knowledge base of social work and share research knowledge and practice wisdom with colleagues.

VI. The Social Worker's Ethical Responsibility to Society

P. Promoting the general welfare. The social worker should promote the general welfare of society.

1. The social worker should act to prevent and eliminate discrimination against any person or group on the basis of race, color, sex, sexual orientation, age, religion, national origin, marital status, political belief, mental or physical handicap, or any other preference or personal characteristic, condition, or status.

2. The social worker should act to ensure that all persons have access to the resources, services, and opportunities which they require.

3. The social worker should act to expand choice and opportunity for all persons, with special regard for disadvantaged or oppressed groups and persons.

4. The social worker should promote conditions that encourage respect for the diversity of cultures which constitute American society.

5. The social worker should provide appropriate professional services in public emergencies.

6. The social worker should advocate changes in policy and legislation to improve social conditions and to promote social justice.

7. The social worker should encourage informed participation by the public in shaping social policies and institutions.

Glossary

Adjudge: to reject or remove by law [rare].

Affidavit: a written statement made or taken under oath before an officer of the court or a notary public or other person who has been duly authorized to so act.

Aggravated assault: an assault where "serious bodily injury" is inflicted on the person assaulted.

Allegations: the statement of the issue that the contributing party is prepared to prove.

Alleged: represented as existing or as described but not so proved.

Appellant: the party who appeals a decision.

Assault: an attempt of unlawful forces to inflict bodily injury upon another, accompanied by the apparent present ability to give effect to the attempt if not prevented.

Battery: the unlawful application of force to the person of another.

Breach of duty: any failure to perform a duty owed to another or to society.

Civil liability: amenability to civil action, as opposed to criminal action; liability to action seeking private remedies or the enforcement of personal rights, based on contract, tort, and so on.

Collective bargaining agreement: mechanism for settling labor disputes by negotiation between employer and representatives of employees.

Common law right of privacy: the right to be left alone based on justice, reason, and common sense.

Compensatory damages: monetary compensation that the law awards to one who has been injured by the action of another.

Conditional privilege: privilege that is dependent upon the happening, or nonhappening, of the condition.

Confidentiality: refers to the ethical responsibility of mental health professionals to safeguard clients by not disclosing information that was given to them in the therapy relationship.

Constitutional right of privacy: the right to be secluded from contact guaranteed by the Constitution.

Contempt of court: an act of omission tending to obstruct or interfere with the orderly administration of justice or to impair the dignity of the court or respect for its authority.

Contention: to maintain or assert.

Contract: a promise, or set of promises, for breach of which the law gives a remedy, or the performance of which the law in some way recognizes as a duty.

Court of appeals: a court having jurisdiction to review the law as applied to a prior determination of the same case.

Covenant of confidentiality: an agreement of promise to keep communication confidential.

Criminal conversation: a tort based upon willful and malicious interference with the marriage relationship by a third party; adultery.

Decedent: a deceased person.

Demurrer: formal allegation that facts as stated in the pleadings, even if admitted, are not legally sufficient for the case to proceed any further.

Deposition: a method of pretrial discovery that consists of a statement of a witness under oath taken in question-and-answer form and cross-examination by an adversary, which are reported and transcribed stenographically.

Discretion: the reasonable exercise of power or right to act in an official capacity.

Disposition: final arrangement settlement; the giving up of, or the relinquishment of, anything.

Foreseeability: a concept used in various areas of the law to limit liability of a party for the consequences of his or her acts to consequences that are within the scope of a "foreseeable risk," that is, risks whose consequences a person of ordinary prudence would reasonably expect might occur.

Gratuitously: without any financial consideration.
Gross negligence: failure to use even slight care.

Holder of the privilege: the person (patient/client) who is authorized to give consent for release of confidential information.
Immunity: a right of exemption for a duty or penalty.
In camera: proceedings that take place privately in the judge's chambers or in court without spectators.
Incarceration: confinement in a jail, prison, or penitentiary.
Inculpatory statements: that which tends to incriminate or bring about a criminal conviction.
Indemnify: to secure against loss or damage that may occur in the future, or to promise compensation for loss or damage already suffered; to insure; to "save harmless."
Intervenor: one who interferes or takes a decisive role, especially with a view to correction, solution, or settlement.

Judicial restoration of his or her competency: court determines individual now has the capacity to understand and act reasonably.

Kelly-Frye: the Frye standard is that, to be admissible, evidence should be generally accepted by the scientific community in which the expert claims membership.

Liable: to be responsible for; to be obligated in law.
Libel: refers to a false and malicious publication printed for the purpose of defaming one alive or marring the memory of one dead (spoken defamation is called *slander*).
Litigation: a judicial contest through which legal rights are sought to be determined and enforced.

Medical malpractice: a special remedial category designed to regulate professional misfeasance.
Militate: to have influence or effect with, against, or, more rarely, for.
Ministerial act: those acts that are performed, according to explicit directions (often embodied in a statute), by a subordinate official.
Miranda rights: the requirement that a person receive certain warnings relating to his or her privilege against self-incrimination (right to remain silent) and his or her right to the presence and advice of an attorney before any custodial interrogation by law enforcement authorities takes place.
Misdemeanor: all indictable offenses below felonies.
Misfeasance: "the performance of a lawful action in an illegal or improper manner."

Negligence: failure to exercise that degree of care that a person of ordinary prudence (a reasonable person) would exercise under the same circumstances.

No privilege: there is no legal basis to resist disclosure of contents of communication.

Ordinary negligence: failure to use ordinary care.

Paradoxical procedure: a contradiction that follows correct deduction from consistent premises that seeks to take advantage of psychotherapy clients' resistance to change or to other therapeutic interventions; may involve directives that the therapist wants a client to resist so change will occur; derived from a process of deliberately prescribing or directing performance of a behavior that appears to be opposed to the client's immediate therapeutic goals.

Patient-litigant: patient is a party involved in a lawsuit.

Pecuniary: relating to money and monetary affairs.

Pending legislation: legislation that is not yet in effect.

Perpetuity: valid for all time; holding for life or an unlimited time.

Prima facie case: a state of the facts that entitles a party to have his or her case go to the jury.

Privileged communication: communications that occur in an air of legal or other recognized professional confidentiality; allows the speakers to resist legal pressure to disclose content.

Proclivity: a natural propensity or inclination.

Proximate cause: that which in natural and continuous sequence, unbroken by any new independent cause, produces an event, without which the injury would not have occurred.

Punitive damages (exemplary): compensation in excess of actual damages; a form of punishment to the wrongdoer and excess enhancement to the injured.

Reasonable care: care governed by reason or sound thinking or common sense.

Remand: to send back, as for futher deliberation; to "send back to the tribunal (or body) from which it was appealed or moved."

Reparation: compensation; the act of making amends.

Res ipsa loquitur: the thing speaks for itself; a rule of evidence whereby negligence of the alleged wrongdoer may be inferred from the mere fact that the accident happened.

Slight negligence: failure to use great care.

Standards of the mental health profession: acceptable quality.

Statute: an act of legislature, pursuant to its constitutional authority, by prescribed means and in certain form such that it becomes the law governing conduct within its scope.

Statute of limitations: "any law which fixes the time within which parties must take judicial action to enforce rights or else be thereafter barred from enforcing them."

Subpoena duces tecum: under penalty you shall take it with you; type of subpoena issued by a court at the request of one of the parties to a suit that requires a witness having under his or her control documents or papers relevant to the controversy to bring such items to the court during the trial.

Summary judgment: a device designed to effect a prompt disposition of controversies on their merits without resort to a lengthy trial, if in essence there is no real dispute as to salient facts or if only a question of law is involved.

Tender: an unconditional offer to perform coupled with a manifested ability to carry out the offer and production of the subject matter (money and so on) of the tender.

Third-party suit: proceeding in a court of justice made by persons who are recognized as having enforceable rights created in them by contract to which they are not parties or for which they give no consideration.

Tort: a wrong, a private or civil wrong or injury independent of contract, resulting from breach of a legal duty.

Undue influence: conscious or unconscious manipulation of transference for their one's own personal gain.

Writ of habeas corpus: a mandatory precept issued by a court to bring a party before a judge with the function to release the party from unlawful restraint.

References

Allen, V. B. (1986). A historical perspective of the AACD ethics committee. *Journal of Counseling and Development, 64*(5), 293.

Allen, V. B. (1987). [To the editor.] *Guidepost, 30*(2), 12.

American Association for Counseling and Development (AACD). (1988a). *Ethical standards.* Alexandria, VA: Author.

American Association for Counseling and Development (AACD). (1988b). *Policies and procedures for processing complaints of ethical violations.* Alexandria, VA: Author.

American Association for Counseling and Development (AACD). (1989). *Ethical standards casebook.* Alexandria, VA: Author.

American Association for Marriage and Family Therapy (AAMFT). (1988). *AAMFT code of ethical principles for marriage and family therapists.* Washington, DC: Author.

American Psychiatric Association (AmPsyA). (1989). *Principles of medical ethics, with annotations especially applicable to psychiatry.* Washington, DC: Author.

American Psychological Association (APA). (1959). *Ethical standards of psychologists.* Washington, DC: Author.

American Psychological Association (APA). (1981). Ethical principles of psychologists. *American Psychologist, 36*(6), 633-638.

American Psychological Association (APA). (1982). *Ethical principles in the conduct of research with human participants.* Washington, DC: Author.

American Psychological Association (APA). (1985). *Ethical standards of psychologists.* Washington, DC: Author.

American Psychological Association (APA). (1987a). *Casebook on ethical principles of psychologists* (rev. ed.). Washington, DC: Author.

American Psychological Association (APA). (1987b). *General guidelines for providers of psychological services.* Washington, DC: Author.

American Psychological Association (APA). (1989). *Ethical principles of psychologists.* Washington, DC: Author.

American Psychological Association. (1990). Ethical principles of psychologists (amended June, 1989). *American Psychologist, 45*, 390-395.

Appelbaum, P. S. (1985, April). Tarasoff and the clinician: Problems in fulfilling the duty to protect. *American Journal of Psychiatry, 142*(4), 425-429.

Appelbaum, P. S. (1988, July). The new preventive detention: Psychiatry's problematic responsibility for the control of violence. *American Journal of Psychiatry, 145*(7), 779-785.

Ard, B. N., Jr. (1976). *Handbook of marriage counseling.* Palo Alto, CA: Science and Behavior Books.

Association for Specialists in Group Work (ASGW). (1980). *Ethical guidelines for group leaders.* Alexandria, VA: Author.

Association for Specialists in Group Work (ASGW). (1989). *Ethical guidelines for group counselors.* Alexandria, VA: Author.

Beauchamp, T. L. (1982). *Philosophical ethics: An introduction to moral philosophy.* New York: McGraw-Hill.

Berman, A. L., & Cohen-Sandler, R. (1983). Suicide and malpractice expert testimony and the standard of care. *Professional Psychology: Research and Practice, 4*(1), 6-19.

Bray, H. J., Shepherd, J. N., & Hays, J. R. (1985). Legal and ethical issues in informed consent to psychotherapy. *American Journal of Family Therapy, 13*(2), 50-60.

Carroll, M. A., Schneider, H. G., & Wesley, G. R. (1985). *Ethics in the practice of psychology.* Englewood Cliffs, NJ: Prentice-Hall.

Cohen, R. J. (1979). *Malpractice: A guide for mental health professionals.* New York: Free Press.

Conidaris, M. G., Ely, D. F., Erikson, J. T., & Levin, S. M. (1989). *California laws for psychotherapists.* Gardena, CA: Harcourt Brace Jovanovich.

Cooke, G. (Ed.). (1980). *The role of the forensic psychologist.* Springfield, IL: Charles C Thomas.

Corey, M. S., & Corey, G. (1989). *Becoming a helper.* Pacific Grove, CA: Brooks/Cole.

Corey, G., Corey, M. S., & Callanan, P. (1988). *Issues and ethics in the helping professions* (3rd ed.). Pacific Grove, CA: Brooks/Cole.

Cormier, S. L., & Bernard, J. M. (1982). Ethical and legal responsibilities of clinical supervisors. *Personnel and Guidance Journal, 60*(8), 486-491.

Cummings, N. A., & Sobel, S. B. (1985). Malpractice insurance: Update on sex claims. *Psychotherapy, 22*(2), 186-188.

Dalglish, T. (1976). *Protecting human subjects on social and behavioral research: Ethics, law and the DHEW rules: A critique.* Berkeley, CA: Center for Research in Management Science.

Dawidoff, D. J. (1973). *The malpractice psychiatrist.* Springfield, IL: Charles C Thomas.

Denkowski, K. M., & Denkowski, G. C. (1982). Client-counselor confidentiality: An update of rationale, legal status, and implications. *Personnel and Guidance Journal, 60*(6), 371-375.

Deutsch, D. J. (1984). Self-reported sources of stress among psychotherapists. *Professional Psychology: Research and Practice, 15*(6), 833-845.

Everstine, L., Everstine, D. S., Heymann, G. M., True, R. H., Frey, D. H., Johnson, H. G., & Seiden, R. H. (1980). Privacy and confidentiality in psychotherapy. *American Psychologist, 35*(9), 828-840.

Farber, B. A. (1983a). Psychotherapists' perception of stressful patient behavior. *Professional Psychology: Research and Practice, 14*(5), 697-705.

Farber, B. A. (1983b). *Stress and burnout in the human services profession.* New York: Pergamon.

Fulero, S. (1988). Tarasoff: 10 years later. *Professional Psychology: Research and Practice, 19*(2), 184-190.

Gabbard, G., & Pope, K. S. (1988). Sexual intimacies after termination: Clinical, ethical, and legal aspects. *Independent Practitioner, 8*(2), 21-26.

Garfield, S. L., & Bergin, A. E. (Eds.). (1978). *Handbook of psychotherapy and behavior change: An empirical analysis* (2nd ed.). New York: John Wiley.

Golann, S. E. (1970). Ethical standards for psychology: Development and revision, 1938-1968. *Annals of the New York Academy of Science, 169,* 398.

Grisso, T., & Vierling, L. (1978). Minors' consent to treatment: A developmental perspective. *Professional Psychology, 9*(3), 412-427.

Gross, B. H., Southard, M. J., Lamb, R. H., & Weinberger, L. E. (1987). Assessing dangerousness and responding appropriately: Hedlund expands the clinician's liability established by Tarasoff. *Journal of Clinical Psychology, 48*(1), 9-12.

Hall, J. E. (1988). Standards for the individual practitioner: A moving target. *Register Report, 13*(3), 3-4.

Halleck, S. (1971). *Psychiatry and the dilemmas of crime.* Berkeley: University of California Press.

Halleck, S. L. (1980). *Law in the practice of psychiatry: A handbook for clinicians.* New York: Plenum.

Handelsman, M. M., & Gelvin, M. D. (1988). Facilitating informed consent for outpatient psychiatry: A suggested written format. *Professional Psychology: Research and Practice, 19*(2), 223-224.

Hare-Mustin, R. T., Marecek, J., Kaplan, A. G., & Liss-Levinson, N. (1979). Rights of clients, responsibilities of therapists. *American Psychologist, 34*(1), 3-16.

Henderson, D. (1987). Negligent liability and the foreseeability factor. *Journal of Counseling and Development, 66*(2), 86-89.

Herlihy, B., & Golden, L. (1989). *AACD ethical standards casebook* (4th ed.). Alexandria, VA: AACD.

Herlihy, B., & Sheeley, V. (1988). Counselor liability and the duty to warn: Selected cases, statutory trends, and implications for practice. *Counselor Education and Supervision, 27*(3), 203-215.

Hopkins, B. R., & Anderson, B. S. (1985). *The counselor and the law* (2nd ed.). Alexandria, VA: AACD.

Keith-Spiegel, P., & Koocher, G. P. (1985). *Ethics in Psychology: Professional standards and cases.* New York: Random House.

Kermani, E. J., & Drob, S. L. (1987). Tarasoff decision: A decade later dilemma still faces psychotherapist. *American Journal of Psychotherapy, 41*(2), 271-285.

Kitchener, K. (1984). Intuition, critical evaluation and ethical principles: The foundation for ethical decisions in counseling psychology. *Counseling Psychologist, 12*(3), 43-57.

Kjervik, D. K. (1984). The psychotherapists' duty to act reasonably to prevent suicide: A proposal to allow rational suicide. *Behavioral Sciences and the Law, 2*(2), 207-218.

Knapp, S., & Vandecreek, L. (1982). Tarasoff: Five years later. *Professional Psychology, 13*, 511-516.

Laing, R. D. (1967). *The politics of experience.* New York: Pantheon.

Leslie, R. S. (1987, January/February). How to handle a subpoena. *California Therapist*, p. 14.

Loewenberg, R., & Dolgoff, R. (1988). *Ethical decisions for social work practice* (3rd ed.). Itasca, IL: F. E. Peacock.

Lyon, M. A., Levine, M. L., & Zusman, J. (1982). Patients' bill of rights: A survey of state statutes. *Mental Disability Law Reporter, 6*(3), 178-201.

Mabe, A. R., & Rollin, S. A. (1986). The role of a code of ethical standards in counseling. *Journal of Counseling and Development, 64*(5), 294-297.

Mappes, D. C., Robb, G. P., & Engels, D. W. (1985). Conflicts between ethics and law in counseling and psychotherapy. *Journal of Counseling and Development, 64*(4), 246-252.

Milgram, S. (1963). Behavioral study of obedience. *Journal of Abnormal and Social Psychology, 67,* 371-436.

Miller, D. J., & Thelen, M. H. (1987). Confidentiality in psychotherapy: History, issues, and research. *Psychotherapy, 24*(4), 704-711.

Mills, M. J., Sullivan, G., & Eth, S. (1987). Protecting third parties: A decade after Tarasoff. *American Journal of Psychiatry, 144*(1), 68-74.

Monahan, J. (1981). *Predicting violent behavior.* Beverly Hills, CA: Sage.

National Association of Social Workers (NASW). (1984). *Code of ethics.* Silver Spring, MD: Author.

National Association of Social Workers (NASW). (n.d.). *NASW standard for the practice of clinical social work.* Silver Spring, MD: Author.

Olsen, D. H. L. (Ed.). (1976). *Treating relationships.* Lake Mills, IA: Graphic.

Paradise, L. V., & Siegelwaks, B. (1982). Ethical training for group leaders. *Journal for Specialists in Group Work, 7*(3), 162-166.

Pope, K. S. (1985, July-August). The suicidal client: Guidelines for assessment and treatment. *California State Psychologist,* pp. 1-2.

Pope, K. S. (1986). New trends in malpractice cases and changes in APA's liability insurance. *Independent Practitioner, 6*(4), 23-26.

Pope, K. S. (1987). Preventing therapist-patient sexual intimacy: Therapy for a therapist at risk. *Professional Psychology: Research and Practice, 18*(6), 624-628.

Pope, K. S. (1988a). Avoiding malpractice in the area of diagnosis, assessment, and testing. *Independent Practitioner, 8*(3), 19-25.

Pope, K. S. (1988b). Dual relationships: A source of ethical, legal, and clinical problems. *Independent Practitioner, 8*(1), 17-25.

Pope, K. S. (1988c). How clients are harmed by sexual contact with mental health professionals: The syndrome and its prevalence. *Journal of Counseling and Development, 67*(4), 222-226.

Pope, K. S. (1989). Malpractice suits, licensing disciplinary actions, and ethics cases: Frequencies, causes, and costs. *Independent Practitioner, 9*(1), 22-26.

Pope, K. S., Keith-Spiegel, P., & Tabachnick, B. G. (1986). Sexual attraction to clients: The human therapist and the (sometimes) inhuman training system. *American Psychologist, 41*(2), 147-158.

Pope, K. S., Schover, L. R., & Levenson, H. (1980). Sexual behavior between clinical supervisors and trainees: Implications for professional standards. *Professional Psychology, 11*(1), 157-162.

Pope, K. S., Weiner, M. F., & Simpson, H. N. (1978). Malpractice in outpatient psychotherapy. *American Journal of Psychotherapy, 32*(4), 593-602.

Rachlin, S., & Schwartz, H. I. (1986). Unforeseeable liability for patients' violent acts. *Hospital and Community Psychiatry, 37*(7), 725-731.

Remley, T. (1985). The law and ethical practices in elementary and middle schools. *Elementary School Guidance and Counseling, 19*(3), 181-189.

Remley, T. P. Jr. (1989). Counseling records: Legal and ethical issues. In B. Herlihy & L. B. Golden (Eds.), *Ethical Standards Casebook* (4th ed., pp. 162-169). Alexandria, VA: AACD.

Roth, L. H., & Meisel, A. (1977). Dangerousness, confidentiality and the duty to warn. *American Journal of Psychiatry, 134*, 508-511.

Rozovsky, F. A. (1984). *Consent to treatment: A practical guide.* Boston: Little, Brown.

Sanders, J. R., & Keith-Spiegel, P. (1980). Formal and informal adjudication of ethics complaints against psychologists. *American Psychologist, 35*(12), 1096-1105.

Schutz, B. M. (1982). *Legal liability to psychotherapy.* San Francisco: Jossey-Bass.

Schwartz, D. (1985, February). *New York State Journal of Medicine*, pp. 67-68.

Schwitzgebel, R. L., & Schwitzgebel, R. F. (1980). *Law and psychological practice.* New York: John Wiley.

Sell, J. M., Gottlieb, M. C., & Schoenfeld, L. (1986). Ethical considerations of social/romantic relationships with present and former clients. *Professional Psychology: Research and Practice, 17*, 504-508.

Sheeley, V. L., & Herlihy, B. (1986). The ethics of confidentiality and privileged communication. *Journal of Counseling and Human Service Professions, 1*(1), 141-148.

Slovenko, R. (1980). Legal issues in psychotherapy supervision. In A. K. Hess (Ed.), *Psychotherapy supervision.* New York: John Wiley.

Snider, P. D. (1985). The duty to warn: A potential issue of litigation for the counseling supervisors. *Counselor Education and Supervision, 25*, 66-73.

Soisson, E., Vandecreek, L., & Knapp, S. (1987). Thorough record keeping: A good defense. *Professional Psychology: Research and Practice, 18*(5), 498-502.

Spielberger, C. (Ed.). (1970). *Current topics in clinical and community psychology*. New York: Academic Press.

Stadler, H. A. (1986a). Making hard choices: Clarifying controversial ethical issues. *Counseling and Human Development, 19*(1), 1-10.

Stadler, H. A. (1986b). *Confidentiality: The professional's dilemma—Participant manual*. Alexandria, VA: AACD.

Stromberg, C. D. (1988). Managing the risks of malpractice. *Register Report Special Supplement, 13*(4).

Stromberg, C. D., Haggarty, D. J., Leibenluft, R. F., McMillian, M. H., Mishkim, B., Rubin, B. L., & Trilbing, H. R. (1988). *The psychologist's legal handbook*. Washington, DC: Council for the National Register of Health Service Providers in Psychology.

Swanson, C. (1983). The law and the counselor. In B. Pate & J. Brown (Eds.), *Being a counselor: Directions and the challenges for the '80s*. Monterey, CA: Brooks/Cole.

Szasz, T. (1986). The case against suicide prevention. *American Psychology, 41*(7), 806-812.

Talbutt, L. C. (1981). Ethical standards: Assets and limitations. *Personnel and Guidance Journal, 60*(2), 110-112.

Tennyson, W. W., & Strom, S. M. (1986). Beyond professional standards: Developing responsibleness. *Journal of Counseling and Development, 64*(5), 298-302.

Turkington, C. (1986). Response to crisis: Pay up or go naked. *American Psychological Association Monitor, 17*(4), 6-7.

Tymchuk, A. J. (1981). Ethical decision making and psychological treatment. *Journal of Psychiatric Treatment and Evaluation, 3*, 507-513.

Vandecreek, L., & Harrar, W. (1988). The legal liability of supervisors. *Psychotherapy Bulletin, 23*(3), 13-16.

Vandecreek, L., & Knapp, S. (1984). Counselors, confidentiality, and life-endangering clients. *Counselor Education and Supervision, 24*(1), 51-57.

Vandecreek, L., Knapp, S., & Herzog, C. (1987). Malpractice risks in the treatment of dangerous patients. *Psychotherapy, 24*(2), 145-153.

Van Hoose, W. H., & Kottler, J. A. (1985). *Ethical and legal issues in counseling and psychotherapy* (2nd ed.). San Francisco: Jossey-Bass.

Wenk, E., Ribison, J., & Smith, G. (1972). Can violence be predicted? *Crime and Delinquency, 18*, 393.

Wexler, D. B. (1979). Patients, therapists, and third parties: The victimological virtues of Tarasoff. *International Journal of Law and Psychiatry, 2*, 1-28.

Wilbert, J. R., & Fulero, S. M. (1988). Impact of malpractice litigation on professional psychology: Survey of practitioners. *Professional Psychology: Research and Practice, 19*(4), 379-382.

Williams, G. T. (1989). Commentary: Responding to Gozman's article "Ethical aspects of psychological therapy." *Journal of Counseling and Human Services Professions, 3*(3), 11-13.

Williams, G. T. (1990). Ethical dilemmas in teaching a group leadership course. *Journal for Specialists in Group Work, 15*(2), 104-113.

Williams, G. T. (in process). *Williams' index of ethical code terminology.*

Woody, R. H. (1988). *Protecting your mental health practice: How to minimize legal and financial risk.* San Francisco: Jossey-Bass.

Woody, R. H. et al. (1984). *The law and the practice of human services.* San Francisco: Jossey-Bass.

Wright, R. H. (1981a). Psychologists and professional liability (malpractice) insurance. *American Psychologist, 36*(12), 1485-1493.

Wright, R. H. (1981b). What to do until the malpractice lawyer comes. *American Psychologist, 36*(2), 1536-1541.

Index

351

American Psychiatric Association
(AmPsyA), 240, 279
disciplinary actions, 258, 260-261
ethics codes, 253, 254, 255, 256, 302-
308
American Psychological Association
(APA)
disciplinary actions, 258, 260
ethics codes, 239-240, 243, 249, 251,
254, 255, 256, 279, 309-320
insurance carriers and, 16
American Rehabilitation Counselors
Association (ARCA), 279
American School Counselor Association
(ASCA), 279
AmPsyA. *See* American Psychiatric Asso-
ciation
Anatomically correct dolls, 158-160
Animal research, APA and, 320
APA. *See* American Psychological Asso-
ciation
Appeals, 22
ASGW. *See* Association for Specialists in
Group Work
Assault and batteries, nontraditional ther-
apy and, 155
Assessment:
AACD and, 294-295
APA and, 317-318
dangerous clients and, 122
diagnosis and, 169-170
misuse of, 248
suicide risk and, 137-138, 140-141
Association for Specialists in Group
Work (ASGW), 240, 279
disciplinary actions, 258, 260
ethics codes, 254, 255, 256, 257, 321-
330
Attorneys:
dangerous clients and, 123
insurance carriers and, 19
Audio, permission to use, 273
Autonomy, ethical decision making and,
248
Aversive techniques, 248

Baker v. United States, 165-167
Behavioral objectives, records of, 40
Bellah v. Greenson, 134-135

Beneficence, ethical decision making
and, 248
Bereavement, suicide risk and, 140
Bernard, J. M., 230, 234
Bills, privacy and, 86
Books. *See* Publication
*Brady, McCarthy, and Delahanty v. Hop-
per,* 115-116
*Bratt et al. v. International Business
Machines Corporation et al.,* 84
Burden of proof, 21
Bystander, foreseeable, 114-115, 119

Caesar v. Mountanos, 51-53
Cairl et al. v. State of Minnesota et al.,
107-108
California:
practicing in, 18
psychotherapist-patient privilege and,
55
suicide risk and, 138
Callanan, P., 45, 214, 246, 247, 253, 254
Call-in system, suicide risk and, 141
Carroll, M. A., 242, 249
Case conference, privacy and, 86
Case notes, 34, 42-43. *See also* Records
Child abuse, reporting, 71, 73
Children:
confidentiality and, 46
informed consent and, 187, 189, 190
isolation and, 174
parental consent to treat, 187, 189,
190-191
record retention and, 38
See also Minors
Child custody, 49-51
Chrite v. United States of America, 110-
111
Civil damages, failure to warn and, 94
Class discussion, privacy and, 86
Clergyman-penitent privilege, 49
Cohen v. State of New York, 134-135,
231-233
Coma, informed consent and, 190
Commitment:
dangerous clients and, 112, 123
diagnosis and, 164
duty to warn and, 94
failure to, 100, 104

About the Authors

Kenneth M. Austin (Ph.D.) is a licensed psychologist and marriage, family, and child counselor in California. He has over 31 years of experience in the mental health field. He served as Director of Clinical Services for the San Bernardino County Probation Department. In 1976, he entered full-time private practice. He has been an instructor in law and ethics at Loma Linda University since 1982. He has also taught courses at San Bernardino Valley College, The University of Redlands, and the University of California, Riverside. He chaired the California State Psychological Association Ethics Committee in 1982, 1983, and 1988. In 1984, he was presented the Silver Psi Award by the California State Psychological Association. Since 1984, he has served as an expert witness for the attorney general in California. During the 1980s, he conducted workshops in law and ethics and in record keeping in California, Nevada, Texas, Oregon, New Mexico, Utah, and Pennsylvania. He is a member of the American Psychological Association, the California State Psychological Association, and the Inland Southern California Psychological Association.

Mary E. Moline (Ph.D.) is Professor and Coordinator of the Graduate Program in Marriage and Family Therapy at Loma Linda University and a licensed marriage and family therapist. She received her doctorate in marriage and family therapy from Brigham Young University. She is a clinical member and an approved supervisor of the American Association for Marriage and Family Therapists. She has taught for nine years at the graduate level and for two years at the undergraduate level (California State University, Fullerton). She has also conduced several workshops on ethical concerns and legal issues for mental health professionals. Her areas of specialty include supervision, AIDS, and group training.

George T. Williams (Ed.D.) is Associate Professor in the graduate Department of Counseling at California State University, Fullerton. He is a national certified counselor and a licensed consulting psychologist in Minnesota. He regularly teaches a course titled "Professional, Ethical, and Legal Issues in Counseling." He also works part-time in private practice, in a hospital, and in an elementary school setting. He has practiced as a certified elementary and secondary school counselor, college counselor, counselor educator, counselor supervisor, and/or psychologist in the states of Pennsylvania, Ohio, Minnesota, Louisiana, and California. He is founding editor of the *Journal of Counseling and Human Service Professions.* Within the past 10 years, he has given over 50 presentations at state, regional, and national conventions. He has also taught over 40 different counseling and psychology courses at the undergraduate, master's, and doctoral levels. He was the recipient of the "Post-Secondary Counselor of the Year Award" for 1986-1987 from the Louisiana School Counselors Association. He chaired the state ethics committee for the Minnesota Association for Counseling and Development (1984-1985) and the national ethics committee for the Association for Specialists in Group Work (1987-1990). He served as state president for the Association for Counselor Education and Supervision in Minnesota (1985) and in Louisiana (1986-1987). Currently, he is state president of the California Association for Specialists in Group Work (1990-present). He is in the process of writing another book, entitled *Ethics in Group Work Casebook.*

NOTES

NOTES

NOTES

NOTES

NOTES